audiences
messages
speakers

AN INTRODUCTION
TO HUMAN COMMUNICATION

audiences

messages

speakers

JOHN L. VOHS   G. P. MOHRMANN

both of the University of California at Davis

HARCOURT BRACE JOVANOVICH, INC.

New York   Chicago   San Francisco   Atlanta

for Shirley and Merilyn

ISBN: 0–15–504286–6

Library of Congress Catalog Card Number: 74-22994

Printed in the United States of America

ACKNOWLEDGMENTS

The authors wish to thank the following for permission to reprint the four speeches in Part 2: Marilyn Hayashi Rye for "My Grandfather"; Margaret S. Boyd for "Shoes"; and *Vital Speeches of the Day* for "Television News Conference." "The Man He Killed" by Thomas Hardy, from *Collected Poems of Thomas Hardy*, is reprinted by permission of the Trustees of the Hardy Estate; Macmillan London and Basingstoke; and the Macmillan Company of Canada Limited. "Freshmen" by Barry Spacks, copyright © 1966 by Barry Spacks from the book *The Company of Children*, is reprinted by permission of Doubleday & Co., Inc.

THE COVER

Soft sculptures by Julie Gildersleeve Hicks.
More of these sculptures are on exhibit at the Webb Parsons Gallery, Bedford Village, N.Y.

preface

We wrote *Audiences, Messages, Speakers* with two related goals in mind. First, we wanted the book to provide students with an increased understanding and appreciation of the oral communication process, and second, we wanted the book to help them develop their skills as speakers. These goals indicate our primary audience, for while we think the book is appropriate for a variety of introductory communication courses, we wrote specifically for students and instructors in the introductory speech class.

In our teaching and in our research, the two of us have emphasized quite different aspects of the communication process, and those very differences convinced us that diversity should characterize our approach. Consequently we drew freely from as many sources and orientations as seemed appropriate, whether modern communication theory, or theory that had long been part of the rhetorical tradition. Such an approach seemed to us the only intelligent way to discuss people in speaking situations, a topic where our differing interests converge.

A word about the overall pattern of the book. As we note in Chapter 1, we realize that the sequence of audiences, messages, and speakers is arbitrary, but we are satisfied with its logic. Speech is a dynamic process, and any point of entry will necessarily be arbitrary. We began with the audience because it is the ultimate rationale for communication. Without an audience—without a someone or someones to receive the message—there is no communication Nevertheless, the sequence of the individual chapters is hardly sacrosanct, and instructors who wish to change it will do no harm to the substance of the book.

Four speech texts appear in Part 2. We chose them because they serve a variety of illustrative purposes in the chapters that follow, and we gave them a prominent position in order to emphasize the role that they play in those chapters. We have also included a number of personal anecdotes and applications that take students outside the confines of the classroom, offering them other angles from which to view and explore the communication process. Some of the applications can be used as specific class assignments;. others simply ask the students to reflect and learn on their own. We hope that the variety and placement of these applications will make them complementary to the instructor's own assignments.

We have already implied that this book is a truly mutual undertaking. Naturally, in the early stages we divided responsibility for the first drafts of individual chapters. Subsequent drafts became joint projects, however, and each chapter of the final product is so cooperative an effort that we used the toss of a coin to decide the order in which our names would appear on the title page.

It is impossible to acknowledge everyone who made some contribution. Edward M. Bodaken commented on the project early; later, Bruce E. Gronbeck, Donovan J. Ochs, and Phillip C. Wander made some helpful suggestions. We are conscious of a debt to all our colleagues in the Department of Rhetoric of the University of California at Davis—particularly for the insistent criticism of Michael C. Leff, F. Eugene Scott, and Harry Sharp, Jr. And we are most grateful to Donna Wilson and Karen Harmon for their assistance with the manuscript. Finally, we owe a special debt to two people at Harcourt Brace Jovanovich: to Matt Milan, who made sure that we got started; and to our editor, Natalie Bowen, who made sure that we got finished.

J.L.V.
G.P.M.

contents

audiences
messages
speakers

PREVIEW: CHAPTER 1

Chapter 1 is concerned with what's happening, both from your point of view and ours. The topics are:

The human being as communicator
Communication and the living of a life
Your expertise
The introductory speech class
Recipes and customizing them
More about your expertise
The speech class and your expertise
The rest of the book

When you have completed this chapter, we hope that you will be aware of your existing skills—your expertise—as a communicator; for the most part, you will be polishing and honing these skills rather than learning dramatically new and different things. And when we couple our comments on your expertise to our comments on the introductory speech course, our aim is to help you get started in making your first speeches. That's all.

what's happening

INTRODUCTION

1

In his famous essay "Self-Reliance" Ralph Waldo Emerson wrote, "Whoso would be a man, must be a nonconformist." Then, emphasizing that each of us must learn to be truly independent and individualistic, he remarked:

> There is a time in every man's education when he arrives at the conviction that envy is ignorance; that imitation is suicide; that he must take himself for better or worse as his portion; that though the wide universe is full of good, no kernel of nourishing corn can come to him but through his toil bestowed on that plot of ground which is given to him to till. The power which resides in him is new in nature, and none but he knows what that is which he can do, nor does he know until he has tried.

This passage has some profound implications, but for the moment we'll stay with the homely figure of the "plot of ground" we are given to till. As we'll point out, the study of communication involves the tilling of a very large plot of ground indeed. But in a narrow sense, if we restrict that plot just a bit, the odds are overwhelming that you are reading this book in connection with an introductory speech course.

If you looked at the course description in your college catalog, you probably found a description similar to one of these:

PUBLIC SPEAKING.
Introduction to the composition and delivery of informative and persuasive speeches.

ORAL COMMUNICATION.
Fundamental principles and methods of selecting, analyzing, evaluating, organizing, developing, and communicating information, evidence and points of view for constructive influence in speech situations.

PRINCIPLES OF SPEECH.
An introduction to the field of speech. Designed to develop confidence, poise, and clarity in the use of the body, voice, language and thought through guided practice in speaking.

Taken from current catalogs, these three descriptions are typical, and the stated goals help explain a good percentage of the enrollment in introductory speech classes. Like many students, you may have enrolled because you feel that speaking ability will be useful to you in business, law, or teaching. Or your primary motivation may stem from a successful experience in a high school class or from a strong recommendation by a friend. Or perhaps you enrolled in the class merely because it is a degree requirement. But whether you arrived out of conviction or were dragged in reluctantly; whether you shopped with care for the instructor and the hour, or simply filled out an IBM card and threw yourself on the mercy of a computer, you are enrolled in an introductory speech class.

So that's the plot of ground. The two of us are convinced that the tilling can be interesting and profitable—even exciting—and we hope this book will convince you too. We feel that there are some compelling reasons for taking a broad and sweeping approach to the study of communication. First, there is no more interesting view of the human animal than the perspective emphasizing the communication process. Second, nothing is more important in the living of a life than skill in communication. And finally—whether you are aware of it or not—you have already achieved remarkable expertise as a communicator.

THE HUMAN BEING AS COMMUNICATOR

When the poet Alexander Pope wrote, "The proper study of mankind is man," he was doing no more than expressing an idea that had gained increasing acceptance after the Renaissance, an idea that is commonplace today. And in discussing that idea, Kenneth Boulding observed, "The study of man is the study of talk. Human society is an edifice spun out of the tenuous webs of conversation." Naturally the two of us are pleased that Pope and Boulding have said it so well for us, but despite their words and despite our claims about communication, we recognize that many and varied points of view help illuminate the human condition. Evidence of the impact that, for example, the natural sciences have upon our lives is everywhere, but we exert little choice or control in those areas—only fools or lunatics think they can alter the second law of thermodynamics, the periodic table, or the orbits of the planets. But most of us are convinced that there are areas where we are more or less in charge of our lives. These areas fall within the compass of the social sciences and the humanities. They center on people in action, people as doers; on people as they act and interact with one another; on people as they attempt to control the quality of their lives; on people as they try to make intelligent choices. Consequently, these broad areas have a special appeal to all.

The nature of that appeal is underlined by the store of knowledge we automatically accumulate in the social sciences and the humanities. Anyone who grows up in our society learns to appreciate people as political, religious, and economic beings long before taking college courses or reading books in those subjects. However, no store of intuitive knowledge approaches the amount we have in the area of communication. The circumstances of time and place determine whether an individual starts out a Christian or a Mohammedan, a capitalist or a socialist, a democrat or a monarchist, but we all have to be communicators. There is no escape, and because there is no escape we are all experts. We *have* to be experts in communication in order to live our lives as human beings.

Our expertise is most useful in the here and now, but it has an interesting historical dimension as well. For example, the most direct and instructive view of the past is gleaned from the written record, from the written remains of a culture. No other artifacts tell us as much as the communicative acts—the letters, diaries, poems, broadsides, novels, plays, speeches, tracts, pamphlets, histories, and so forth—of which the written record is comprised. This record tells us what people thought about, what they considered important and why they considered it so, what they did, tried to do, hoped to do. This record also helps us get hold of the individual mind.

All of us can compile an extensive list of famous historical figures— explorers, philosophers, athletes, generals, politicians, scientists, or whoever—but no matter how much we know *about* them, we seldom know them very well as people without reading either their own words or those written about them by others. To say that Plato was a philosopher, Marie Curie a scientist, and Jim Thorpe an athlete is to identify areas of special competence and to indicate standards of excellence, but such statements carry little or no awareness of personality as personality. No doubt there are times when the deed is enough;

in hitting home runs, the total number is the overriding concern, and no matter how interesting, the personalities of Babe Ruth and Hank Aaron are incidental. But the fact remains that communication acts are of the utmost significance when it comes to a genuine perception of an individual personality.

COMMUNICATION AND THE LIVING OF A LIFE

Certainly, all of us find communication most vital to use here and now, because communication is intimately associated with the living of our lives. Communication tells us almost everything we know about everybody we know, including ourselves. Imagine if you can that our elaborate systems of symbolic behavior had been stripped from us. What would be left? Our cells would continue to divide, we would continue to reproduce offspring, and the planets would continue to wheel in their orbits. As animals, we would have a social structure worth studying—perhaps a hierarchy of dominance and subservience such as that illustrated in the pecking order among chickens or in the fact that one cow always leads the herd in at milking time. Our survival would require some rudimentary form of communication, such as the elaborate dance the bee does to indicate a source of honey to its fellow-workers. But without a symbol system such as we have in language, these phenomena could not be studied. Can you imagine dancing out all that is involved in fermentation? Socialism? A pizza recipe? Furthermore, we just wouldn't *care* about fermentation, socialism, or pizza. Caring is human. And caring emerges from a concern with the quality of life, from a sharing of attitudes and values—and the sharing depends on an intricate system of symbolic interaction. Without such a system, the social fabric as we know it today quite simply would not exist.

There would be no social fabric because there would be no people as we know them today. There would be no people because, as we have suggested earlier, communication is a dominant element in the development of personality. Some impressions—often accurate ones—may be formed in ways that do not rest upon conscious communication; we may learn important things about people by discovering what they do with their leisure time, by watching them perform certain tasks, or merely observing the clothes they wear. Yet fullest knowledge demands understanding of people as communicators. Although his characterizations are broad and stereotyped, Shakespeare illustrates our point in *As You Like It* in Jaques's comment on the seven ages of man (Act II, Scene 7):

> And then the lover,
> Sighing like furnace, with a woeful ballad
> Made to his mistress' eyebrow. Then a soldier
> Full of strange oaths, and bearded like the pard,
> Jealous in honour, sudden and quick in quarrel,

> Seeking the bubble reputation
> Even in the cannon's mouth. And then the justice,
> In fair round belly with good capon lined,
> With eyes severe, and beard of formal cut,
> Full of wise saws and modern instances.

We can form an abstract judgment about a soldier who recklessly seeks "the bubble reputation," but how much better we know him when we know how he argues and what oaths he uses. Of course, any clue or set of clues may be misleading: the length of a man's hair may be a very poor index of his voting behavior, and the fact that a woman never wears a skirt may reveal nothing about her sexual inclinations. Certainly communication itself can be most misleading. People lie and dissemble. They even change their minds. But whatever the shortcomings in the process, our impression of other people's individual personalities depends, in large part, on interacting with them in communication, and observing them interact with others.

These interactions also form the basis for finer distinctions. Whether or not we live through seven separate ages, we all regularly fill several different roles at any given period of life. In a room with friends, a college student acts one way; another way when attending classes; still another at home during vacation. But when we say that people act one way in one situation and differently in another, we usually include a large piece of linguistic behavior in that determination—people *talk* differently in different situations. In addition, differences in linguistic behavior indicate responses to differing expectations. That is, our language use is shaped, in some measure, by what we perceive to be appropriate, which, in turn, is partially shaped in a given situation by previous experience in communicative interaction. So, much of what we are and much of what we know of ourselves is a function of communication. As Robert Burns wrote:

> O wad some Power the giftie gie us
> To see oursels as ithers see us!
> It wad frae monie a blunder free us,
>   An' foolish notion.

If, then, we get to know others through the medium of communication, and if we get to know ourselves in the same way, then surely the communication process is vital to the living of every life. One more reason, we think, for an occasional glance at the horizons rather than an exclusive concentration on the narrow plot of ground.

YOUR EXPERTISE

The third reason for a broad approach to communication, as we mentioned, is that you already are expert with the language; if you weren't you would be unable to read this book. Asked to discuss the topic of communication, a college student who had no special training wrote the following paragraph:

> Communication isn't simply a matter of one person speaking to another. Something has to happen at the other end. Just as a quarterback needs someone to catch his pass, so effective communication requires the action of a receiver. First of all, the receiver needs to be in the same game as the speaker. The receiver simply has to be there. Secondly, he must evade all aggressive suggestions that would interfere with the reception. Finally, he must take in what is thrown to him by the speaker. This is the involvement a listener must have with a speaker if any real communication is to take place.

The football metaphor is a bit oversimplified, but it is indicative of the knowledge we all unconsciously assimilate about the communication process. Born with the potential for language acquisition and thrust into a linguistic environment, we all achieve a remarkable degree of skill in communication in only a few years. We soon learn that the noises people make with their mouths are quite important—they are patterned and regulated; they serve many purposes—and it isn't long before we adjust to and exert mastery over the norms of our linguistic environment. Entering kindergarten or the first grade, we are blissfully ignorant of the differences between smooth and striated muscle, or about the tides in the Bay of Fundy, or how many parts Caesar divided Gaul into, but by that time we are all communication experts. In truth, the ability to communicate cannot be separated from the living of a life, cannot be separated from the maturation process of the human animal.

We'll return to your established expertise later in this chapter because we want to build on it throughout the book. Your communication skill makes it difficult for us to tell you anything really new and startling, but it does create a tremendous stock of explanatory and illustrative material. With communication playing a dominant role in our lives, insights are available everywhere. To put it another way: anyone interested in communication will find that the world can be both classroom and laboratory, and we intend to range freely, sampling as suits our purposes.

V. One aspect of our sampling requires an explanation and introductions. First the introductions. The V indicates me, John Vohs, and an M will indicate Jerry Mohrmann. We settled on this procedure because we realized that there were times when we had to speak as individuals and not as joint authors—personal experiences are, after all, personal. Thus the first person singular, rather than the indirect and cumbersome "one of your authors."

Jean-Jacques Sempé. © Denoël

"I will be brief."

THE INTRODUCTORY SPEECH CLASS

We haven't forgotten the small plot of ground you're tilling—the introductory class in which you are enrolled. We will take a brief look at it right now, surveying what is likely to happen in the course so that you will have a better idea of what to expect during the coming weeks.

To begin with, most classes concentrate on extemporaneous speaking. Don't be misled. Whatever you have heard or read to the contrary, an "extemporaneous" speech does *not* mean a spur-of-the-moment or an off-the-cuff speech. The word still retains a bit of that flavor, but when instructors and textbooks refer to extemporaneous speeches, they mean speeches that are carefully prepared and practiced; they use "impromptu" to signify the entirely spontaneous speech, the speech given without previous notice or specific preparation. The element of spontaneity is expected in the extemporaneous speech, however; although extensive preparation may be required, exact wording and expression await the moment of delivery, and although the speakers may use notes, they do not memorize the speech or read it from a manuscript.

In addition, you will probably find that your first speeches will be quite short, running to only a few minutes in length, while later assignments will be much longer. Furthermore, the earliest speeches may focus on communicating information, and while that task is far from simple, it is less psychologically complicated than attempts to alter attitudes or change opinions, assignments you are likely to encounter later.

Whatever the assignment, several things are involved in getting ready. You will have to settle on some goal, choose your topic, gather your materials, select and arrange your ideas, practice aloud, deliver your speech, and evaluate your performance. Sometimes the general purpose or goal will be indicated early, as when you are asked to give an informative speech, but there will still be a wide latitude within which to choose a specific topic to develop.

You may find that adequate development will require no more from you than memory, for you may be able to find enough substance in what you already know about a hobby, a job, travel, or some other experience. Many subjects, however, will require an investigation that extends beyond remembering what you know, and whether you rely on memory or make a systematic inquiry, it will not take long for you to assemble more materials than can be kept in mind. Consequently, you will need a notebook or file, or some other system for recording information and ideas.

Once you have gathered your materials, you need to put them into coherent order. An outline will help, giving structure to the speech as a whole, before you develop the various sections within the overall framework. After you have satisfied yourself with the substance, you will find it useful to practice aloud. Then you present the speech in class, receive the critique, and move on to greater triumphs. Nothing to it, right?

RECIPES AND CUSTOMIZING THEM

The difference between a recipe and a prescription is that a prescription must be filled exactly as it is written, while many recipes can be varied and adapted in any way the cook likes. In helping you carry out the sequence above, we will offer you no set prescriptions, but we will tuck in some recipes along the way.

Take this one, for example:

1 package active dry yeast	3 tbs. olive oil
¼ cup lukewarm water	¼ tsp. salt
1 tbs. sugar	1 cup warm water
5 cups flour	

Dissolve yeast and sugar in lukewarm water. Place 4 cups flour, oil, salt, and warm water in large bowl. Mix well and add yeast mixture.

> Mix until smooth and knead, adding remaining flour as needed. Let rise until double in size.

Fairly commonplace and not very exciting ingredients, but the recipe produces a good pizza dough, though thicker than that served at most pizza parlors. In different proportions, the same ingredients go into a thinner dough, and for both, different results are produced by varying the sauces, cheeses, meats, and other adornments that are served with them. The point is this: given the same materials and the same instructions, cooks still introduce imaginative innovations. The skillful cook uses the recipe as a point of departure and blends materials and methods into an original final product. Like any other analogy, this one cannot be pressed too far, but the comparison is instructive—although we will list some basic communication ingredients and suggest a few combinations, you'll find no packaged cake mix or frozen TV dinners here. You'll have to be your own creative chef.

The kind of creativity we're thinking of is happily and quickly illustrated by Russell Conwell and his speech, "Acres of Diamonds." Traveling the length and breadth of this country at the turn of the century, Conwell gave the same speech over eight thousand times, and he earned enough from these presentations to found Temple University. In some ways it was always the same speech, but in other ways it wasn't. Conwell invariably used certain examples over and over again, but he always customized his lecture, always adapted it, in ways we'll let him describe himself:

> I visit a town or city, and try to arrive there early enough to see the postmaster, the barber, the keeper of the hotel, the principal of the schools, and the ministers of some of the churches, and then go into some of the factories and stores, and talk with the people, and get into sympathy with the local conditions of that town or city and see what has been their history, what opportunities they had, and what they had failed to do—and every town fails to do something—and then go to the lecture and talk to those people about the subjects which applied to their locality. "Acres of Diamonds"—the idea—has continuously been precisely the same. That idea is that in this country of ours every man has the opportunity to make more of himself than he does in his own environment, with his own skill, with his own energy, and with his own friends.*

The idea remained constant, but Conwell went to great lengths in customizing his speech for particular audiences. Maybe that helped him succeed.

Customizing leads to creativity. A pleasant illustration appears in the essay *Farewell My Lovely,* a bit of nostalgia that Richard Strout

---

* These comments and one version of the speech appear in Russell H. Conwell, *Acres of Diamonds* (New York, 1915). Later quotations from the speech are from the version in this book.

and E. B. White wrote about the disappearance of the Model T Ford from the American scene:

> There was this about a Model T: The purchaser never regarded his purchase as a complete, finished product. When you bought a Ford, you figured you had a start—a vibrant, spirited framework to which could be screwed an almost limitless assortment of decorative and functional hardware. . . . First you bought a Ruby Safety Reflector for the rear, so that your posterior would glow in another car's brilliance. Then you invested thirty-nine cents in some radiator Moto Wings, a popular ornament which gave the Pegasus touch to the machine and did something godlike to the owner. For nine cents you bought a fanbelt guide to keep the belt from slipping off the pulley.

We're still doing the same things to our automobiles, though on a much grander scale—such as those magnificently customized Chevrolets of the 1950s—and the idea of customizing is all about us. Some imagination and effort turns a plain T-shirt into a dramatic example of tie-dying; inventiveness and plain old sweat create a charming landscape around a standard subdivision dwelling; thought and attention to detail give a dormitory room character and individuality. Perhaps the T-shirt, the subdivision lot, and the dormitory room rank with a basic pizza dough for lack of excitement, but all can become interesting when approached with thought, imagination, and creativity. We can make suggestions, but only you can create, create for yourself.

We hope we can get you thinking about the many dimensions in the communication process, and we hope that the thinking will eventuate in greater appreciation, understanding, and skill, but these goals will be best accomplished if you learn to build upon what we say rather than relying upon it for specific directions. When all is said and done, maybe the most important thing you can learn from this book is how to get along without it.

Perhaps the same can be said about much of the reading associated with formal education, but learning to rely on yourself is especially critical in communication study. Since communication is so personal and so much a part of your life, you must start with yourself. Since communication is a process that does not yield a tidy bundle of all-purpose rules, you must start with yourself. You'll *have* to start with yourself, combining your existing skills with your imagination and inventiveness in order to tinker with our recipes, to customize our suggestions. In this connection, you may not want to accept the burden of Conwell's optimism in his closing lines, but it might be worthwhile to think about the ideas in the passage from Emerson's "Self-Reliance," remembering that you do have considerable skill upon which you can rely and build.

MORE ABOUT YOUR EXPERTISE

Compare your existing expertise with language with another common-place human activity—walking. Most of us walk well enough to get from place to place, but do you ever think to yourself, "Oh, how wonderful it is that I can walk! What a graceful walker I am!" No, you just walk along without giving any thought to the process, and of course it is a very complicated one. Only problems capture your attention. Slipping on ice or snow, twisting an ankle when climbing over rocks, stumbling on the stairs, banging a shin on the leg of a chair. But when these things occur, you certainly don't decide you are a second-rate walker and begin to doubt your ability.

Involving attitudes and feelings, communication is an even more complex and complicated business, but none of us should be misled by the icy spots, rocky places, or sudden obstructions along the way. Ordinarily, we communicate well enough to live our lives, and we ought to concentrate on that accomplishment. Of course we have all said something and wished it immediately unsaid; of course we have all misunderstood instructions, missed a directional sign on the highway, distorted a friend's meaning—these blunders are important. But we should not be greatly distressed by the current fretting about generation gaps and communication breakdowns. Naturally, it is important that we be aware of genuine problems in communication, but little is accomplished by wallowing in the difficulties, by elevating them to some undeserved status. A much better point of departure for improving your skills in all forms of communication is the frank recognition of your language ability.

The precise nature of language readiness and language acquisition still are matters of debate, but it is clear that we gain skill by engaging in the process, by using the language. It is all so deceptively easy and natural: with no choice about the particular linguistic environment into which we are born, we assimilate the words, syntax, and inflectional patterns that we hear about us. The nature of that accomplishment is easily demonstrated. Remember the story about the girl who meets a wolf while she is carrying a basket of food to her grandmother? She's wearing a little red riding hood, right? But she could not be wearing a red little riding hood because that is not the normal order in English; in English, words describing more general attributes ordinarily precede words describing color. Thus, we say "a large white house" not "a white large house." Of course all languages have their own special quirks, but adults learning English as a second language must study such things, though we have assimilated them as part of our intuitive knowledge.

Similarly, we all have learned that inflection of words alters meaning. We know for instance that a green house is not the same as a greenhouse, that all black birds are not blackbirds, and the difference in the printed words represents a vocal difference of minute but important character. We also learn that inflectional emphasis can alter meaning significantly. The question "Are you walking to campus today?" takes on different meanings, depending on which of the words is stressed and how.

In addition to learning about inflection, we also learn that there is a certain flexibility in words and their combinations, although we cannot be entirely arbitrary, as Humpty Dumpty is in *Through the Looking Glass,* when he says to Alice:

> "There's a glory for you!"
>
> "I don't know what you mean by 'glory,'" Alice said.
>
> Humpty Dumpty smiled contemptuously. "Of course you don't—till I tell you. I meant 'there's a nice knockdown argument for you.'"
>
> "But 'glory' doesn't mean 'a nice knockdown argument,'" Alice objected.
>
> "When *I* use a word," Humpty Dumpty said in rather a scornful tone, "it means just what I choose it to mean—neither more nor less."
>
> "The question is," said Alice, "whether you *can* make words mean so many different things."
>
> "The question is," said Humpty Dumpty, "which is to be master—that's all."

We learn to exert mastery over words and their uses but never can we become dictatorial masters over their meanings. Much of the learning occurs through direct imitation. Some of it takes place as the result of trial and error. A sound or word that creates a neutral or negative response may be quickly abandoned. In a supermarket, a young child points at a stranger, smiles happily, and says "Daddy." The stranger's reaction may discourage repetition, and the mother will probably tell the child that "man" is the correct word. Eventually the child learns that "daddy" is a "man" but that not every "man" is "daddy," and that "daddy" may be lumped together in a group of "men." So the learning goes, from the meaning and pronunciation of individual words and combinations all the way to the subtle states of linguistic consciousness suggested in Ecclesiastes: "To every thing there is a season . . . a time to keep silence, and a time to speak." It seems so easy and natural, but it isn't. Society nurtures the process, first in the family, then in the school. Our parents correct us; so do our sibling rivals—sometimes with a vengeance—and teachers continue the process. But after we have learned our ABCs, most of the correction and direction has to do with writing, with sins like split infinitives and dangling participles.

As we get older, both direct and indirect instruction fall off rather drastically, for two reasons. First, our expertise seems to serve us well enough, and second, our egos get in the way. Our self-image is so much a part of us as communicators that we are sensitive about correction.

It is bad enough to be misunderstood, but when someone tells us that we ought to communicate differently, even in matters of pronunciation, we can't help feeling that we are being attacked as people. Sensitive about this in ourselves, we sympathetically project our reaction to others—even in the formal study of communication, in classes devoted to speech and writing.

None of these classes can remake you as a communicator, but the introductory speech class can help you improve. It can help you become more aware of the entire communication process, it can show you how to analyze your skills objectively, and it can promote further learning, both through the observation of others and through direct participation.

THE SPEECH CLASS AND YOUR EXPERTISE

When we said that we would include some recipes along the way we meant that any helpful hints, practical suggestions, or advice about making speeches would appear whenever they seemed appropriate in the text. In this section, we will discuss some fairly basic problems that speakers encounter—particularly in the introductory class—and we will talk about them in terms of using your expertise to solve them. After all, some communication problems are problems only because people fail to capitalize on what they already know as communicators.

Choosing the subject

Oddly enough, the choice of something to talk about can be a problem. It shouldn't. By definition, any intelligent young adult has lived a rich life—a life rich in experiences and ideas, a life with an almost limitless set of subjects worth discussing. The book on the shelf, the newspaper on the floor, the conversation last night, the poem in class yesterday, the movie last week, the trip last year—but why go on? The world, especially the world of the college campus, is alive with ideas. The topic need not be earth-shaking; it need only reflect your alertness to the possibilities, your alertness to what you are as a human being. You communicate with others every day, and many of the things that you communicate about in the living of your daily life are eminently suitable subjects.

Research

Being self-reliant in picking the subject for a speech is enough if the assignment asks only for your opinion on the subject, or if your knowledge of the subject enables you to develop the entire speech from what you remember about it. But sometimes to rely on yourself will mean that you will want to use the library card catalog, the *Reader's Guide to Periodical Literature,* or some other index.

But there are sources of information other than books, magazines, and newspapers. A speech about advertising might involve monitoring television and radio commercials, billboards, and even the cans and boxes on the shelves at the supermarket. Then there are interviews and samplings of opinion. These can be exceedingly complex, but you don't have to be a Harris or a Gallup to accumulate useful information from these methods. Some speeches will need a variety of research activities, but again it is a matter of being alert; to some degree, the potential resources are limited only by your imagination and inventiveness.

Composing the speech

Outlining may not be a part of your expertise that evokes pleasant memories, but you've been there before probably, and that counts for much. It will count most if you make it an integral part of your speech preparation, something that you keep in mind all the time you are doing your initial preparation. Usually, it is best to keep that structure simple, restricted to a very limited number of main ideas. In fact, one main idea may be quite enough for a short speech. How long, for instance, do you think it would take to give a satisfactory definition of patriotism, drugs, or art? More than a few sentences' worth, certainly.

The notion of defining takes us to other things that count in your experience. Being a communicator—that is, a human being—you have learned to define, describe, use personal experiences, cite examples, make inferential leaps. In the process, you have learned to express yourself in ways that work in public speaking as well as in conversations. You have more time to plan and to exert control when preparing a speech, but the raw materials are those that you use every day.

Rehearsal

How long has it been since you practiced for a conversation with a friend, a teacher, or some member of your family? Even if such practice was part of a daydream, it was intended to produce control, and the same goal dictates practice sessions for the extemporaneous speaker. As we noted earlier, the extemporaneous speech is *not* completely and exactly memorized; rehearsal is a memory exercise, however, and it is to be expected that many words, phrases, and longer sentences will finally appear as practiced. But the main point of rehearsal is to establish general control over the ideas. It is also important for control of the time, whether it be five, eight, ten, or fifteen minutes. If you haven't done much public speaking, it will probably be difficult for you at first to estimate how long you have been talking. As the course moves along and you gain experience, you will learn how much or how little rehearsal you need to feel comfortable with your speech, to know when you are in command.

Delivery

Like most people without much experience in public speaking, you may be nervous at first, and it may seem to you that all your communication expertise has flown out the window. It really hasn't, even though some adrenalin may make it seem otherwise. A natural reaction, the release of adrenalin in your system will affect your pulse, your respiration, and other aspects of physiology. But please try to remember that though these manifestations may be obvious to you, they may never be noticed by most of your listeners. In truth, the sensations you feel at the beginning of a speech are not that different from those associated with the excitement you may have felt at the start of an athletic contest, a piano recital, or even an important test. When these sensations are tempered with experience, the result can be a more exciting performance.

Experience is crucial, of course, but the most effective way to build confidence is to attack the problem through your expertise: pick a subject that interests you, do the necessary research, develop your ideas carefully, and spend some time rehearsing. Even then, there will be no magic transformation, but positive results are likely to be in direct proportion to the effort expended. After all, Emerson was right.

THE REST OF THE BOOK

Any discussion of the communication process is arbitrary, but it is both intelligent and convenient to separate the various elements of communication for the purposes of study and learning. When communication occurs, however, the speaker, the speech, and the audience are inextricably interwoven in a single process. Ironically, vocabulary is not adequate here. No single word will do. "Confluence" has some of the right flavor because it suggests that merging which takes place when one river joins with another. Far upstream, differentiation is no problem, but where, precisely and exactly, does the Missouri become the Mississippi—or better still, where do the Monongahela and Allegheny become the Ohio? Each river makes a significant contribution, as does each element in communication, and in both cases the confluence is important only in terms of the ultimate unity.

So to start with the audience is arbitrary, and a good case could be made for starting with the speaker or the speech. If speech is so personal a thing in our lives, and if it is correct to assume that people have some selfish interests when they study communication—want to improve for what it means to them as individuals—why not begin with the speaker? Or why not the speech? If communication is to take place, there must be some kind of message. There must be words or other stimuli that carry meaning.

But where does meaning exist? It exists inside our heads, and that is one of the reasons we choose to start with the audience, with the place where meaning *means,* even if we are only talking to ourselves. The medium may be the message, but only because the mind makes it so. If you have a book of poems in your room, meaning exists as a potential on its pages, but until the poems are read—until you actively engage in the process of communication—the meaning is no more than unrealized potential. It is the same with the words on this page as your eyes scan the lines of type. It is the same with a speech: communication takes place as the result of audience perception of the message. There simply has to be a receiving audience. Consequently, we turn first to that perception.

And there's another reason for beginning as we do: we hope that we can help encourage objectivity in your study. The personal dimension in communication cannot be denied, nor should it be, but we think that you can most readily accomplish a systematic and objective examination of your skills if you start by looking outside yourself, by standing back and being as impersonal as you can. In that way, you will be better able to determine where you are as a speaker, where you want to be, and how to go about getting there. Besides, if we told you right off how to be an elegantly eloquent speaker, why should you want to read the rest of the book?

1

audiences

PREVIEW: CHAPTER 2

Chapter 2 is concerned with receivers—those to whom communication is directed. The topics are:

Receiving habits
The receiver's image
    Time and space
    Social anchors
    Valuation
Sharing images
Images and behavior

When you have completed this chapter, you will appreciate how much a part of our lives the business of receiving messages is. In fact, who we are is largely determined by the messages we receive. You will also appreciate the importance of the private image we all have of the world—how we share it with others through communication, and how a change in the image affects us. These points are important for you to keep in mind as you get ready to prepare and present a speech. They should influence what you may expect from your receivers and what they, in turn, may expect from you. The receiver is, after all, the rationale for communication.

tuning in on the world

RECEIVING MESSAGES

What does it mean to be a receiver of a message? That may seem an obvious, even simple-minded question, but so do many important questions. So let us begin to answer it at an appropriately obvious level, by asking you to examine your own behavior.

At the moment, the second paragraph of Chapter 2 of this book is the message you are receiving. The fact that you are reading this book represents a choice on your part, even though it may be a forced choice. But unless you have isolated yourself in a soundproof room, many other messages vie for your attention. The distant sound of traffic, a dog barking, guitar music, or the hum of conversation compete. Perhaps the light changes as the sun moves behind a cloud, or perhaps someone enters the room, or perhaps the aroma of coffee drifts in the air. Most of us are barraged with messages most of the time.

For short periods, we may shut everything else out and become totally absorbed in a single message—a great novel, an athletic contest, or a favorite piece of music. Usually, however, we are at least partially aware of several competing messages, and sometimes we are compelled to change our focus of attention. For example, the phone rings, someone touches our arm, or someone walks past wearing an irresistible perfume. At other times, we simply drift away from a message for one reason or another. We've all had the experience of suddenly becoming aware that the last few bars of some favorite music were being played and wishing that we had been listening from the beginning. And we've all tried to concentrate on important reading only to find that we have been reading one or two sentences over and over again without any awareness of their meaning, because our thoughts have been elsewhere, responding to other messages.

So what does it mean to be a receiver of a message? It means that we are doing something so natural that we are hardly aware of it: we are tuning in on our surroundings. Psychologists have demonstrated —if there was ever any doubt—that we all have a strong drive to stay in touch (note the sensory metaphor) with our environment. We need to tune in on our world, and we have some sophisticated monitoring instruments—our eyes, skin, ears, nose, and taste buds.

Stop reading for a moment. Make a quick inventory of all you can see and hear. Some distant sounds may be hard to identify, making only slight demands on your attention. Other sounds may be so loud that you will be surprised you had suppressed them. Your sight will also pick up "loud" and "quiet" messages about you; some items in your visual field may demand attention while others are relatively unobtrusive. Since we rely so much on sight and hearing, the other senses may not seem as important. Focus your attention, though, and you'll feel a message from whatever it is you are sitting on at the moment. And, right now, are there any messages directed to your senses of smell and taste?

If we have overstressed the obvious, it is only to remind you of the wide array of messages potentially available, even though you have learned to tune most of them out at any given moment. And if you have taken a psychology course, you know that the "messages" we have been talking about might more appropriately be termed "stimuli." There are differences between messages and stimuli, but for the present, we will continue to use the terms interchangeably, postponing until later a refining of the meaning of "message."

As receivers, then, we are exposed to a constant volley of stimuli, a constant barrage of messages. Since we can't even begin to process all the information we are receiving at any one instant, we learn to tune out many of the messages. We are taught, and we teach ourselves, to select only those messages that are important to us at a given time. As infants and children, our attention span is very limited—much to the amusement, amazement, and annoyance of our parents and older sisters and brothers—because we have not yet learned what to tune out. The infant and the child respond indiscriminately to anything and everything in this "blooming, buzzing confusion," as William James described the world about us. As we mature, we learn to ignore most of the messages that come to us, to focus on what is important to us.

Naturally, what is important varies, depending on what our parents, our peers, and our society deem important.

V. Eager to have our son and daughter get a close-up look at some of the wild animals they had seen on television, my wife and I took them to a large zoo. At the bear grotto, a male grizzly paced back and forth with an impressive, menacing look, while his mate showed off her repertoire of tricks. Next door, a mother lion brought her cub out of the cave for some sun, while father lounged in the shade. To us adults, the bears and lions seemed the most important, but not to my four-year-old daughter. She had no time for bears and lions because of her absolute fascination at the chickens roaming freely about the grounds. Plain, ordinary chickens, but she was so absorbed in following them and feeding them that she missed what we thought was important. No doubt we missed what *she* thought was important too!

As we mature, the demands of both physical and social survival require that we learn to keep up with the world as it exists around us, even at the loss of something precious—our childhood innocence. We must learn to be effective, fairly efficient receivers of information, and we must therefore learn to tune out some of the most attractive messages. That last notion is worth the exploring, worth considering for its personal implications, because it raises the issue of the significance in all we learn to ignore, but you'll have to think about this interesting side issue on your own, because it would take us too far from our main purpose to discuss it.

It sounds awesome to say that an important part of our growing and learning involves the development of our abilities to select those messages which are pertinent and reject those which are not—we rarely think of ourselves and our reception of messages at this truly profound level. Yet, while driving an automobile, isn't is virtually automatic for you to ignore a horn honking in the distance as you concentrate on the messages from the officer ahead who is directing traffic? And does it take a lot of thought for you to realize that you may suffer severe consequences if you don't tune out the attractive member of the opposite sex nearby and listen to the instructor's remarks about the upcoming examination?

RECEIVING HABITS

Gradually—sometimes happily, sometimes painfully—we learn to screen out the unimportant messages that our environment presents from moment to moment. Though this screening is a never-ending process, we finally develop *receiving habits* to help us cope; that is, we learn to handle the routine day-to-day messages almost automatically. Of course our criteria for what is important may change in an instant, so we must always be ready to acquire new receiving habits when confronted with new situations. On an unfamiliar thruway, for example, you may feel some mild anxiety as you try to find the signs leading to your destination. Much of this anxiety comes from the fact that there is so much new information to respond to—speed limit signs, highway signs, off-ramp signs, billboards, and so forth. You must process all this information while searching for the few messages that are important in getting you to your destination. Furthermore, some situations may cause even greater anxiety because you may not know what to search for—you may not know what messages are important.

Let's assume, for example, that you are a chemistry major and you have enrolled in a course in art history. Now in your home territory, chemistry, you have pretty well learned what is important in the subject matter and you have adjusted your receiving habits to the particular styles of your chemistry instructors. You have learned to respond to their mannerisms of presentation, emphasis, and so forth. You know when to stay tuned in and when you can afford to tune out. You have developed and you are refining receiving habits that work. (If you haven't and if you aren't, you are in big trouble!)

But the art history course may pose a problem. Pretty much compelled to rely only on whatever general habits you have acquired, you watch and listen, you take notes, you hope you have captured the important things, but it's a different ballgame in some respects. While you may have learned what to look for in a chemistry lecture, you haven't developed a similar set of habits for a lecture on art history. Until you do, you may be taking notes on the "wrong" things as far as your art instructor is concerned. Some instructors can make your task easier by providing "importance clues" in their presentation which make it easy to receive their messages. Aided by your study and their lectures, you'll soon develop a new set of receiving habits for art history. Again you'll learn when to tune in and when you can afford to tune out.

No doubt we have an incredible capacity for receiving messages, but there is a limit to this capacity, and that limit regularly confronts us in our daily lives. We cope by learning to monitor several messages simultaneously. It is not too difficult to read the newspaper and, at the same time, extract the important nuggets from the evening TV newscast. Both these sets of messages are relatively easy to follow and we can readily shift our primary attention from one medium to the other without any great loss of information. Similarly, once we have developed the proper receiving habits, we can listen to many lectures or speeches and still process other messages. But some receiving requires real concentration. For example, it would be difficult to keep up a brisk conversation and try to comprehend a set of directions or an involved story or a poem at the same time.

An intelligent conversation, too, contains quite a bit of information. It's not likely that many of us can handle it and some other message both at once without experiencing a lot of information loss in each. So, usually, we focus harder and try to absorb ourselves in only one message, not both. Some reading—a detective story, for example —is easy to stay focused on, because other messages do not become distracting; but reading of greater difficulty or less interest value may require that you stay far away from distractions. For one reason or another, some messages can't stand any competition.

Having started with this what-does-it-mean-to-be-a-receiver question, we have proceeded to tease out some of the implications in rather elaborate fashion. If you have not been distracted from this message, perhaps you have reexamined some things about yourself and others as communicating beings. We know we can't produce any new and startling information in this area, but we hope you have gained some insights that you may not have had when you started. Our present needs don't require that we take the subject much further, but if you are interested you should look into such areas as information theory as well as attention and perception studies. These subjects are extremely important, and if you are inclined to explore them, you will find an extensive body of worthwhile material that bears directly on the study of human communication.

We want to conclude this section by reemphasizing the general concept of the human being as receiver. To repeat: *Who we are is largely determined by the messages we receive.* As sensing, perceiving, processing, interpreting beings, we come to know our world, and we begin to define our place in it. We fill our lives with the receiving of messages, and we build our lives on the basis of the messages we receive, as Walt Whitman suggested in "Leaves of Grass":

> There was a child went forth every day,
>> And the first object he looked upon and received with wonder
>> or pity or love or dread, that object he became,
> And that object became part of him for the day or a certain part
>> of the day . . . or for many years or stretching cycles of years.

Along the way Whitman notes impressions made by flowers, newborn animals, other children, a drunkard, "all the changes of city and country," "the family usages, the language, the company, the furniture," and he concludes:

> The strata of colored clouds . . . the long bar of maroon tint
> away solitary by itself . . . the space of purity it lies motionless in,

The horizon's edge, the flying seacrow, the fragrance of saltmarsh
and shoremud;
These became part of that child who went forth every day, and
who now goes and will always go forth every day,
And these become of him or her that peruses them now.

Although autobiographical, Whitman's statement applies to us all.
That we are all shaped by messages received is a fact that has implications for self-awareness beyond skill in oral communication, because
we all can benefit from—perhaps need—visions of ourselves and others
from different angles. However, since this book does center on oral
communication, the human being-as-a-receiver-of-messages orientation
is especially significant. Receivers are, after all, the rationale for communication, the somebody to talk with, even if the somebody is yourself.

*

It is worthwhile for any student of speech communication to reflect
occasionally on these general notions of receivers and their receiving
habits. When you face an audience as a speaker, in a very real sense
each of your listeners is a unique product of all the previous messages
he or she has received. To be sure, our social systems have arranged
things so that there is a lot of overlap, both in messages received and
in receiving habits. This is extremely important, but so are the individual
differences. Later in the book we will talk more specifically about audience analysis, but at this point we will ask you to do something very
ordinary for a specific purpose.

The next time you are a member of an audience during a speech
or a lecture, observe the other listeners closely for a few moments. You
should readily be able to identify those who are not listening to the
speaker. You might find it interesting to speculate whether they have
dropped out just momentarily or whether they have tuned out altogether.
Where is their attention at the moment—focused on the program or a
book, or miles away in a private dream world of their own? (The trouble
is, this exercise can be so absorbing that you might not get back to
the speaker yourself!)

*

THE RECEIVER'S IMAGE

Time and space

Before narrowing our focus further, we want to extend our general
considerations of receivers, and we want to insert some of the notions
we have been discussing into a larger scheme of human behavior. We

think this approach will prove useful as you continue to examine the communication process and work at your own communication skills.

The conception of human behavior that seems most workable for our purposes appears in a book we quoted from earlier, Kenneth Boulding's *The Image.** Since this readable and profound book was first published, its impact has been felt in fields ranging from psychology to international relations. Boulding's ideas have two refreshing virtues: first, they are relatively free of jargon, and second, they make a lot of sense. We think that his ideas are particularly effective as a backdrop against which to study the communicative behavior of others and ourselves, so we'll use them.

Boulding's notion of the image is an ambitious, encompassing one. The image, as he conceives it, is a unifying construct which, he thinks, offers insight into complex systems ranging from the lower organisms through highly elaborate social institutions. Along the way, people are involved, and, naturally, our use of the image will concern its relationship to individuals and groups as receivers of communication. According to Boulding, the image is the "subjective knowledge structure" that each person has, a conception—complete with its gaps and uncertainties—of the world that is unique to every individual. Extending from its broadest and most general sense to its narrowest and most discrete details, the image comprises a personal knowledge and belief system. It is the individual's picture of the way things are, and it develops largely as a result of past experience. Experience helps the individual to define the world, identify a place in it, and give it fullest meaning by adding increments of emotion and value. For example, experience helps each of us define our spatial world, so that we know where we are located in space. If we are sitting in a room, for instance, we know it. And we perceive where the room is in the building, where the building is in its neighborhood, where that neighborhood is in relation to the larger community, and where that community is with respect to other communities. Our images vary in clarity and certainty, of course. We usually have a rather clear image of our immediate surroundings and a less clear image of our more distant environment. For a young child, the total image of the world may not extend much farther than his or her immediate surroundings.

Travel, television, education, and other experiences will continue to broaden and sharpen the child's image of space, just as they have for all of us. Nevertheless, maturation does not remove all the hazy edges, even in geography; despite the years of conflict in Vietnam, most of us would have difficulty in drawing an accurate map of Southeast Asia. Or, closer to home, a map of the countries in Central America. We can survive well enough without accuracy in distant parts of our spatial image, and we do, but our immediate needs are illustrated in

---

* (Ann Arbor, 1956). Subsequent brief quotations from Boulding are also from this book.

Joseph Farris. Copyright 1970 Saturday Review, Inc.

"Every now and then Roger likes to cut himself off from all media."

M. I was driving with a friend one day, with his five-year-old son riding in the back seat. Some political signs prompted comments on a coming election and the candidates for county supervisor. Suddenly a voice from the back asked, "What is a county?" We mumbled something about towns and cities, and even had a word or two about states before lapsing into uncomfortable silence. After a pause, the voice asked, "Is that all you're going to say?" We tried again, stumbled about, and gave up. The voice came again, this time tinged with disgust. "Is that all you're going to say?" Somehow we changed the subject. . . .

the old story about the drunk lurching down the street. Walking erratically, he reels smack into a lamppost. Backing off a few unsteady steps, he pauses and then staggers forward again, smack into the lamppost. Again he backs away, again moves forward, again the same result. This time he backs off, peers blearily into the night sky, shakes his head sadly, and sighs, "Lost. Lost in the midst of an impenetrable forest!"

Knowing where we are in space is only part of our image. Other interrelated parts of our subjective knowledge structure are such things as our image of time, our image of nature and natural laws, our image of personal relationships, our images of values, emotions, certainty, reality.

In western culture, time, for example, is an important part of the image for most people, and we use the past, present, and future in sorting out this element. Here, recent events have a clear temporal sequence, and the details of that sequence may be quite specific. But as with space, we are less certain about events far in the past, and our image of history may be very spotty. Here and there will be sequences and details that stand out vividly—such as the Civil War—but large parts of the time picture are empty, except for the knowledge that *something* fills the gaps, and the belief we could discover what, if we wanted to take the trouble.

Social anchors

Another dimension of the image, one that bears more directly on our concern with the human being as a receiver of messages, has to do with the area of human interaction and social relationships. We all have a picture of our own position in the human social arena, and this is what we mean by the expression "social anchors." In truth, a very persuasive case can be made that most identity questions are answered in a context of social relationships. The who-are-you/what-are-you questions are phrased in many ways, but they usually evoke a socially oriented response, consisting of one or more social anchors: "I'm a Republican," "I'm an anthro major," "I'm a Sigma Chi," "I'm Dana's roommate." "I'm a Scorpio."

Questions which tap our social images are important ones in our culture. The two of us live in an area where someone called "Captain Delta" is the host on a morning television show for children, and he almost invariably asks the preschool members of his studio audience what they want to be when they grow up. College students are not the only ones under this pressure, and you can almost see some of the children straining to give an answer that will please and impress the Captain. The social dimension of the image is not that complicated at such a young age, but there often is a premium placed on this facet of the identity question.

Our image of place and direction in the social maze becomes fundamental as we mature—becomes perhaps the broadest foundation for our sense of self. Some of our social anchors are only incidental to our sense of who we are, but others are absolutely vital to that sense. Any threat to one of these vital anchors can be disturbing or frightening. It can be distressing to be required to change one of our central social anchors or even to initiate a radical change on our own. Students who go to college with no set career goals ("I'm in sociology but it's no big deal.") may shift from one major to another with no adjustment problems. On the other hand, students who find they are unable to handle basic courses in a field central to long-standing aspirations ("All my life I've wanted to be a doctor but I can't handle chemistry.") will have to make a drastic and painful change of image. College campuses have always been notoriously disorienting places for many students—and these days even for some faculty. Society continues to put a premium on the "right" answers to who-are-you/what-are-you questions at the very time when the "right" answer may be hard to come by—when trying one major after another may be the most personally satisfying activity. Most students are faced with new concepts of social roles, social goals ,and social definitions, with the old images seeming out-of-date, superficial, or naive, and although students are assured that they are now adults, many parents and teachers seem happiest when these "adults" behave like obedient children.

*

Think about the members of your speech class in terms of their social anchors. How do you suppose they would define themselves in social terms? How many social definitions do you suppose they would give you? Of these definitions, which would you say are incidental? Which would you say are vital to them?

If you had some answers to these questions, would they influence what you choose to talk about in your next speech or how you might present it?

*

Valuation

By now you know that Boulding's concept of the image comprises all the subjective knowledge we have—all that we as individuals believe to be true about ourselves and the world. We can add another dimension to this definition that sheds still more light on our conception of human beings as message receivers—the dimension of individual value systems. Not only do we have an image of an object or event, but we attach a valuation to it, which is a very different thing. For example, we have an image of our home town at some particular time in the past, but we also have an image of the value of our home town. As Boulding puts it, the value-related images involve "the *rating* of the various parts of our image of the world, according to some of betterness or worseness." Thus, our image of our home town will include buildings, streets, cars, children, neighbors, and maybe trees, lawns, and driveways. Each of these components has a value image too, although some will be more important than others. In memory, we may value our neighbors for being either friendly or discreet, or devalue them for being either snoopy or aloof. We may prize the house we first lived in for its snug warm rooms, or devalue it because it had no lawn. In addition, we have a general value image of the old neighborhood, one which can be thought of as a weighted sum of the smaller, individual components. As you can readily appreciate, other people from the same neighborhood could have essentially the same components in their image and yet place an entirely different value on them.

Although we have value scales for many things in our personal knowledge structures, we don't have them for everything. For example, you probably don't value one kind of carpet tape over another kind, unless you install carpets for a living. And most of us, including the carpet installer, don't have a strong preference for Jupiter over Saturn, unless we happen to be devoted to astrology. But on matters that are close to our daily lives, we develop clear and sometimes rigid scales of valuation. These value scales in an image play a dominant role in determining whether we will receive a message at all, how we will receive it, and what effect it will have on the rest of our image of the world. As we mature, essential parts of our image become stable and resistant to change. Messages and events in the world get filtered through our value image; those that are favorable to the consistency of the image we tend to receive easily, and those that are unfavorable we receive with difficulty, or not at all. Consider your parents' political affiliations, for example. Don't they ordinarily find it easier to listen to members of their own party than to members of the opposition? We all get more and more that way—it is part of being alive. We have seen how Whitman noted the development in his poetry, and Tennyson expresses a slightly different version of the idea in his *Ulysses*:

> I am become a name;
> For always roaming with a hungry heart
> Much have I seen and known—cities of men
> And manners, climates, councils, governments,
> Myself not least, but honored of them all—
> And drunk delight of battle with my peers,
> Far on the ringing plains of windy Troy.
> I am a part of all that I have met;
> Yet all experience is an arch wherethro'
> Gleams that untravelled world, whose margin fades
> For ever and for ever when I move.

Living and experience lead us on to other worlds, but they color what we see in those worlds. Boulding puts it unforgettably when he says, "There are no such things as 'facts.' There are only messages filtered through a changeable value system." This statement seems profoundly accurate, given the validity of Boulding's concept of the image.

SHARING IMAGES

How, then, can we ever break through the private knowledge structures of our own differing images? The answer is deceptively simple:

we *share* our images with others. As Boulding maintains, a part of our image of the world is the conviction that other people have had or are having experiences similar to our own, and hence have similar images. Consequently, our private knowledge of the world can be shared and made public through communication with others. The accuracy of this notion is most clearly demonstrated by the people we deal with in our day-to-day living. Since their experiences parallel ours in critical ways, we know that their images also do, and as time passes, we learn where our images overlap. We could even go so far as to say that the more similar people's images are, or the more similar they become, the less the need for communication. Think about that for a moment.

M and **V.**   The two of us, for example, are ten years apart in age, but we have similar economic and educational backgrounds, and we both grew up in relatively small towns. Now we have been working together for several years, and we know there are places, both significant and insignificant, where our images correspond. Substantial segments of those images have developed and been refined in the time we have worked together, so there are some remarkable points of duplication. As a result, a word or phrase from one of us may be enough for the other to recall and recapture at least some portion of an earlier event. The sharing goes further. We have attended conferences and meetings to hear speakers say things that pleased us or irritated us, and we have exchanged glances that shared the pleasure or irritation. Those glances were all that we needed to know we shared the same **image.**

No doubt you can think of similar experiences of your own within your family or with your friends. Such experiences make up a small fraction of the total time we spend communicating, and they are rare because they occur on those relatively infrequent occasions when images are in close correspondence.

If a similarity of images reduces the need for elaborate communication effort, it should follow that very different images will require the greatest effort, that the need to learn how to share images becomes most complex and demanding when images are most disparate. Obviously, people raised in different cultures—with different upbringing, different socialization, and different languages—will be able to communicate with each other in only a very limited way. In fact, it is hardly an exaggeration to say that when the holders of disparate images encounter the same situation, it is not one situation, it is two. History records countless examples. In the late nineteenth century, for example, the U.S. Government's image of agricultural "productivity" was completely at odds with that of the Sioux Indians, who saw themselves as hunters and warriors—in other words, as anything *but* farmers. And during the Vietnam War, not everyone's image of "protecting" a territory was to level it with bombs. In the light of such examples, Boulding's concept of the image may seem discouraging and frustrating in its implication that communication is a frail reed, but one to which we must cling in the hope that people can finally come to understand, share, and respect each other's images, no matter how disparate.

Fortunately, our daily lives are shaped so that there is a good deal of image overlap. That is, our pictures of the world are similar enough to those of the people we work and associate with so that we can get on with the business of living. When we suspect that our images differ significantly, or when we discover that they definitely do, we commonly engage in communication in the hope of sharing images and reducing any existing discrepancies. By making the images public, we stand a better chance of clarifying the issues involved. At the very least, we can discover what the differences are, and that discovery itself may offer the solution. No wonder that communication—this sharing of images—has been regarded by thoughtful people throughout history as the most marvelous and distinctive trait of the human species.

IMAGES AND BEHAVIOR

Before concluding our discussion of image, we want to touch on two more points, both of which are implicit in much of what we have already said. First, our behavior depends on our image of the world—a point that should be apparent. What people do in a given situation depends on what their image tells them about themselves, about the situation, and about the world in general at that moment. Furthermore, we expect people's behavior to change as their images of the world change. There are exceptions, of course; you may know a few people with one image of the world, but who behave consistently as though they entertained another image altogether. Many of us have fit this description at times, when we act outwardly as though nothing is wrong even though inwardly we are troubled or disturbed. And, as we noted earlier, we all have a tendency to resist changes in our image. An extreme or prolonged conflict between the image and behavior can lead to or be a sign of a mental disorder.

The second point we want to stress relates to behavior and messages because it deals with messages and their effect on image. As Boulding wrote, "*The meaning of a message is the change it produces in the image.*" We can explore that statement by considering some of the kinds of changes that might take place in an image when a message is received. Suppose, for example, that you are interested in learning about buying and serving wines. You already know a little, but you are certainly not an expert. One day you hear a professional talk on the subject. For the first time, you hear that though red wines improve with age, white wines do not. Red wines can be stored for years, but white wines should be drunk while they are young. Immediately, your image of wines alters slightly—not so much alters, really, but expands and is refined. This addition to your image should change your behavior: you certainly will never keep white wines around for the purpose of aging them, and you can take satisfaction from your more complete image of wine—maybe even be a little smug about being able to explain these matters to the uninitiated.

This kind of change involves the completeness or detail of an image. Another kind of change in the image is produced when a message affects the clarity or vagueness, the certainty or uncertainty of an image. Our images of the future probably offer the best illustration of this kind of change. Of necessity, our images of what lies ahead are vague and uncertain, and in many unfamiliar but unthreatening situations, we search for messages to help clarify the images. As we already have indicated indirectly, this happens over and over again to students in the classroom during the search for what is important to their instructor, when the tests will be, what kind will they be, etc. Some messages, in class and out, have the opposite effect—they confuse rather than clarify. Do you remember the succession of stories and broadcasts that followed the kidnapping and slaying of Israeli athletes during the Munich Olympiad, the tangle of events and reports surrounding the Watergate affair, or the prolonged siege at Wounded Knee? In these and other momentous events, the mass of bewildering, often contradictory information we received compounded our confusion as to what was happening, and our images lost clarity in the process.

Additions to or clarification of an image does not require any drastic revision in its organization; an individual's picture of the world remains much as it was before, in spite of any such refinement. However, there is a third kind of change, one that can have dramatic and far-reaching consequences. If a message reaches deep into the center of an image, a revolutionary alteration may take place, and important aspects of the image may change radically. Religious conversions fit in this category; so does the drastic reorientation of those who have quit drinking, or withdrawn from drugs, or discovered some new and overwhelming purpose in life.

Most of us may know someone whose image has changed dramatically, and we can readily observe the corresponding changes in their behavior. Usually, though, such profound and sudden changes of the image do not occur. Conversions of any kind are, in fact, extremely rare in the normal lives that most of us live. Our images are resistant to drastic changes—a point that is most pertinent to the study of communication. We'll have much more to say about this later, but we want to stress here that changes in people, alterations in their images, are more likely to be the result of *erosion* rather than conversion. Though conversion may be more fascinating to talk about, changes in the image—especially as a result of communication—are more likely to be of the smaller types that we discussed earlier.

This is a particularly important insight for you as a student of communication. It is not often that a speaker can stand before a group of people and bring about monumental changes in an audience as the result of a single, short speech. After years of organizing values and experiences into what seems a coherent system, most people are not about to make abrupt and extensive changes in their images. As we said earlier, there are no magic formulas that guarantee success in communication. If anything, our discussion of the image should have reinforced this point. In the next chapter, we will consider a means of looking at the ways in which a speaker *can* affect listeners, a means that should be useful in helping you identify and achieve your goals as a speaker.

*

In preparing for a speech on some particular topic, think about your goals and purposes in terms of the receiver's image. If the goal of your speech is to change a part of the listener's image in some way, what kind of a change would you like to bring about? What kind of a change would you settle for, given the subject matter and time limitations that you face? Should you try to convert your listeners or would a strategy of erosion be more appropriate?

*

SUGGESTED READINGS

Kenneth Boulding, *The Image* (Ann Arbor, 1956). This readable book has a broad, interdisciplinary perspective and a clear emphasis on communication.

Colin Cherry, *On Human Communication*, 2nd ed. (Cambridge, Mass., 1966). This volume provides a detailed and rather technical treatment of communication. Readers who are interested in a more advanced study of some of the issues raised in this chapter will find Cherry's Chapters 1 and 7 helpful.

C. David Mortenson, *Communication: The Study of Human Interaction* (New York, 1972). This thorough survey examines communication from both psychological and sociological points of view.

Wilbur Schramm, *Men, Messages, and Media: A Look at Human Communication* (New York, 1973). This book provides a survey of the process of communication, with some emphasis on mass communication.

PREVIEW: CHAPTER 3

Chapter 3 presents a conceptual framework for the positive effects that a speaker can have on a listener. These effects, which occur in five identifiable stages, are:

Awareness
Willingness
Understanding
Acceptance
Behavior

Influencing a listener's behavior is usually the ultimate goal of a speaker, and the first four effects are very often important in achieving this goal. In many speaking situations, in fact, any of these effects may serve as goals themselves. It is important for you to know rather specifically what effect you would like your speech to have on your listeners. When you have completed this chapter, you will be able to clarify your goal as a speaker in terms of these five effects, and you can use this information in the preparation and presentation of your speeches.

influencing listeners

AUDIENCE EFFECTS

3

In Chapter 2, we talked generally about the ways in which communication affects receivers and their images. In this chapter, we will begin to focus more sharply on listeners and audiences because, after all, they are the object of a speaker's efforts. Compared with the various other things that people do, listening is usually regarded as a rather passive process. But we can be, and often are, misled by this simple diagnosis. Most of us have fallen short of our communication goals often enough to know that listeners have minds of their own. One of the reasons that speakers fall short of their goals is their incomplete understanding of what happens when listeners respond to a speaker's efforts. This chapter will present a preview of the different communication effects that can be identified in listeners.

We saw in the preceding chapter that people's images and behavior do change in various ways as a result of communication. An important question from our viewpoint, of course, is *how* they change. That is the question in its neutral form. Here is the same question in a more focused and urgent version: "How can I succeed with my audience?" Every student of communication, whether amateur or professional, must come to grips with this question sooner or later. This issue probably binds us all together in our interest in communication—regardless of our roles, our situations, our lots in life, or our goals—more than any other. It is tempting to stop here and discuss at length the countless specific versions the question can take. It is asked by teachers, politicians, sons, students, daughters, presidents, mailmen, mothers, lovers, preachers, salesmen, fathers, butchers, bakers, candlestick makers—in short, by every human being. And if anyone could come up with a single specific answer to this question, the whole complex of human social relations would no doubt be revolutionized. Does all this mean that there is no answer? We trust you are not surprised when we say that in our view there is no *universal* answer, and we doubt there will ever be one. We are prepared to argue, though, that there are *approaches* to an answer which *you* can apply to *your* communicative needs and goals. To borrow a notion from Chapter 1, you can "customize" these approaches and increase the likelihood of success with your audience. At the very least, you should be able to phrase your "How can I succeed . . . ?" question in such a way that you will know how to begin to work out your own informed approach. You may even arrive at an "answer," but then only you and your audience can be the judges of that. It probably means something different to each of us to be an "effective" communicator, to "succeed" with an audience, and even the meanings of these two terms will vary with the situation. Yet in spite of these individual differences, there are some general concepts about listeners and audiences which may be applied to almost any communication situation. Specifically, we can think of a speaker's efforts as having a positive effect on listeners at five identifiable stages:

1. the listeners' awareness
2. the listeners' willingness (to listen)
3. the listeners' understanding
4. the listeners' acceptance
5. the listeners' behavior

Communication is, of course, a dynamic and complex process, and you must recognize that we are distorting the whole thing when we isolate the stages of communication in this way. But this kind of analysis can aid in the understanding of all kinds of complex and subtle processes—the growth of a flower, the migration of birds, or the cycles of a nation's economy, for example. Taking a separate and close look at each stage of the communication process should give you a better idea of what goes on in listeners when they accept the influence attempts of a speaker.

AWARENESS

Before a communicator can influence people's images or behavior on any issue, the people must be made aware that the issue exists. This point is so elementary that it seems unnecessary to mention it—except that it is important, and it is overlooked by communicators every day. Until a few years ago, for example, there was no large public awareness of an impending ecological crunch; in fact, the very word "ecology" was not a part of the popular vocabulary until around 1969. Efforts then (and, to some extent, even now) to get the public to conserve the earth's resources were met with a variety of reactions, most of them bordering on indifference. It is pretty difficult to get people to change their views on conservation until they are at least aware that it *is* an issue. And it should be particularly obvious from this example that once people are aware that an issue exists, it does not mean that a behavior change will follow. Simply put, all it means is that people are aware of an issue! To an avid ecologist this fact must be frustrating; to a communicator this fact is simply Stage 1 of a communication effect on a receiver of a message. As a communicator, you may be after more advanced effects than just a listener's awareness, but it is important for you to note that awareness is a significant stage for a listener, and that sometimes it may be all you can hope for at that time. It is possible that your efforts to bring your listeners to more advanced stages of communication may be wasted efforts until you are satisfied first that your audience is at the awareness stage. In most cases, though, awareness is the starting point in a speaker's efforts to bring listeners to more advanced stages. Of course many of the people you see regularly share your awareness of a great number of issues and events. Nothing surprising about that, since we all read the same papers, watch the same TV programs, and move about in essentially similar general environments.

*

A worthwhile exercise for you would be to list a variety of issues about which some audience of yours has little or no awareness. These may include any number of matters which involve your own personal life—your interests, your plans and decisions, your goals, etc.—about which others probably have little or no awareness. They may also include issues at a larger social level; many listeners may share your awareness of many social issues, but there are certainly areas where their degrees of awareness will differ a great deal.

From the items on this list, make a smaller list of the items your audience should be *made* aware of. What are the reasons for your decision? Can you expand this smaller list? Here is a good starting place for choosing a speech topic. Maybe you would merely like to make your listeners aware of how interesting the topic is, or maybe you hope to bring about some specific change in their image or behavior. (Notice that this approach defines your subject matter in terms of your audience, not so much in terms of you as a speaker.)

*

WILLINGNESS

Once people are aware of an issue, they decide, one way or another, if they are willing to receive further information on the subject. The process is analogous to your turning on your TV set to find something that you might like to watch. Once you discover what is on TV at that moment—that is, once you become aware—you may decide to watch one of the programs, or you may decide to turn the set off and read a book instead. Maybe the programs just weren't interesting, or maybe you've seen them before. Listeners may make similar judgments about the high or low interest value of what is being said, or the importance or the triviality of the message. Depending on these judgments, they may or may not be willing to listen. Suppose, for example, that you hear some unpleasant views about a very special friend; now that you are aware of these views as an issue, you will have to do some serious thinking about whether or not you are willing to hear any more about this issue. Or look at the area of communication between young people and their parents. Say a college girl wants to spend her spring vacation with a group of her friends at some popular beach resort. She makes her parents aware of the issue by requesting permission to go, but they turn her down because they feel she isn't old enough. From her point of view, this may not be a satisfactory reason but if her parents are not willing to hear any further discussion on the subject, not willing to receive further information or hear further arguments, the issue is probably as good as dead.

You can easily think of numerous other examples which illustrate this willingness-to-listen stage. As with the awareness stage, you should

*

It is fortunate for a speaker that people apparently are willing (though not always eager) listeners in a wide variety of communication situations over an extensive range of subjects. The challenge to a speaker often becomes one of *sustaining* the willingness to listen. Some subjects seem to be almost inherently interesting, while others are made so by a speaker's interesting treatment of them. Also, if a subject is important or useful to the listeners, a speaker can be assured of a willing audience.

If you suspect that the audience which you face may be less than willing to hear what you have to say, you will want to devote extra care in preparing and presenting your speech. You may want to try to find some new slant in dealing with your subject matter, or you may want to think about some special treatment of the topic you have chosen. You will often be surprised at how many options you will have in handling your speech, if you give some extra consideration to these matters.

*

note that efforts to bring listeners to more advanced stages than willingness to listen may be inappropriate because they are premature—listeners must first be willing to receive further information on the issue. Furthermore, it is possible that the communication tactics that you would use to bring listeners to the willingness stage will differ from those you would use to get listeners to the further stages of communication. As the previous examples indicate, to bring listeners to the willingness stage may be an accomplishment in itself.

UNDERSTANDING

The third communication stage—more advanced than awareness and willingness—is understanding. The idea of understanding, as it relates to communication, is a bit difficult to deal with, partly because it is a common notion having a number of slightly different interpretations. We've often heard students say of their parents, "They just don't *understand* where I'm at . . ." (and, just for the record, we've heard a number of parents make the same point about their children). The word packs a heavy burden in this kind of context. It usually amounts to an equivalent to agreement—if they "understood" they would agree. The understanding we are talking about here is more modest, in the sense that it is possible for someone to understand you and still not accept your position. In the way we are using the term—as one of the stages for listeners—"understanding" means that the listeners see the relevant facts, know the implications of those facts, and have some emotional grasp (such as empathy or concern) of the issue.

You can see that our use of the term "understanding" is obviously still quite loose, but we are content to leave it like that for the moment. The extent to which a listener understands is still a matter of degree, and to us this seems a sensible way of thinking about it. The important thing for you to see is that it is possible for listeners to understand you and still not be ready to do as you wish them to do. Hence, from the speaker's point of view, listeners' understanding entails a good deal more than awareness and a good deal less than total cooperation. Let's turn to ecology again for an example: suppose you, as a speaker, want an audience to support certain air pollution regulations. It is possible that your listeners have the same facts about air pollution that you have (whether they got them from you or from somewhere else); you may get the listeners to see the implications of those facts, and you may even succeed in getting a suitable emotional reaction (alarm or concern). In this case, the listeners were *aware* of the issue, they were *willing* to receive further information on the issue, and now you know that they *understand* the issue. Viewed in this sense that's real communication progress—but it still doesn't follow that the listeners will support the pollution regulations. This may be the furthest stage to which you can bring your listeners, or it may be that you can get them to still more advanced stages with additional communication efforts or tactics.

*

In preparing your speeches, you should clarify your own goals as they relate to your audience's understanding. Think for a minute: what is it that you want your listeners to understand? Have you chosen a topic that they will reasonably be able to understand? Most often it is not the subject itself, however, but the *treatment* of the subject that will determine whether understanding occurs or not. As a speaker, you should therefore be especially concerned that the level of your presentation is appropriate to the level of the audience's capabilities. For some topics examples and illustrations will be essential; for other topics they may not be necessary.

Another important factor involved here, of course, is time. Many topics are understandable if you have enough time to present them fully, but often a speaker doesn't have that luxury. A speaker's effort to cover a subject completely in a short time may be costly in terms of an audience's understanding.

In education, one common measure of "understanding" is an exam of some sort, such as a multiple-choice test. Most of us would agree that this is a fairly shallow indicator of understanding. But just for the sake of argument, how well would your audience do if they were given a multiple-choice test after your speech?

*

ACCEPTANCE

As a speaker, you may find that your audience's position on a given issue may be consistent with your own value system, or you may even be able to change the audience's value system so that it is in line with yours on this issue. In either instance, your communication with the audience is at the acceptance stage. To continue with the air pollution example, if the audience meets the general requirements we sketched for understanding the issue, *and* if the facts, the implications of those facts, and the audience's own feelings are consistent with your value image on the subject of pollution and the ways to control it, then the audience has accepted your position on the issue. Many listeners receive and process messages in this common, sensible sequence. At some point they become *aware* that an issue exists, they are *willing* to receive further information on it, they *understand* it, and they evaluate it with respect to their own value images. On this latter basis, they may or may not *accept* the issue. Perhaps unfortunately, though, the communication sequence in a listener which leads to the acceptance stage is

Drawing by McCallister; © 1973 The New Yorker Magazine, Inc.

*"He defended my right to say it.
Then, foolishly, I said it again."*

not always this rational or this orderly. You may recall from our discussion of value images in Chapter 2 that many people filter the "facts"
of the world through their value systems. The psychologist Carl Rogers,
who has made some important contributions to the study of communication, observes this same tendency in many of us: we have a habit of
judging issues and the things people say before we understand them.
Indeed it is not unusual for many of us to have formed some evaluative
conclusions about something we hear even before we are halfway
through hearing it! No doubt this unhappy practice is the cause for a
number of "barriers to communication"—as Rogers entitles an article
on this subject.* And no doubt some kind of ongoing judgment is a
natural part of what it means to be a listener. We can probably all
agree, though, that when listeners are in the accept/reject frame of
mind—that is, before they understand what the speaker is saying—the
speaker faces a particularly demanding challenge.

As we know from our earlier consideration of the way people
develop and support their images, it is not at all unusual for people to
accept or reject an issue before they understand it. We even have a
label for it. When people are particularly blind to certain sides of a
given issue, or when they consistently react in the same way to a wide

---

* Carl Rogers and F. J. Roethlisberger, "Barriers and Gateways to Communication," *Harvard Business Review*, Vol. 30, No. 4 (July-August, 1952), pp. 46-50.

range of issues, we call them closed-minded (among other things). The use of communication tactics to bring such people to an acceptance stage in their listening is often useless—perhaps even irrelevant. The best a speaker can probably do in cases of this sort is to concentrate on getting such an audience to the willingness or understanding stage.

In many situations if you, as the speaker, can bring more open-minded listeners to the acceptance stage of communication, you will have accomplished a great deal, whatever your goals. To the extent that people behave in ways that are consistent with their values, your listeners have now been persuaded/sold/converted/influenced/changed—you can choose the appropriate term. But, as we shall see in examining the next stage, there are times when people do not behave consistently with their values. Thus, in spite of having brought a listener to this important stage, if your goal as a speaker is to change your listeners' behavior in some way, your communicative task is not yet finished.

*

There are two basic strategies you should consider when your goal is to get the acceptance of your listeners. The first of these is to find a way to satisfy them that what you propose is consistent with the values they already hold. The second strategy is to change the listeners' value images so that they are in line with your goal.

As we know from our consideration of the image, it is usually more difficult to change a listener's value image than it is to connect a speech topic with an existing value image. It stands to reason that the more familiar you are about your listeners' value images, the more options you will have in trying to gain your listeners' acceptance. So for the present, at least, concentrate on preparing and presenting speeches for an audience whose values you are confident you know.

*

BEHAVIOR

Often, in communication transactions, the ultimate test of success is whether the listener behaves in a way that is appropriate to the speaker's goal. If you ask someone to pass the salt to you, for example, the obvious test of your effectiveness as a communicator is whether, in fact, the person hands you the salt. Similarly, as any politician knows, while it may be gratifying to have voters tell you that they understand your position and that they share your value image of the issues, the politician's real concern is whether the voters will translate their understandings and values into the appropriate behavior—that is, will they vote for you? In a relatively free society such as ours, people quite often behave in ways that are consistent with their images of the world. Still, there are times when we all face constraints and conflicts that make it difficult or awkward or costly to behave in ways that are consistent with our values. We know that you will have no trouble in thinking of many examples of this human phenomenon. In fact, we would be surprised if you were unable to find at least one or two instances involving your own conflicts and constraints. Our central point here is that the behavior of listeners is for perhaps the vast majority of communication situations, the final criterion for a speaker's efforts. To get listeners to *think* or *say* they support you and accept your position (that is, to express their acceptance) and to get them to *behave* as though they accept your position are very often two different things.

*

In many communication situations, all that you or any other speaker can reasonably hope to get from listeners beyond their acceptance is their *commitment* to behave in a certain way at some later, appropriate time. No matter how stirring and convincing a politician's speech, for example, the listeners can't cast their ballots until election day.

Salespersons know that it is important to show their customers how easy it is or how rewarding it will be to engage in the appropriate behavior—that is, to buy the item under consideration. Similarly, as a speaker, you would do well to think about the kind of behavior you want from your listeners when, in fact, you do have certain behavior in mind. It is often a good idea to mention the desired behavior explicitly in your speech. If, for instance, you want your listeners to take part in a blood drive, tell them where and when they can do it. Better still, tell them to come with you when you go to give blood. Speakers sometimes forget to spell this out, perhaps because they think it is "too obvious" to do so. Occasionally this is a wise bit of judgment; at other times it's an important oversight. A significant part of any speech you make may include an assessment of the behavior you are asking for: how demanding will it be for your listeners? How rewarding?

*

We should note here also that a person's acceptance/behavior consistency is often a matter of degree. It may depend on how demanding the person perceives the behavior involved to be. For example, you may understand and accept the politician's position and agree to vote for him or her. This behavior would certainly be consistent and, in the privacy of the ballot booth, it would probably not be too demanding. Congruent with your attitude, you may even agree to put the candidate's bumper sticker on your car. This is slightly more demanding—now your own position would be more public—but you may still be willing to behave in this way also. If, however, the candidate asked you to drop your classes for a month and help out with the campaign, you would probably feel that this was quite an extreme demand, no matter how consistent such behavior would be with your values. Even though your value support is strong, your behavioral support might fall short of this last request. If you felt that you were unable to comply with this appeal, it would probably be because it finally came into conflict with a set of values that you held more strongly, such as completing your college year successfully.

Although we have listed these five effects in a certain order, you should note that listeners do not always respond in this same sequence. Behavior does not always follow the understanding or acceptance stages; it may precede either or both of them. Listeners may accept a speaker's influence and behave as the speaker wishes, for example, not because they understand the issue but because they have a great deal of trust in and respect for the speaker. If you think about this for a moment, you should be able to find several examples in your own experience.

V.   One rather discouraging illustration of a short-circuited communication effect occurred when I was invited to speak to a group of about 1300 high school students who were attending a leadership conference sponsored by their organization. My topic was "Communication and Leadership." I began by telling them about a book called *20 Days to Power, Influence and Control Over People,* which promised its readers a vast amount of personal power and ability if only they would read the book and follow its prescriptions. Then I proceeded to show in some detail that such "magic formula" approaches were unrealistic and ineffective.

Apparently, a number of my listeners were quite impressed with part of my presentation—the part they wanted to hear— even if they failed to understand the point of my speech. I found this out later when an employee of the campus bookstore called to find out where they might order this book that I had criticized. Several of the young people at the conference had come in wanting to buy it! And so it goes.

On the other hand, listeners may behave as the speaker wishes in spite of the fact that the required behavior is contrary to their own values. Often, children will grudgingly follow parental demands, students will quietly (but resentfully) comply with their instructors' assignments, and friends will go along with each other even though they don't agree. This kind of behavior is usually grounded in some kind of power relationship; it occurs not because of value orientation but because of reluctance to suffer the consequences of not complying. Behavior by the listener which would be appropriate to the speaker's goals may be the result of a rational, orderly succession of communication effects on him, or it may be the product of some "short-circuited" process such as those we have just discussed. Often it may be difficult or even impossible for the speaker to know which of these processes has occurred in the listener. Given the realities of the situation, a speaker may not care how or why the desired behavior has occurred, just so long as it does. Ideally, of course, most of us would no doubt prefer it if our listeners' behavior were based on an understanding and acceptance of our message.

We hope it is apparent to you now—if it wasn't before—that we think listeners deserve particular attention in any study of speech communication. This complex and challenging process would be impossible without them; they are the object of our communication efforts. For now, we will be content if you have a decent working grasp of the points we have been discussing, and if the orientation we have provided has sharpened your already rewarding, intuitive image of the communication process. Many of our points will be expanded further as we draw on them throughout the book, and as we consider the ways in which they can be applied to the communication situations in which you find yourself.

SUGGESTED READINGS

Wilbur Schramm, *Men, Messages and Media: A Look at Human Communication* (New York, 1973). Chapters 11 and 12 of this book contain further discussion of communication effects. This section also has a number of worthwhile leads for those interested in further study.

Philip Zimbardo and Ebbe B. Ebbeson, *Influencing Attitudes and Changing Behavior* (Reading, Mass., 1969). This little paperback is more readable than most of its kind. It deals with both theoretical and practical issues which directly involve communication. It also contains a short treatment of attitude measurement.

PREVIEW: CHAPTER 4

Chapter 4 is devoted to audience analysis—what they know and how much they care. After discussing several specific ways of analyzing an audience, we turn to the ways in which listeners resist messages. The topics are:

Reasons for audience analysis
Types of audience analysis
    Demographic analysis
    Motive analysis
    Range-of-receptivity analysis
Polar responses
    Audience readiness
    Audience resistance

The ability to analyze audiences is part of your skill in communication, and it is an ability that you can improve. Toward that goal, we talk about demographic analysis, motive appeals, and range of receptivity —topics that are important for you in estimating the knowledge and attitudes of your listeners. As listeners are active participants in communication, the discussion of listener resistance is most important in this estimate. We'll be satisfied if the chapter makes you more appreciative of the significant role that audience analysis plays, and if you learn some things that will improve your ability in this respect.

what you see is what you get

AUDIENCE ANALYSIS

4

As we have noted, the tendency to talk, to converse, to communicate, is very, very human. Before turning to audiences directly, however, we suggest that you ask yourself why you want an audience, why you should want to make a speech in the first place. We all know people, of course, who turn this natural human tendency into an ego trip, who have to have an audience primarily for the purpose of gratifying ego needs. These people always have a few words for any audience; sometimes they even give orations in the midst of what you think ought to be a conversation. Some of them are behind the microphone at most rallies on campus, and many of them are the ones who regularly stand up to ask a question of another speaker in a forum, the question often being a speech disguised as a search for information. Speech being human, the ego is always there, but there are other, more important reasons for communicating. You may be prompted to speak because it appears that other people are doing or not doing something. You may not really want to speak at all, but you may feel compelled to, or you may be asked to do so. Such cases probably involve some issue about which you want to influence the images and behavior of your audience. But regardless of your motive, whatever may prompt you to speak can be summarized like this: *you are going to give somebody else a piece of your mind.* Whether you succeed or not is another way for you to view what this book is all about. But who is it who's getting a piece of your mind? Why? Who isn't? Why? Those who are and those who aren't may be sitting side by side, so let's talk about audiences and audience analysis.

REASONS FOR AUDIENCE ANALYSIS

Part of your expertise as a communicator is skill in audience analysis. This is another component that is so natural, so habitual, that you use it without thinking. Within your family you generally know the best time and the worst time to bring up certain subjects—things like using the car, grades, and money. That's just good audience analysis. But now let's go a step farther. Within the past few days, the chance is excellent that you have *thought* about talking with someone about something important before the talking took place. It would be surprising if you hadn't, and it would be equally surprising if you hadn't given some attention to details. Perhaps you thought about the physical surroundings, or the mood the other person might be in, or how receptive the person would be to you and your ideas, or what the response might be. Many times, people just don't respond in the way we worked it out in our planning, but the fact that our plan goes awry doesn't mean that we don't rehearse the next time. The amount of rehearsal is a function of the importance that the communication has in our minds, but any kind of prior preparation of this sort is a form of audience analysis. Certain previous preparations may stand out in our minds—either because they failed or succeeded—but, ordinarily, communication analysis of listeners and potential listeners is so much a part of our lives that we don't give it conscious attention.

But why do we intuitively perform these analyses, why do we anticipate? A large part of the explanation lies in the very process of learning the language, because learning the language includes learning how and when to speak for some particular effect. By trial and error, most of us learn, for example, that the timing of our communicative efforts makes a difference in the effect we get. We get more satisfying

*

Can you recall a recent instance when you prepared for a conversation or an interview? Try to list all the things that entered into your rehearsal. Obviously, the subject and the person were controlling elements, but *how* did they exert control? And what differences can you isolate if you compare preparations for talking to a member of your family, a close friend, one of your instructors, or someone interviewing you for a job? These and any other questions are all interrelated, and some reflection on them can clarify the place of audience analysis in your everyday uses of communication. That clarification, in turn, will help you in the public-speaking situation.

*

responses more often, say, if we don't interrupt an ongoing conversation, or if a potential listener doesn't appear preoccupied. And we learn that certain ways of expressing ourselves are superior than other ways with certain audiences. We find out that being too blunt may be unwise, that it may lead to an unwanted effect on our audience; in other situations, we find that being too familiar or too formal with listeners causes a negative reaction. The point is that much of what our culture rewards us for in the areas of custom and courtesy is the development of our communication sensitivity toward other people. So, simply as a matter of growing up in our culture, we develop a habitual practice of audience analysis, and a persuasive case can be made that we have very little choice in the matter.

Actually, it is not very often that any one of us can communicate effectively *without* making use of some intuitive habits of audience analysis. In fact, the communication point of view gives us an interesting, if distressing, insight into the egocentric personality: communication egocentrics speak only on their own terms, without real awareness of their listeners' varied states of mind and needs; furthermore, they don't much care about the communication situation and how it might influence the whole process. Few people are so self-centered that they have utter disregard for everyone, and you undoubtedly can think of some very egocentric individuals who still manage to be very careful in adapting their messages to their audiences. We all know how Hitler, for example, skillfully exploited the defeat Germany suffered in World War I, the worldwide depression, and the threat of Communism to create the Nazi regime and exterminate six million Jews.

Undoubtedly there are times when the audience is receptive, and willing to buy anything a speaker has to sell, just as you may be willing to forgive a television comedian who is not quite up to your expectations or an excellent instructor who is having a bad day. But everyday people in everyday life are not always in such happy circumstances, and most speakers do not find that they encounter an ideal audience situation. As speakers, we may not be able to choose a warm, friendly, receptive group of listeners, and the time and place may leave much to be desired. Actually, to borrow an old phrase, the best that can be said of an audience is very often "what you see is what you get."

It hardly needs to be said that what you see and what you get will be many and varied kinds of audiences. They may be incredibly diverse or quite homogeneous. Did you ever attend a meeting at an elementary or secondary school where the teachers spoke to both the parents and the students? If that isn't diverse enough, what about the audience listening to an address by the President on television?

With over a hundred million people listening, the huge number of different images makes the problem of audience analysis almost imponderable, and perhaps it is little wonder that most presidents speak in a predictable and abstract way, presenting a little something for everyone. In contrast, presidents have a much more homogeneous audience when they address their Cabinet, and, despite their differences, college students comprise a rather homogeneous group of listeners. As a speaker, however, you should not assume that you will always be talking to audiences with similar interests and attitudes. As we have seen, many audiences have diverse images, and the more diverse they are, the greater the problem for speakers in adapting their speeches. In extreme cases, speakers may be talking over the heads of some of their listeners, at an appropriate level for others, and beneath the understanding of the rest.

M. The problem of adaptation was evident one Sunday morning some years ago. I was in church with my children, and a visiting minister gave us such a hellfire-and-damnation sermon that I thought I detected the odor of sulphur. I was also thinking that his approach was much too heavy and fundamental for this audience in a college community. My youngest child provided the clincher, though, by bursting out in a ringing voice, "Daddy, he's shouting at us!"

There is no ready solution to the difficult problem posed by a diverse audience. Every effort necessitates compromise, but you should keep in mind that you have choices about the kinds of compromise to be made. You may provide a little something for everyone—an approach that many politicians have to take—or you may try to direct your speech to a particular group of listeners within the audience at large. Whatever strategy you choose, the important thing is to be aware that choices exist. And the most important thing is to *make* a choice, not let communication be a matter of chance and luck.

Clearly, though, audience diversity is a relative concept. One criterion may suggest that some particular audience is most homogeneous, but another criterion will indicate a rich mixture of images and attitudes in that same audience. For example, a PTA audience may be nearly unanimous in supporting a broad, liberal education, but it may be quite varied in regard to the school lunch program or the question of sex education. Even if these particular issues are of no concern to you now, they—or some other issues—will certainly concern you someday, and whatever the issues, your audience's relationship to them will be important to you. That's what listener homogeneity is all about—how listeners stand in relation to the topic. It comes down to these two questions: *How much does the audience know? How much does the audience care?* We will discuss procedures for audience analysis that are more elaborate than these two aspects, but virtually all of them can be traced to these questions about what the audience knows and how much it cares. Obviously, we are right back with the image and its valuation.

*

In relation to knowing and caring, think about free speech, for example. Certainly we prize it, but what do we really know about it? As a speaker, you could start with the knowing by exploring the historical bases. You could talk about our inheritance from Great Britain and trace its development in this country since the Revolution and Bill of Rights. Or you might want to explore some recent considerations. Free speech—or the lack of it—is involved when an audience shouts down a speaker. It is also involved in some obscenity cases that have come before the courts. Now, of course, we're moving into the caring. Some audiences may care so much that they don't want to entertain any discussion, but seldom will you find people who are not willing to add to what they know, and you may find that caring is a useful springboard for the presentation of further information.

*

So that you can get a better grasp on the question of image and its valuation in your audience, thereby expanding your intuitive methods of audience analysis, we'll now turn to approaches commonly used by teachers and students of speech communication, approaches that merely elaborate on common-sensical ways of examining audiences. We hope that this elaboration will put you in a better position to prepare and present speeches, and that it will steer you away from unnecessary and costly errors by centering your attention on the choices that you can make. After all, vital as we think it is, audience analysis is no more than the art of making intelligent choices, and we hope you will develop the habit of working on this art.

TYPES OF AUDIENCE ANALYSIS

Demographic analysis

Demography is the science of vital statistics, and vital statistics is the most common approach to audience analysis. Information about age, sex, occupation, group memberships, residence, religion, marital status, political affiliation, income, education, and so forth, is the stuff on which the Census Bureau thrives. So do Gallup, Harris, and the other survey researchers who base their analyses on demographic profiles. That the number of these polling organizations is increasing in the country is probably the best evidence that demographic information is useful. Political candidates rely on polls to help them chart their strategies, and for years, people in marketing have used demographic information to help them determine what products might sell to what consumers, using what approach. Does that sound very sophisticated and up-to-date? It was in the fourth century B.C. that Aristotle wrote his *Rhetoric,* and in explaining "how to compose our speeches so as to adapt both them and ourselves to our audiences," he noted how critical the features of "various ages and fortunes" were. As Aristotle explained, "By ages I mean youth, the prime of life, and old age. By fortune I mean birth, wealth, power, and their opposites —in fact, good fortune and ill fortune."

These are broad categories, but almost any kind of demographic information will put you in a better position in regard to the preparation and presentation of speeches. Such information will assist you in making informed judgments about the *experiences* of the audience and about audience *attitudes*. If you know that your listeners are college-educated, or that most are parents, or that most go to church, or any other bit of demographic information suggesting what they know and what their attitudes might be, you are establishing a basis for making intelligent choices. You are in a position to talk to them on *their* terms, rather than exclusively on your own. The failure to give careful thought to ways in which your materials can be shaped so that the audience can accept and relate to them entails obvious risks; what appears to you to be a happy illustration or a perfectly good argument may not be understood or accepted by some or all of your listeners.

Research in oral communication has not yet identified any demographic information so crucial that a speaker will always find it useful. That may be because there isn't any. If this possibility is a trifle disappointing, it shouldn't be disillusioning. It simply means that each new audience and each new speech calls for fresh thought about the demographic properties that are important in the particular situation. It simply means the habitual cultivation of the art of audience analysis. Very often, just a few moments of thought and reflection from this general perspective will be enough to suggest intelligent choices.

Motive analysis

Another popular way of analyzing listeners is to study the various motive forces that are operative in any audience. It certainly seems only natural that students of speech communication should be interested in motives and the related notions of needs and drives, since these appear to be the forces which compel human beings to act. An understanding of them should therefore be of value to speakers who want to influence the thoughts, attitudes, and behavior of their audience.

Generally, an emphasis on motive appeals indicates an approach to communication that is more concerned with persuading listeners than informing them, and it is an ancient approach. To show how long it has been around, we'll return to the section of Aristotle's *Rhetoric* that we cited in connection with demographic analysis. Most interested in persuasion, Aristotle combined two modes—demographic and motive analysis—and he directed much of his speculation to emotional appeals. In this connection, he described the character of the young, saying, among other things:

> They think they know everything, and are always quite sure about it; this, in fact, is why they overdo everything. If they do wrong to others, it is because they mean to insult them, not to do them actual harm. They are ready to pity others, because they think every one an honest man, or anyhow better than he is: they judge their neighbour by their own harmless natures, and so cannot think he deserves to be treated in that way. They are fond of fun and therefore witty, wit being well-bred insolence.

Interestingly, these character sketches were lifted by the Roman poet Horace and became the basis for stock characters in drama, but Aristotle's purpose was to ascertain the psychological make-up of listeners. Perhaps it is only fair to the young to include a fragment from one of his other descriptions:

> The character of elderly men—men who are past their prime—may be said to be formed for the most part of elements that are the contrary of all these [the young]. They have lived many years; they have often been taken in, and often made mistakes; and life on the whole is a bad business. The result is that they are sure about nothing and *under-do* everything. They "think," but they never "know"; and because of their hesitation they always add a "possibly" or a "perhaps," putting everything this way and nothing positively. They are cynical; that is, they tend to put the worse construction on everything.

Although these descriptions became prescriptions for actors in their interpretation of roles, the orientation to motive appeals is plain. If people do "put the worse construction on everything," then you have to be alert to that fact as a speaker. The basic idea is this: If you can link the goals and purposes of your speech to the motives and needs of your audience, you can increase your effectiveness as a speaker.

Knowing your subject, you ordinarily can think of ways to relate your materials to the motives of your listeners. Depending upon what appear to be the important needs or motives, a speech can be developed in a variety of ways. Suppose you want to attract your listeners to the idea of bicycle riding. A health motive might appeal to some listeners ("Exercise is good for you"); others might be attracted by convenience reasons ("They're easier to park"); others by an appeal to economy ("It certainly is cheaper than driving"); and still others by social reasons ("Your kind of people are riding bikes"). The parenthetical expressions may seem gross, but many attempts to create needs or to capitalize on existing ones—such as so many television commercials and newspaper ads—are anything but subtle.

*

Try a survey of some television advertising, with an eye to its motive appeals. You could concentrate on kinds of products—automobiles, household appliances, or furniture, for example. The commercials for any one kind of item will vary in motive appeal, but you are likely to find some similarities within each type. The differences within types can be as instructive as the similarities, and you might find it interesting, too, to check across types for similar appeals. From the point of view of those who made the commercials, what motives seem basic to all humans? Which seem culturally acquired?

*

If you consider all the possible motivational links you can use in a given situation, you should come up with some clues for developing a particular speech for a particular situation. Nevertheless, the value of such analysis is mainly for the *kinds* of approach that might be effective; situations, subjects, and audiences differ so much that hard and fast rules can be misleading. There are no certainties here, any more than there are in demographic profiles. Psychologists have produced long and impressive lists of human motives, lists which turn up in discussions of public speaking, but the research on motivation reveals no constant, universal conclusions about motives that can be invariably applied by students of speech communication. People and situations are too various. However, motive analysis, alone or combined with demographic analysis, can be extremely useful. They both illustrate the importance of knowing and caring in an audience, and they both can help you appreciate the images your listeners have and their valuations of those images.

Range-of-receptivity analysis

Certainly it is impossible to categorize knowing and caring neatly, separating them into distinct and different compartments. Even seemingly neutral symbols can be freighted emotionally—perhaps you remember a mathematics teacher who got obvious aesthetic satisfaction from the way in which an equation worked out on the blackboard,

M. I have two examples appropriate to this section. Several years ago, in an introductory communication course at the University of Florida, a student decided to make a three-minute informational speech about the most rudimentary aspects of water-skiing. After the speech, the discussion revealed that everyone in the thirty-person audience had water-skied before, and that most of the audience skied with some regularity.

The second example took place at a meeting of parents whose sixth-grade children were going to participate in an "outdoor education" program, a week of camping that was integrated into the curriculum. After welcoming the parents, the coordinator immediately explained the care with which the program had been developed, and the first thing he mentioned was insurance coverage. Not only did he mention it, he went into specifics, describing the dollar value assigned for the loss of one leg, one arm, one arm and one leg, two legs, and so on through all the gruesome possibilities. Sitting near the back of the room, I could see people begin to squirm, and I could hardly blame them because I was doing the same. Our youngest son was one of those sixth-graders!

despite the fact that he had worked through the same problem with countless other classes. In truth, knowing and caring are direct functions of each other, and they often develop together. Someone who knows may start to care more, and someone who cares may start to learn more.

But no matter how inextricably knowing and caring are interwoven, they can help you "locate" your audience in relation to your subject. We think that the locating will be simplified if you think of these two cognitive and emotive dimensions as intersecting somewhere in a *range of receptivity*. This term includes every possible audience response to a message—responses that are influenced by the knowledge listeners have acquired and the attitudes they have developed toward a topic. To talk of "locating" potential responses within the total range of receptivity suggests spatial relationships, and we think the spatial notion is a useful approach.

As an illustration of locating audience response, let's use a subject that seems most appropriate—barbed wire. The topic of barbed wire probably finds most of us located in a rather central and neutral position. We have some vague familiarity with it, but we don't care all that much. Most audiences, then, can probably be moved from this relatively neutral location without much difficulty. For example, you should find most people receptive to a speech that takes them to greater understanding, and an obvious possibility is a speech treating the role that barbed wire played in the American West during the nineteenth century.

Some audiences, however, would not be neutral, and they would be located elsewhere. Odd hobby though it seems, there are people who collect barbed wire, for instance. These people have a considerable store of knowledge, not only about the historical role of barbed wire, but about its manufacture and production as well. And that they care is demonstrated clearly by the prices they are willing to pay for samples of old wire. At still another location in the broad range of audience response would be those ranchers today who need barbed wire and find supplies dwindling while prices spiral upward. What they know and the nature of their caring would intersect at yet another place, with many of them doubtless highly impatient with any talk of barbed wire in the days of the Old West. What we are trying to suggest here is that you, as a speaker, should determine where your listeners are located before you decide where you can relocate them.

The notion of space in reference to ideas is very old, and it is reflected over and over again in our language. "Where does she stand on that issue?" "What position should we take?" "They were on solid ground with that argument." "He's way out in left field." You have heard or used such expressions, just as you have heard or used "I couldn't tell where she was coming from," or "His head was in a funny place," or "I didn't know where he was at"—all referring to communication, not geography. Our position (note the word) is that this spatial notion is natural and useful—as natural and useful as the idea of movement that frequently is involved in such usages. Not only do "message" and "epistle" come from words that mean "to send," but action is suggested in some of the expressions above, and "grasp," "lead," "follow," "press," "hold," and "guide" are only a few of the words commonly used in connection with mental activity and communication. Most appropriate, we think. The notion of movement goes hand in hand with the location metaphor, implying that if the location of the mind is to be altered, then the place must first be determined.

The young man who talked to experienced water-skiers erred because he failed to determine how much his listeners knew. He failed to locate them in relation to their prior experience. Their enthusiasm for the subject differed, no doubt, but that was beside the point when he told them what they already knew too well. On the other hand, the parents of the sixth-graders learned more than they wanted to know about the details of the insurance policy. Concerned about their children, they would have been satisfied to hear that an insurance policy was in effect. Concerned about their children, they did not need to have that concern intensified by gruesome possibilities. They were moved, it is true, but not in a direction that was productive to the ultimate goals of the speaker.

Knowing and caring are the crucial determinants of audience

location, so that all the other questions you ask about an audience will eventually center on finding out how much they know and how much they care. Sex, age, educational background, or any other factor in analysis is useful only insofar as it helps you know those clusters of knowledge and attitude that enable you to proceed intelligently in planning for your speech. We don't mean to suggest that any group of people will be entirely homogeneous in knowledge and attitude, nor that they can be located with pin-point precision. Furthermore it is not simply a matter of deciding whether the audience is favorable, neutral, or antagonistic.

POLAR RESPONSES

The extremes of response are clear enough: there are messages we like to receive and those that we don't. That's why we change channels on the television and stations on the radio. And when you have finished an examination, knowing how well you have done, aren't you still pleased with the A marked on the top of the paper when it is returned? But what if a C appears when you expected an A? And have you ever waited for the message that is the grade, fearful that you have not done well but hopeful that you have been lucky? Such reactions fall on a continuum running from eagerness through apathy to resistance, but for the moment we will restrict the discussion to the extremes, to the polar responses.

Since your first speech assignments may encourage you to avoid polarity, it might seem that the areas of neutrality would make the best point of departure, but we believe the extremes give us the best grasp on the subject. In the first place, these responses are the most fascinating. Though they may demonstrate human frailty and weakness, though they may show that all of us are noodles and ninnies at one time or another, extreme reactions emphasize the active nature of the receiving mind in the communicative process. Furthermore, the activity of the mind in receiving messages has lent itself to study; social psychologists and others have made considerable headway in delineating its components, particularly in regard to the ways in which we resist communication. Finally, discussion of the extremes will pave the way for a discussion of the myriad but more subtle possibilities that lie between.

Much of the research in the area of extreme response is comparatively recent, but the basic ideas are far from novel. Richard Whately, an Irish clergyman of the nineteenth century who was keenly interested in communication and who wrote a book called *Elements of Rhetoric*, remarked in an annotation to one of Francis Bacon's essays:

> It may be noticed here that the effect produced by any writing or speech of an argumentative character, on any subjects on which diversity of opinion prevails, may be compared—supposing the argument to be of any weight—to the effects of a fire-engine on a conflagration. That portion of the water which falls on solid stone walls, is poured out where it is not needed. That, again, which falls on blazing beams and rafters, is cast off in volumes of hissing steam, and will seldom avail to quench the fire. But that which is poured on woodwork that is just beginning to kindle, might stop the burning; and that which wets the rafters not yet ignited, but in danger, may save them from catching fire. Even so, those who already concur with the writer as to some point, will feel gratified with, and perhaps bestow high commendation on an able defence of opinions they already held; and those, again, who have fully made up their minds on the opposite side, are more likely to be displeased than to be convinced. But both of these parties are left nearly in the same mind as before. Those, however, who are in a hesitating and doubtful state, may very likely be decided by forcible arguments. And those who have not hitherto considered the subject, may be induced to adopt opinions which they find supported by the strongest reasons. But the readiest and warmest approbation a writer meets with, will usually be from those whom he has *not* convinced, because they were convinced already. And the effect the most important and the most difficult to be produced, he will usually, when he does produce it, hear the least of. Those whom

he may have induced to reconsider, and gradually to alter, previously fixed opinions, are not likely, for a time at least, to be very forward in proclaiming the change.

It is possible to quibble with some of this account, but Whately was speculating over a century ago, and it is a tribute to his analysis that it is substantially correct.

Audience readiness

So let's begin with eagerness to receive a message, with those happy to "bestow high commendation on an able defence of opinions they already held." In fact, this is an understatement because people some-times will bestow that commendation without either having read or heard the message. For them, just to know it exists is to support it. A classic example of this phenomenon occurred on November 3, 1969, when President Nixon appeared on television to discuss the Vietnam War. On the following day, newspapers carried an Associated Press dispatch reporting that congratulatory telegrams began arriving at the White House before the President's television appearance, and before the text of the speech had been released. Partisan politics is responsible for such a response, and most of us react similarly at one time or another.

However, the eagerness to receive a message can be illustrated in less volatile contexts. The speech "Acres of Diamonds," mentioned earlier, is a case in point. We quoted Conwell's purpose, his thesis that people have the opportunity to make more of themselves than they do. This was something people were eager to hear. Touring the country in a time of economic and social turmoil and in a time when Social Darwinism made survival of the fittest applicable to all facets of life, Conwell offered reassurance. He told his listeners that "the foundation principles of business success and the foundation princi-ples of Christianity itself are both the same," and he told them, "You ought to make money. Money is power. Think how much good you could do if you had money now. Money is power and it ought to be in the hands of good men. It would be in the hands of good men if we complied with the Scripture teachings."

Giving example after example of financial success, he insisted that "no man has the right to go into business and not make money. It is a crime to go into business and lose money, because it is a curse to the rest of the community." And he wrapped all this in the flag of patriotism, saying,

> Never in the history of God's government of mankind was there a nation stepping upward more certainly toward all that is grand and beautiful and true than is the nation of America today. Let the poli-

ticians say what they will for personal greed, let them declaim with all their powers, and try to burden the people, you and I know that whichever way the elections go, the American people are not dead, and the nation will not be destroyed.

It would be terribly simple-minded to conclude that Conwell achieved his remarkable success merely because he told people what they needed to hear. Nevertheless, audiences did attend because they knew they would carry away some inspiration, some greater hope for a brighter day.

Audience resistance

The reference to "Acres of Diamonds" serves, paradoxically, as a transition to the other extreme—to the idea of resistance to messages. Many people who went to hear Conwell went because they were eager to expose themselves to his message. They enthusiastically participated in the communication process and helped make it a success for him. On the other hand, we are all expert in avoiding messages that we do not want to hear. On that basis, it is safe to assume that liberals are not inclined to subscribe to the *National Review,* nor conservatives to the *New Republic;* atheists don't go to church much, and members of the American Legion can't be counted on to attend Communist Party rallies. Too much shock for the images!

But while we are all expert at avoiding the possibility of exposure to unwanted messages, we are also skilled at shunting them aside. We can all click off the processing equipment, though retina and eardrum continue to function, and we are so adroit in this regard that we can appear to be attending as we engage in avoidance. This "hearing but not listening" is really no different from physical avoidance, and it is something that we all engage in, for a variety of reasons. There are times when we simply cannot concentrate and keep drifting away. This may well happen to you in the speech class on those days when you give a speech; somehow, you'll find that it is difficult to concentrate on the speakers who precede you! Then there are the times when we intentionally tune out a message, times when we are part of a captive audience or when we couldn't care less about what we are hearing. Whatever the reason, we may continue to give the impression that we are courteous, willing listeners, all the while letting our minds drift and wander to more interesting thoughts and ideas.

We all have minds that are tremendously sophisticated in resisting messages, and merely drifting away is perhaps the simplest method. The available means of resistance—the ways in which we are all part of an "obstinate audience," as Raymond Bauer so aptly put it—are many. Resisting a message is a perfectly natural aspect of the communication process. In fact, it is resistance to messages that gives some stability to our lives. How unstable life would be if we were influenced by every message sent our way! We would be tossed on the breeze of whimsy like dandelion seed in a high wind, with no control available to us. So if the following list of the ways in which we all resist messages seems to make the speaker's task a rough one, be happy that you have such capability in your being.

Counterarguing. This technique is deliberately cultivated in formal debate and in parliamentary procedure where one speaker responds directly to the argument of another. We all often use a less formal version in conversations or discussions, challenging or disagreeing with something that has been said. We also respond aloud to visual messages; we may read part of an editorial to a friend before pointing out its weaknesses, and almost everyone makes some disparaging remark about a television commercial while it is in progress. Watching television, we may also counterargue aloud while a politician is making a speech, but, if we are members of a live audience, an audible response would be in bad taste. In such situations social pressure usually forbids members of the audience to heckle a speaker. The social norms tend to insist that speakers be given their time, and most counterargument is therefore covert. But whether overtly or covertly, as listeners we may reject a message for a variety of reasons. We may tell ourselves that the speaker's information is out of date, incomplete, a violation of common sense, or in conflict with the ideas of the truly significant authorities in the field. The precise nature of the counterargument is not important; what *is* important is that we all ward off threats to our public and private images by this method.

*

You need not be chagrined, however, at the thought that listeners may counterargue. This mode of resistance means that you should know what you are talking about and know how well informed your audience is. A mastery of the subject will help you know where you can expect counterargument and suggest ways in which you might anticipate. No message can prevent extremely irrational counters, but a strong argument often will earn respect, even from some who might be on the other side.

*

Derogating the source. Another common way in which we ward off threats to our image is to reject the speaker's influence by rejecting the speaker as a person. This kind of resistance may have little or nothing to do with the merits of the case, but we can resist by deciding that a speaker or writer is stupid or dishonest—or both. In this connection, you probably have watched speakers on television who were assailed as untrustworthy scoundrels who couldn't possibly be on the right side of any issue. And you may have heard an argument dismissed because of the clothing or appearance of the speaker. On that irrational basis, many of us would have rejected Abraham Lincoln, who was physically most unimpressive.

Yet derogation of a speaker is not necessarily an irrational response. We all know from experience that it is entirely legitimate to reject a speaker's proposal if we suspect his or her competence. We all have learned that some people have marvelous gaps in their credibility, and if some speakers strike us as being generally incompetent and untrustworthy, then we have a right to suspect their arguments, or at least to take them with a grain of salt.

*

If someone doesn't like the way you look, you can't do much about it, but you can make your message work for you in ways that will make it more difficult for a listener to derogate you as a source. If you are competent, if you can be trusted, and if you can convey these qualities to your audience, you stand a greater chance of being effective against this latter kind of resistance. We'll be paying particular attention to these traits in Chapter 10. Meanwhile, though, you might consider what it is that makes for competence and trustworthiness in a speaker.

*

Social support. If the grain of salt won't do, social reinforcement may. As we noted in Chapter 2, society plays a dominant role in the creation of our images. Consequently, one of the most significant forces in anchoring us to a position is the confirmation we get from others, the reinforcement and support that other people supply. One of the best-established notions in the social sciences is that our beliefs, attitudes, and behavior are socially derived. Peer groups, respected authorities, and others hold up our positions as root systems maintain a tree, and the system of social support can deter an attempt to change us. When such an attempt is made, we may resist change via social support. During a speech, we may check for physical clues from our friends, noting whether they are reacting favorably or "sitting on their hands," and we may exchange knowing glances or whisper to those close by. This reinforcement may be enough, but the challenge to our beliefs may be so strong that we will need to seek social confirmation from our peers after the communication is over. The confirmation and support we receive from others will help counteract the pressure to change the image.

*

Despite any examples of hostility from audiences, most speakers can expect that the audience will at least pretend to hear them out, and it is seldom that you will meet with overt social resistance to any speech that you give. Your listeners' search for social support is more likely to come after the speech, but the time for their resistance is during the speech. Perhaps the best way for you to deal with this is to consider what social anchors seem to predominate in the audience. If you can locate some of the most important and relate your message to them, you may go far toward blunting some of the resistance that might otherwise emerge.

*

But suppose that the techniques described so far are not enough. Many times a speaker's appeal will have such an impact on us that we will at least temporarily be compelled to adjust our image in some way—even if only temporarily—so as to avoid making a larger change. Two rather common means of resistance which involve this kind of adjustment are (1) bolstering an insecure part of the image, and (2) devaluating the importance of the issue. Although these are different, they are similar in that an adjustment of the image takes place.

Bolstering the image. When a speaker exerts pressure on us to change, we may beef up (or bolster) the basis for our beliefs and behavior. If we smoke, for example, despite the fact that we are aware of the connection between smoking and lung cancer, we can still bolster our image so that we can go on smoking. We may rehearse for ourselves all the reasons why we should continue to smoke: smoking helps to relieve tension, smoking helps keep weight down, and, besides, the odds against getting lung cancer are in our favor. By amplifying or enumerating reasons for our present behavior, we make an adjustment in our image, bolstering it in such a way that we can avoid making any drastic and unwelcome change—even though that change might add twenty years to our lives.

Devaluating the issue. This tactic involves downgrading the importance that we assign to an issue on which a speaker pressures us to change. Faced by an insurance salesman and agreeing with his line of argument, you could resist by deciding that while insurance definitely was worthwhile for a lot of people, it simply isn't necessary for you right now. After all, you have no family to provide for, no huge debts to cover, a long life ahead of you; so you may be impressed, but you still conclude that life insurance is not for you at this moment. Again, a relatively minor adjustment in the image can defer or eliminate the need for a drastic change in behavior.

*

Think of ways in which your listeners might either bolster their images or devaluate the importance of the issue in response to a particular speech you are preparing. By anticipating these things, you will be in a better position to make your message one that will minimize both forms of resistance. Can you think of a way to make bolstering impossible? Can you think of a way to make it very difficult for your listeners to devalue the issue?

*

Differentiating. Given a general category of things or events, differentiating is the drawing of finer distinctions within the category. Often it can be seen in the way words or terms are defined. For example, many people who are against relaxing the laws on marijuana do not feel that their martinis fall into the category of "drugs." On the other hand, many of the people who grumble about the "materialism" of the present day clearly do not include expensive leather jackets or stereo equipment in that term. Richard Whately, whom we quoted earlier, gives us a delightful example of differentiating; in the sixth edition of his *Bacon's Essays,* he comments on a review of an earlier edition:

> My Annotations were, by one of the reviewers, described as *"slipshod gossip."* This description, though not designed to be complimentary, is one which perhaps there is no reason to complain of. By "gossip" is probably meant, discussions not of deep metaphysical questions, but of the concerns of every-day-life, such as men are accustomed to converse about: and by a "slipshod" style, language simple, perspicuous, and homely, without any attempt at high-flown declamation. Now all this is precisely what I have aimed at.

Like the other means of resistance, differentiating is a familiar technique, and, also like the others, it may or may not meet the standards of logic. Whether logical or not, what this method generally amounts to is that the listener concedes some specific instance but will not accept the larger more encompassing issue. By differentiating, we can leave our image as we want it to be.

*

Any time you find yourself making a speech that involves general issues or trends, you may be vulnerable to resistance through differentiation. What you have to do is figure out what path the differentiation will take and develop arguments to show that any instance your listeners might cite is consistent with the general case. Careful definition will also help you prevent some uses of differentiation.

*

Transcending the issue. A listener may be able to resist persuasion by finding a higher or more encompassing reason for maintaining his present position. This response can be illustrated with an example from the current controversy over the busing of school children to achieve racial integration. Attempts to change our attitude and perhaps our voting behavior if we are listeners who favor busing could run as follows: busing violates the rights of the children, deprives parents of the right to base their residence on the quality of schools, destroys the concept of the neighborhood school, and adds tremendously to the tax burden. We might grant some or all of these points and still maintain our original position. We could transcend the issue by contending that the social and material costs of busing are not as great as the costs of segregation, and that integration is a goal to be pursued in spite of any immediate costs.

Historically, the proponents of slavery transcended the issue in their response to the abolitionists. When the abolitionists charged that slavery was a social and moral evil, the economic motive of those who favored slavery seemed a shallow argument. John C. Calhoun therefore responded in his speech "On the Reception of the Abolition Petitions" in 1837:

> But I take the higher ground. I hold that in the present state of civilization, where two races of different origin—distinguished by color and other physical differences, as well as intellectual—are brought together, the relations now existing in the slaveholding States between the two, is, instead of an evil, a good—a positive good.

This position retained its vitality for a long time; twenty years after Calhoun spoke, the Senate heard James Hammond reiterate the argument in his Mud-Sill speech. The long life of this argument indicates something of the importance that transcending the issue can have in resisting persuasion. This form of resistance probably is not as common as others, but it may be especially potent; if listeners are forced to "take the higher ground," they may well assume a position that is very difficult to shake and change.

*

As a speaker, one of the best ways for you to minimize the tactic of transcending the issue is to make the immediate case vivid and urgent. That doesn't mean you can make the lower ground appear the higher; it simply means that you should make the best argument possible. In that regard, you should be well aware of what ground any listener might take, and you might find that a comparison with that ground is your best line of argument. At times, too, you will find it possible to link your message with other transcendent issues by tying your speech to some generally important and accepted value or institution in our culture.

*

We have listed the more common means by which listeners can resist influence efforts from speakers. These are tactics we all use at one time or another, and it shouldn't be difficult for you to recall when you have used one or more of them yourself. Of course, we don't use all of them all of the time, but all are generally available, and most of us learn to rely on a certain few, in preference to others, that have served us well in the past and are comfortable for us to use. In a very real sense, we develop a style of resisting in the same way that it can be said we develop a style of language, or develop a style in other aspects of our lives. No doubt you know people who seem always to be the persistent counterarguers, who cling to their positions no matter how strong the opposition, and no matter how much their position may appear to be at odds with the persuasive force of reality.

There is some of that in all of us, and as we noted earlier, resistance efforts are more pronounced when the consequence of a change involves some relatively important element in a listener's image, or when the change would lead to some significant reorganization of the image. Research in persuasion seems quite clear in regard to this point, and it also confirms a common sense understanding. Bauer phrases the notion as well as anyone when he says that a listener's "resistance to persuasion probably increases in proportion to the efforts made to persuade him against his own perceived interest." As resistance increases, the listener may turn to a variety of tactics in responding to a single communication. A listener who favors capital punishment, for example, might begin counterarguing internally while hearing someone attack the issues of justice and deterrence, but if the force of the speaker's arguments is strong enough, the listener might maintain his or her position through differentiating, by admitting that capital punishment should be made more selective.

You have also doubtless encountered people who will clutch frantically for one strand of support after another in an attempt to find *some* way of sustaining their position, and the clutching may become desperate when the speaker methodically cuts every strand, one after the other. Even then these people can resist change, but without any visible means of support, they may have to suffer the consequences of looking a bit foolish. (As a matter of fact, almost all of us have been there at one time or another.)

We have seen that listeners use a variety of tactics to resist persuasion, and—whether rationally or irrationally—they use these tactics to avoid being influenced by the efforts of speakers and other communicators. But an equally important notion is present in these facts: listeners are active. Listeners are not passive targets like the little ducks in the shooting gallery or the bull's-eye at the end of the archery

V. One of the strongest sales pitches I ever heard came from a freezer-plan salesman as we sat at my kitchen table one evening. Taking my weekly food budget, he proceeded to show me reasonably and logically that the same budget would permit my family to eat more food, to eat better food, and *at the same time* to make payments on the large freezer his company would happily place in my home. I couldn't argue with the economics because I had furnished the budget figures and watched him work out the details to the penny—he was a whiz with small figures. Obviously a skilled mathematician, he also had an impressive folder of documents testifying to his authority and credibility, so I could not attack him as an unreliable source. And he had a response of some kind for every other defense I tried. Nevertheless, when he finally pushed the contract across the table, I told him I couldn't sign. He seemed stunned for a moment, and then he wanted an explanation. With a fair amount of embarrassment, I sighed and said, "I don't know—I guess I'm just irrational." To my great relief, it was the one reply he wasn't prepared to cope with.

range. Listeners are living, feeling, thinking, acting beings, and they have a significant piece of the action in the communication process. We all know that, don't we? But don't we also see speakers every day in lecture halls, classrooms, meeting places, and on television acting as though they were not aware of the point? No doubt there are audiences so eager and so uncritical that anything the speaker says will be greeted with roars of approval—just watch the televised broadcasts from the next national political convention for a demonstration. Furthermore, we have seen that a great deal of communication takes place in a generally cooperative atmosphere. Think how surprising it would be if you were to ask someone what time it was, and the response was "Go to hell!" Surely our humanity makes us willing listeners much of the time, so we do not mean to suggest that the speaker always encounters resistance or even reluctance. But we do want to reemphasize the potential responses of listeners within the range of receptivity are active and not passive. In Chapters 5 and 6, we'll return to the effects we introduced in Chapter 3, expanding this idea of the active listener and relating it to specific speaking tasks. But first, we ask you to read the four speeches that follow from the perspective of what we have said so far about the nature and uses of communication, listener effects, and audience analysis.

SUGGESTED READINGS

Raymond A. Bauer, "The Obstinate Audience: The Influence Process from the Point of View of Social Communication," *American Psychologist* 19, No. 5 (May, 1964), 319-328.

Theodore Clevenger, Jr., *Audience Analysis* (New York, 1966). This is a pleasantly unpretentious book, but it is also very thorough, with especially useful material on the measurement of listeners' responses.

Paul D. Holtzman, *The Psychology of Speakers' Audiences* (Glenview, Ill., 1970). As the title indicates, the discussion places primary emphasis on the role of the audience in the communication process, and much of the book's material extends our commentary.

four speeches

PREVIEW: PART 2

Part 2 consists of four speeches; the texts are:

"My Grandfather" (1968)	Marilyn Hayashi Rye
"Television News Coverage" (1969)	Spiro T. Agnew
"Shoes" (1955)	William Boyd
"The Cooper Institute Address" (1860)	Abraham Lincoln

The first speech is a statement by a college student about Japanese relocation during World War II; the second is a challenge to the major television networks about their handling of the news; the third is a very positive treatment of the role that life insurance can play; and the fourth is a speech that was part of a campaign to win a presidential nomination. Each of the speeches is highly individualistic, but all of us can learn much from the responses these four speakers made to four different situations.

We chose these particular speeches to serve a wide variety of illustrative purposes, and that is why we introduce them at this point. In subsequent chapters, we will include extended quotations from some of the speeches, but for the most part we will simply allude to them. We do not expect you to read them so closely that any passing reference will be immediately intelligible, but the rest of the book does rest on the assumption that you will have given these speeches more than a passing glance. In truth, anything more than a cursory examination should help you go beyond anything we can do in using these speeches to illuminate various aspects of public speaking. We use them, but we necessarily use them in limited fashion, and you should find it easy to amplify what we have to say.

Whether it be a matter of audience analysis, pattern of organization, evidence adduced, or minute stylistic considerations, we cannot begin to exhaust the possibilities in our discussion of the specific examples to be found in these speech texts. As an intelligent human being, you will perceive possibilities that we do not mention, and—more important, perhaps—that have not even occurred to us.

All four speeches show human beings being human beings who happen to be making a speech. We like all our examples. We think they show speakers achieving the effects they set out to produce, and we are convinced that the texts can help you improve your own communication skills.

A final suggestion about reading the speeches: it would be helpful for you to read at least some of the passages aloud. In different ways, all the speeches reveal that one human being is speaking to others face to face, and reading aloud will give you a better awareness of this immediacy. In addition, you may acquire a sharper appreciation of the way the ideas develop, the way they fit together, and the way they build in the speaking situation.

"MY GRANDFATHER"

MARILYN HAYASHI RYE

Marilyn Hayashi Rye was a sophomore at the University of California at Davis when she presented this speech in an introductory public speaking class. It was an extemporaneous speech, which she delivered a second time as part of a videotape exercise. She then wrote the manuscript reprinted below, trying to keep the written version as close as possible to the original extemporaneous speech. This happens to be one speech in a series that she gave on a general topic, but it stands well by itself. Since it is short, and since it is the kind of speech you might well hear in a classroom situation, we feel no need for further explanation.

In 1883, a man named Hirokichi Hayashi sailed from Fukuoka, Japan to America. Perhaps he had heard that the opportunities for success were far more abundant in America than in Japan. Perhaps he had heard that the streets were paved with gold or that the Golden Gate Bridge was really made of gold. But for some reason, he came. When he arrived in California, he settled in Alameda where he started a little nursery. He grew rose bushes, azaleas, and seasonal plants. By 1905, he was rich enough to afford on of the greatest personal luxuries for a Japanese immigrant—he sent for a picture bride.

In 1910, my father was born. By this time, my grandfather had a nursery in Oakland. In Oakland, my father grew up and went to school. Now this may not seem to be too remarkable a statement, except that in San Francisco, in 1906, a measure was passed by the school board which prohibited all Japanese from attending public schools. This attempt to keep foreign influences away from American children was initiated by District Attorney Abe Ruef and Mayor Eugene Schmitz. They were under indictment at the time for graft and corruption, and they wanted to draw attention away from themselves. Of the measure, President Theodore Roosevelt said, "Those infernal fools in California! Insult the Japanese, and in case of war, it will be the nation as a whole who will have to pay."

But back to my grandfather. An aerial photograph of his nursery in 1925 showed that it covered three blocks of Oakland. It was about a mile away from what is now the Oakland Coliseum. My grandfather owned this land. Now that may not seem to be too remarkable a statement, but in 1920, the California Legislature passed a bill which stated that no Japanese immigrant could own or lease land for more than three years, or hold more than 49 percent stock in any land. Japanese got around this law by buying land in their children's names, but the legislature amended the 1920 land law in 1923. It stated that no Japanese alien could own or lease agricultural land at all, and that no Japanese alien could act as the guardian of minor children.

You may be thinking, "Why didn't your grandfather become a citizen?" Well, he couldn't. Part of the Gentlemen's Agreement of 1908 stated that no Mongolian, Polynesian, or race native to the Western Hemisphere was eligible to become naturalized. The Gentlemen's Agreement also limited immigration of Japanese to those who were the parents, children, or spouses of American residents, and to those who had been in America before. But, in 1908, there were very few Japanese in America, so the immigration of Japanese was severely limited.

But my grandfather was a lucky man. He had come to America before the Gentlemen's Agreement. He had bought his land before the land laws of 1920 and 1923. He managed to run a prosperous business and to send his two sons to fine schools. In fact, my father graduated from the University of California at Davis, in 1933. But in 1942, along with 127,000 other Japanese, my grandfather was subjected to one of the greatest forms of racial injustice that ever happened in America. His land was sold for ten cents on the dollar, and he was herded into a concentration camp in the middle of Utah. In a space 20 by 25 feet, he had to live with his family for four years, and his family included my grandfather, grandmother, father, mother, uncle, two brothers, and a little baby brother who was born there. My grandfather watched his wife receive careless hospital treatment in the prison hospital and remain crippled for the rest of her life. And the biggest irony happened when my uncle joined the United States Army and left for Europe. It must have been a very moving scene to see him in his army uniform waving good-bye to his family who were behind barbed wire fences being guarded by the United States Army.

After the war, my grandfather went back to Oakland where he found that the original three blocks of land had shrunk to a narrow strip down the middle of one block. In 1964, he died at the age of 96. He never became a citizen because before the war he couldn't, and after the war he felt he was too old. But he never lost his faith in the United States that he had heard of in Japan. He had heard the legends of freedom and truth and justice. He had plenty of reasons for doubt, but he never did.

Those barbed wire fences of twenty-five years ago are gone now. I imagine that men with wire cutters went up to the fences and just cut them down. However, there are still people behind barricades. They are behind these barriers because they happen to be of a different color, or because they happen to be poor, or because they happen to be Indian. The barriers aren't physical. You can't see or touch them. But, they do exist. They exist in people's minds as a tangled mass of prejudice. The only wirecutters that will work on this kind of barbed wire is the wirecutter of your conscience. How many of us can honestly say that we have no masses of wire in our minds, and that we have never said or done anything to put the wire in a child's mind? How many of us can honestly say that we let our wirecutter do its work?

TELEVISION NEWS COVERAGE

SPIRO T. AGNEW

Later events have removed Spiro Agnew from the national spotlight, of course, but while he was Vice President he caused considerable furor by his attacks on the news media. At Des Moines, he lashed out at television; a week later in Montgomery, Alabama, he returned to the same general theme and included both television and the press in his indictment. The debate was quite lively for a few months—evidence, as we will point out later, that Agnew had achieved some significant effects. In anticipation of that discussion, you might keep in mind the many and different audiences that were available to Agnew for the Des Moines speech that we reprint, a speech that was televised nationwide.

The debate is less heated now, but some of its issues keep bubbling up regularly. Similar issues have in fact been argued for decades—since the advent of radio and the Federal Communications Commission—and the role of television assures that they will continue to be debated. Whether you agree or disagree with Agnew's position, you will find that his ideas are current. And it might be profitable for you to give some thought as to *why* you agree or disagree.

Tonight I want to discuss the importance of the television news medium to the American people. No nation depends more on the intelligent judgment of its citizens. No medium has a more profound influence over public opinion. Nowhere in our system are there fewer checks on vast power. So, nowhere should there be more conscientious responsibility exercised than by the news media. The question is, Are we demanding enough of our television news presentations? And are the men of this medium demanding enough of themselves?

Monday night a week ago, President Nixon delivered the most important address of his Administration, one of the most important of our decade. His subject was Vietnam. His hope was to rally the American people to see the conflict through to a lasting and just peace in the Pacific. For 32 minutes, he reasoned with a nation that has suffered almost a third of a million casualties in the longest war in its history.

When the President completed his address—an address, incidentally, that he spent weeks in the preparation of—

his words and policies were subjected to instant analysis
and querulous criticism. The audience of 70 million
Americans gathered to hear the President of the United
States was inherited by a small band of network
commentators and self-appointed analysts, the majority
of whom expressed in one way or another their hostility
to what he had to say.

It was obvious that their minds were made up in
advance. Those who recall the fumbling and groping that
followed President Johnson's dramatic disclosure of his
intention not to seek another term have seen these men
in a genuine state of nonpreparedness. This was not it.

One commentator twice contradicted the President's
statement about the exchange of correspondence with Ho
Chi Minh. Another challenged the President's abilities
as a politician. A third asserted that the President was
following a Pentagon line. Others, by the expression on
their faces, the tone of their questions and the sarcasm
of their responses, made clear their sharp disapproval.

To guarantee in advance that the President's plea for
national unity would be challenged, one network trotted
out Averell Harriman for the occasion. Throughout the
President's message, he waited in the wings. When the
President concluded, Mr. Harriman recited perfectly. He
attacked the Thieu Government as unrepresentative; he
criticized the President's speech for various
deficiencies; he twice issued a call to the Senate
Foreign Relations Committee to debate Vietnam once again;
he stated his belief that the Vietcong or North
Vietnamese did not really want military take-over of
South Vietnam; and he told a little anecdote about a
"very, very responsible" fellow he had met in the North
Vietnamese delegation.

All in all, Mr. Harriman offered a broad range of
gratuitous advice challenging and contradicting the
policies outlined by the President of the United States.
Where the President had issued a call for unity, Mr.
Harriman was encouraging the country not to listen to
him.

A word about Mr. Harriman. For 10 months he was
America's chief negotiator at the Paris peace talks—a
period in which the United States swapped some of the
greatest military concessions in the history of warfare
for an enemy agreement on the shape of the bargaining
table. Like Coleridge's Ancient Mariner, Mr. Harriman
seems to be under some heavy compulsion to justify his

failure to anyone who will listen. And the networks have shown themselves willing to give him all the air time he desires.

Now every American has a right to disagree with the President of the United States and to express publicly that disagreement. But the President of the United States has a right to communicate directly with the people who elected him, and the people of this country have the right to make up their own minds and form their own opinions about a Presidential address without having a President's words and thoughts characterized through the prejudices of hostile critics before they can even be digested.

When Winston Churchill rallied public opinion to stay the course against Hitler's Germany, he didn't have to contend with a gaggle of commentators raising doubts about whether he was reading public opinion right, or whether Britain had the stamina to see the war through.

When President Kennedy rallied the nation in the Cuban missile crisis, his address to the people was not chewed over by a roundtable of critics who disparaged the course of action he'd asked America to follow.

The purpose of my remarks tonight is to focus your attention on this little group of men who not only enjoy a right of instant rebuttal to every Presidential address, but, more importantly, wield a free hand in selecting, presenting and interpreting the great issues in our nation.

First, let's define that power. At least 40 million Americans every night, it's estimated, watch the network news. Seven million of them view A.B.C., the remainder being divided between N.B.C. and C.B.S.

According to Harris polls and other studies, for millions of Americans the networks are the sole source of national and world news. In Will Rogers' observation, what you knew was what you read in the newspaper. Today for growing millions of Americans, it's what they see and hear on their television sets.

Now how is this network news determined? A small group of men, numbering perhaps no more than a dozen anchormen, commentators and executive producers, settle upon the 20 minutes or so of film and commentary that's to reach the public. This selection is made from the 90 to 180 minutes that may be available. Their powers of choice are broad.

They decide what 40 to 50 million Americans will

learn of the day's events in the nation and in the world.

We cannot measure this power and influence by the traditional democratic standards, for these men can create national issues overnight.

They can make or break by their coverage and commentary a moratorium on the war.

They can elevate men from obscurity to national prominence within a week. They can reward some politicians with national exposure and ignore others.

For millions of Americans the network reporter who covers a continuing issue—like the ABM or civil rights— becomes, in effect, the presiding judge in a national trial by jury.

It must be recognized that the networks have made important contributions to the national knowledge— for news, documentaries and specials. They have often used their power constructively and creatively to awaken the public conscience to critical problems. The networks made hunger and black lung disease national issues overnight. The TV networks have done what no other medium could have done in terms of dramatizing the horrors of war. The networks have tackled our most difficult social problems with a directness and an immediacy that's the gift of their medium. They focus the nation's attention on its environmental abuses—on pollution in the Great Lakes and the threatened ecology of the Everglades.

But it was also the networks that elevated Stokely Carmichael and George Lincoln Rockwell from obscurity to national prominence.

Nor is their power confined to the substantive. A raised eyebrow, an inflection of the voice, a caustic remark dropped in the middle of a broadcast can raise doubts in a million minds about the veracity of a public official or the wisdom of a Government policy.

One Federal Communications Commissioner considers the powers of the networks equal to that of local state and Federal Governments all combined. Certainly it represents a concentration of power over American public opinion unknown in history.

Now what do Americans know of the men who wield this power? Of the men who produce and direct the network news, the nation knows practically nothing. Of the commentators, most Americans know little other than that they reflect an urbane and assured presence seemingly well-informed on every important matter.

We do know that to a man these commentators and

producers live and work in the geographical and intellectual confines of Washington, D.C., or New York City, the latter of which James Reston terms the most unrepresentative community in the entire United States.

Both communities bask in their own provincialism, their own parochialism.

We can deduce that these men read the same newspapers. They draw their political and social views from the same sources. Worse, they talk constantly to one another, thereby providing artificial reinforcement to their shared viewpoints.

Do they allow their biases to influence the selection and presentation of the news? David Brinkley states objectivity is impossible to normal human behavior. Rather, he says, we should strive for fairness.

Another anchorman on a network news show contends, and I quote: "You can't expunge all your private convictions just because you sit in a seat like this and a camera starts to stare at you. I think your program has to reflect what your basic feelings are. I'll plead guilty to that."

Less than a week before the 1968 election, this same commentator charged that President Nixon's campaign commitments were no more durable than campaign balloons. He claimed that, were it not for the fear of hostile reaction, Richard Nixon would be giving into, and I quote him exactly, "his natural instinct to smash the enemy with a club or go after him with a meat axe."

Had this slander been made by one political candidate about another, it would have been dismissed by most commentators as a partisan attack. But this attack emanated from the privileged sanctuary of a network studio and therefore had the apparent dignity of an objective statement.

The American people would rightly not tolerate this concentration of power in Government.

Is it not fair and relevant to question its concentration in the hands of a tiny, enclosed fraternity of privileged men elected by no one and enjoying a monopoly sanctioned and licensed by Government?

The views of the majority of this fraternity do not— and I repeat, not—represent the views of America.

That is why such a great gulf existed between how the nation received the President's address and how the networks reviewed it.

Not only did the country receive the President's

address more warmly than the networks, but so also did
the Congress of the United States.

Yesterday, the President was notified that 300
individual Congressmen and 50 Senators of both parties
had endorsed his efforts for peace.

As with other American institutions, perhaps it is
time that the networks were made more responsive to the
views of the nation and more responsible to the people
they serve.

Now I want to make myself perfectly clear. I'm not
asking for Government censorship or any other kind of
censorship. I'm asking whether a form of censorship
already exists when the news that 40 million Americans
receive each night is determined by a handful of men
responsible only to their corporate employers and is
filtered through a handful of commentators who admit to
their own set of biases.

The questions I'm raising here tonight should have
been raised by others long ago. They should have been
raised by those Americans who have traditionally
considered the preservation of freedom of speech and
freedom of the press their special provinces of
responsibility.

They should have been raised by those Americans who
share the view of the late Justice Learned Hand that
right conclusions are more likely to be gathered out of
a multitude of tongues than through any kind of
authoritative selection.

Advocates for the networks have claimed a First
Amendment right to the same unlimited freedoms held by
the great newspapers of America.

(But the situations are not identical. Where *The New
York Times* reaches 800,000 people, N.B.C., reaches 20
times that number on its evening news. [The average
weekday circulation of the *Times* in October was
1,012,367; the average Sunday circulation was 1,523,558.]
Nor can the tremendous impact of seeing television film
and hearing commentary be compared with reading the
printed page.)

A decade ago, before the network news acquired such
dominance over public opinion, Walter Lippman spoke to
the issue. He said there's an essential and radical
difference between television and printing. The three or
four competing television stations control virtually all
that can be received over the air by ordinary television
sets. But besides the mass circulation dailies, there

are weeklies, monthlies, out-of-town newspapers and books. If a man doesn't like his newspaper, he can read another from out of town or wait for a weekly news magazine. It's not ideal, but it's infinitely better than the situation in television.

There if a man doesn't like what the networks are showing, all he can do is turn them off and listen to a phonograph. Networks he stated which are few in number have a virtual monopoly of a whole media of communications.

The newspapers of mass circulation have no monopoly on the medium of print.

Now a virtual monopoly of a whole medium of communication is not something that democratic people should blindly ignore. And we are not going to cut off our television sets and listen to the phonograph just because the airways belong to the networks. They don't. They belong to the people.

As Justice Byron White wrote in his landmark opinion six months ago, it's the right of the viewers and listeners, not the right of the broadcasters, which is paramount.

Now it's argued that this power presents no danger in the hands of those who have used it responsibly. But, as to whether or not the networks have abused the power they enjoy, let us call as our first witness former Vice President Humphrey and the city of Chicago. According to Theodore White, television's intercutting of the film from the streets of Chicago with the current proceedings on the floor of the convention created the most striking and false political picture of 1968—the nomination of a man for the American Presidency by the brutality and violence of merciless police.

If we are to believe a recent report of the House of Representatives Commerce Committee, then television's presentation of the violence in the streets worked an injustice on the reputation of the Chicago police. According to the committee findings, one network in particular presented, and I quote, "a one-sided picture which in large measure exonerates the demonstrators and protesters." Film of provocations of police that was available never saw the light of day while the film of a police response which the protesters provoked was shown to millions.

Another network showed virtually the same scene of violence from three separate angles without making clear it was the same scene. And, while the full report is reticent in drawing conclusions, it is not a document to inspire confidence in the fairness of the network news.

Our knowledge of the impact of network news on the national mind is far from complete, but some early returns are available. Again, we have enough information to raise serious questions about its effect on a democratic society. Several years ago Fred Friendly, one of the pioneers of network news, wrote that its missing ingredients were conviction, controversy and a point of view. The networks have compensated with a vengeance.

And in the networks' endless pursuit of controversy, we should ask: What is the end value—to enlighten or to profit? What is the end result—to inform or to confuse? How does the ongoing exploration for more action, more excitement, more drama serve our national search for internal peace and stability.

Gresham's Law seems to be operating in the network news. Bad news drives out good news. The irrational is more controversial than the rational. Concurrence can no longer compete with dissent.

One minute of Eldridge Cleaver is worth 10 minutes of Roy Wilkins. The labor crisis settled at the negotiating table is nothing compared to the confrontation that results in a strike—or better yet, violence along the picket lines.

Normality has become the nemesis of the network news. Now the upshot of all this controversy is that a narrow and distorted picture of America often emerges from the televised news.

A single, dramatic piece of the mosaic becomes in the minds of millions the entire picture. And the American who relies upon television for his news might conclude that the majority of American students are embittered radicals. That the majority of black Americans feel no regard for their country. That violence and lawlessness are the rule rather than the exception on the American campus.

We know that none of these conclusions is true.

Perhaps the place to start looking for a credibility gap is not in the offices of the Government in Washington but in the studios of the networks in New York.

Television may have destroyed the old stereotypes, but has it not created new ones in their places?

What has this passionate pursuit of controversy done to the politics of progress through local compromise essential to the functioning of a democratic society?

The members of Congress or the Senate who follow their principles and philosophy quietly in a spirit of compromise are unknown to many Americans, while the loudest and most extreme dissenters on every issue are known to every man in the street.

How many marches and demonstrations would we have if the marchers did not know that the ever-faithful TV cameras would be there to record their antics for the next news show?

We've heard demands that Senators and Congressmen and judges make known all their financial connections so that the public will know who and what influences their decisions and their votes. Strong arguments can be made for that view.

But when a single commentator or producer, night after night, determines for millions of people how much of each side of a great issue they are going to see and hear, should he not first disclose his personal views on the issue as well?

In this search for excitement and controversy, has more than equal time gone to the minority of Americans who specialize in attacking the United States—its institutions and its citizens?

Tonight I've raised questions. I've made no attempt to suggest the answers. The answers must come from the media men. They are challenged to turn their critical powers on themselves, to direct their energy, their talent and their conviction toward improving the quality and objectivity of news presentation.

They are challenged to structure their own civic ethics to relate to the great responsibilities they hold.

And the people of America are challenged, too, challenged to press for responsible news presentations. The people can let the networks know that they want their news straight and objective. The people can register their complaints on bias through mail to the networks and phone calls to local stations. This is one case where the people must defend themselves; where the citizen, not the Government, must be the reformer; where the consumer can be the most effective crusader.

By way of conclusion, let me say that every elected leader in the United States depends on these men of the media. Whether what I've said to you tonight will be heard and seen at all by the nation is not my decision, it's not your decision, it's their decision.

In tomorrow's edition of The Des Moines Register, you'll be able to read a news story detailing what I've said tonight. Editorial comment will be reserved for the editorial page, where it belongs.

Should not the same wall of separation exist between news and comment on the nation's networks?

Now, my friends, we'd never trust such power, as I've described, over public opinion in the hands of an elected Government. It's time we questioned it in the hands of a small and unelected elite.

The great networks have dominated America's airwaves for decades. The people are entitled to a full accounting of their stewardship.

SHOES

WILLIAM BOYD

William Boyd's speech is a very personal statement, and its autobiographical references provide a good deal of information about the speaker, including the fact that he was in the life insurance business and that he lived in the Pacific Northwest. A few things need to be added, however. Boyd was working for the Aetna Life Insurance Company in Seattle, Washington, when he developed this speech, which he gave many times to members of the Aetna staff and to prospective employees.

The version reprinted here was taken from an audiotape that was made when he delivered the speech to a regional meeting in San Francisco. Although the text did not vary much from one occasion to the next, you will find that he introduces some specific references to time and place—that he customizes the presentation for the occasion. You will also find that the general tone of the speech differs from the other three. (In this respect, we particularly call your attention to the things that we already have said about audiences and effects.) The speech is similar to "Acres of Diamonds" in that the listeners are not told what they do not want to hear; in other words, Boyd seems most interested in reinforcing existing ideas and attitudes.

Well, gentlemen, after an introduction like that I can't help but feel pretty good. Mrs. Boyd and I have just had two weeks in Phoenix and Palm Springs, and I'm glad that my credit's good with the general agent when I get home. Thank you also, Denny, for mentioning my family.

You've met Mrs. Boyd. I'm very proud of my family, especially of that granddaughter of mine, and I have a particular reason to be very proud of her, because for over a period of years I've been looking at pictures of grandchildren of my customers and friends. In fact I've counted 592 pictures of grandchildren that I've looked at. And now at least I have a chance to get even and inasmuch as I just happen to have a picture of my granddaughter I'll give you all a chance to look and now I'm almost even.

WILLIAM BOYD   87

The first job that I had as a youngster was working as a clerk in a wholesale footwear firm, and it was my job to keep the shoes all in order. They all had bins and we filled orders from them, and I learned that there were many different types of shoes. Well, just think of it a minute. You fellows and ladies have on your business shoes today. On the weekend I don't know what you do in San Francisco, but I assume you could have on your fishing boots or your yachting boots or tennis shoes or different types of recreational shoes.

There seem to be shoes for every purpose, for every use, just like there are life insurance policies for every use and purpose. A great deal has been written in the various papers and journals and company bulletins about this subject of advanced life underwriting. Now that is the subject wherein we talk about insurance for businesses, sole proprietorships, partnerships, corporations, pension plans, where we study the use of life insurance as it applies to estate planning, inheritance taxes, probate costs, and where we study the use of trust services, and various options to be used within the policies.

All of this matter is advanced, but really it's basic because I've found that there is one common denominator in all of this study and that is that somebody is going to receive some money. And the "somebody" is usually, in the majority of cases, a widow or children or a senior citizen of retirement age. And the "some money," portioned in an ever increasing number of cases, is in the form of a monthly income check.

Well, really isn't that the basic fundamental of life insurance? Isn't that the reason why life insurance was invented, to provide money for widows and children and for old people in retirement years? So no matter how far we advance in this advanced life underwriting theory we always seem to come back to the basic fundamentals of life insurance, or the use of life insurance. Every year our agency devotes a few meetings, a few hours of study just to fundamentals so we don't get overburdened with all the highfalutin' ideas of advanced life underwriting.

Let's get right back to fundamentals. And over a period of years I have come to believe that there are three main theories surrounding your activity and my activity. The first theory is that any man, any man worth his salt, does have an economic value to somebody— maybe to a business or to his family. The second theory is that for a man with a family, his earnings over the family dependency period can readily be capitalized for the protection of the family members. And the third theory, which I believe is growing in importance, is that the use of the lifetime income option of life insurance policies does have a very important place in man's financial portfolio. Now those are the three theories that I personally have been trying to develop in my business. Since we usually understand theories in the light of our own knowledge and experience, my message to you today is to tell you in the light of my personal experience why I believe that there is no substitute for life insurance.

I have here a board—I usually bring a board from my own workshop, but they wouldn't let me across the Columbia River South with any Washington wood going into Oregon or California, so somebody was kind enough to get me this board. Pretend with me a few minutes that this board represents a house. Now it's a good house. It has a foundation, walls, roof, floors, rooms, closets, windows, inside plumbing and it's wired for electricity. This is the kind of house that my wife Margaret and I decided that we wanted as a home. Now the only way I know how to convert a house into a home, especially for a young fellow, is that somebody's working shoes must support it. So inasmuch as this represents our home I'm going to put my working shoes under this board and now this becomes our home.

Well, the first thing you have to do with a home is to furnish it, and we buy rugs, tables, chairs, beds, dressers, mirrors, linens, drapes, curtains, kitchen utensils, dishes, silverware—well, you know, all kinds of gadgets that make up a home. Well, we furnish our home and now we have a place in which to raise our family. From our storeroom I have brought you the first pair of shoes that I ever purchased for our family. These shoes, just the way I put them away nineteen years ago, were worn by all three of our children, and during that period of life, you know, where they get into kitchen cupboards and pull out all the canned goods and the pots and the pans and the lids, and which made walking across the kitchen floor quite an occupational hazard for Ma. But these shoes represent a great deal to me and bring back many happy memories, as I'm sure your baby shoes will bring back memories to you. I'm going to place these at this end of the board to illustrate the

beginning of that period called family life. Now I'll
show you the last pair of shoes that I bought for my
family—wedding slippers. That was a great day in our
life—when I walked down the aisle with my daughter, and
that day brings back many happy memories. I place these
at this end of the board to represent the end of the
period called family life.

Along with those shoes I should have brought you a
great big pair of black shoes which I didn't buy, but
which were allotted by the Navy to our son in the Air
Reserve. And a bigger pair of brown shoes worn by our
University of Washington senior. But we don't want to let
those fellows go barefoot so I couldn't bring 'em, and
anyway there wouldn't be room on the board.

But the point I want to make is that this period
between the first pair of shoes which I purchased and the
last pair of shoes or these grown-up shoes is the period
which I emphatically indicate as the family period.

Now, let's see what went on during this period. The
first thing we needed was a lot of food. And there's
probably nothing more indicative in our house than a can
of beans to represent food.

Our grocer, no, our milkman indicates that during this
period we have consumed 27,000 quarts of milk. Now I
don't know how much work that is for a San Francisco cow,
but if your milk comes in glass bottles, quart bottles,
like ours it would reach, if they stood side by side,
from here almost down to your famous ferry dock—and
that's a lot of milk.

Our grocer tells me that we have consumed 44,000
pounds of food during this period. Well, that's 20 long
tons or 22 short tons, whichever way you calculate in
California, and that's a great deal of meat and potatoes
and gravy and chicken and dumplings, and turkey, and
fruits, and vegetables, and bread and butter and jam,
and cereals and sugar and spices and catsup, and ice
cream and cookies and a lot of birthday cakes with
pretty little candles on them. That's a lot of food,
fellas. But evidently it takes that much to raise 23
pounds of brand new babies into 495 pounds of grown up
kids. So much for food.

We also needed clothing. Starting in with the three
cornered variety of underwear—the old fashioned variety
because my daughter tells me they don't fold them that
way "no more." But we had underwear and rompers and
shirts and shoes and socks and pants and blouses and

boots and skirts and overshoes and raincoats and corduroys and suntans, and sweaters, topcoats, dresses, suits, and party dresses, scarves, ties, hats, and dress-up clothes. And all this time we feel that we've always had an adequately dressed wife and mother although at times I've heard her say she had nothing to wear. So we needed clothes.

We've had transportation. Starting with the baby buggy we've had kiddy cars, scooters, little red wagons, roller skates, tricycles, skis, bicycles, and we've always had a family car. And any of you with teenage children learning to drive the family car know and appreciate the fact that the depreciation factor really enters into the family budget.

We've had health factors. And I've a vitamin box to illustrate that. And looking over the record we've had four tonsillectomies and four adenoidectomies, we've had bumps, sprains, bruises, gauze, bandages, vitamins, measles, chicken pox, pills and shots for allergies and hay fever, tooth cavities filled, doctors' fees, hospital fees, four minor operations, nurses' fees, three major operations, one broken arm, and three orthodontias.

Well.

Now, there's another factor which I enter in which I call advancement and recreation. There have been pre-school classes, dancing lessons, piano lessons, clarinet lessons, and trumpet lessons until the neighbors were ready to scream. There have been Church activities, Girl Scouts, Cub Scouts, Boy Scouts, high school clubs, YWCA, YMCA, college organizations, a cumulative nine years of college expense for a total of $49\frac{1}{2}$ years of education for the kids. We've had all kinds of sports equipment like baseballs, volleyballs, basketballs, footballs, golfballs and tennis balls and rackets and all the other equipment. We've always had radios and now a TV. Books and magazines, summers at the beach. A wonderful trip to California with the whole family one year. Many camping trips and picnics. Oh yes, we've had pets too—two dogs, four cats, thirteen kittens, a little white rabbit, three pigeons, two turtles and a duck. So that illustrates something of what's gone on in our house, approximately, and you can fill in all the little details about it.

Oh, I suppose that sometimes during these years we have been a little bit extravagant, but usually the

expenditure for all these items has been somewhat
controlled by the earnings from the working shoes. We
have developed three million-dollar kids, although my
financial statement, my banker, says they are non-
admitted assets. In talking about the expense of raising
children one of my customers made the comment that
having a child is just like having a twenty-year non-
taxable mortgage. With little bitty payments to begin
with and great big payments the last six years. I
thought that was a pretty smart observation from a
customer, and I hand that to you as a real seller's tool
in trying to describe to your prospects the meaning of a
family protection period during this dependency period.
I use it a great deal.

It is true that with all these items—phone calling,
transportation, medical fees, advancement and
recreation—they take a great deal of money. And I'm not
ashamed to say that in some years it took more money
than the earnings from the working shoes. But isn't that
money the price that we pay for all the joys, the
concerns, the worries, and the happiness of children? I
think any of us are willing to spend the money to have
that happiness that they bring.

Now during this period, Margaret and I have tried to
save money. And every time we accumulated 100 or 200
dollars or more something always seemed to happen. Maybe
orthodontia, or an operation, or the car broke down, or
the furniture needed replacing. You know what happens to
money. Always some place to put it. So, we, at no time,
during this period from baby shoes to grown-up shoes
have ever had any substantial money to invest. But we
decided many years ago that it would be necessary for us
to accumulate some type of a financial reserve. So we
budgeted each month a few dollars—10, 20, 30, 40, 50,
75, 100 dollars—as the working shoes earned it and we
bought life insurance.

And here are the very policies that we purchased—
ordinary life, family income, family income, ordinary
life, ordinary life, ordinary life, December 1965 paid
up group insurance pension plan. And along with my
policies I had to place my agency contract because the
guaranteed renewals within this contract really act as
though they were a life insurance policy under option.

Now I take these policies, and I put them right
alongside of my working shoes. And in this position, I
have always felt that they gave effectiveness to these

working shoes. Now, during this period, being human I hope, being an individual, I could have been killed by an accident or I could have died. Some of my friends and customers were killed in accidents and some just up and died. Well, suppose it had happened to me. So what.

Well, here's what. Take these working shoes out of the picture. And the policies support the home. That's what. All during these years from the pots and pans period of babyhood through the childhood years of twist, wiggle and squirm, and fun, food and fight; through the adolescent years marked by those incessant telephone conversations—all during those years these policies would have provided money to pay for the food, the clothes, the transportation, the medical fees and the advancement and recreation. Oh, probably not to the extent of that provided by the working shoes, but, essentially, family life would have been maintained. There is no other investment in all the world that could have provided so much for just a few dollars a month. Is it any wonder therefore that I believe that there is no substitute for life insurance?

Well, this family life period is about over. In four more months our youngest is scheduled to graduate. But the working shoes are still going. And although the terrific expense of raising a family is over, these working shoes still have a job to do. Margaret and I have developed a very expensive habit of eating. We want to wear clothes. We want a car to go places. We'd be foolish not to provide for the contingency of medical expense or possible store teeth. And we want our share of advancement and recreation. So these shoes have a job to do.

And after we get a few mortgages paid, maybe we'll have money to do things that we have heretofore postponed. Instead of two weeks in Phoenix and Palm Springs, maybe we could make it three weeks or a month, or travel to other places. No use leaving the Pacific Northwest in the summer time. That's when you fellows come up there. Perhaps Margaret can have that greenhouse she wants out in the backyard. I don't know what she wants it for but she does. Perhaps I can have that woodworking machine for down in my workshop. She doesn't know why I want it, but I do. Or perhaps we can do a lot of other things. I don't know.

But all the times these working shoes have gone along, maybe not so efficient as they used to be or effective,

maybe a little slower than they used to be, but
nevertheless they've gone along and we'll keep putting
these few dollars a month into these policies. Because
they still have a job to do. They are now arranged so
that when I die Margaret will receive an income check
each and every month for as long as she lives.

Well now, I don't know how long she's going to live.
Her parents pushed into the eighties, aunt and uncle
into the nineties. She might live to be 100 or 125. I
don't know.

But I do know, that every month she does live she
will receive an income check. It says so right here:
"The proceeds of this policy shall be payable in monthly
installments, for years certain and as long thereafter
as the payee lives." And Margaret is the payee. There
just is no other investment that contains that type of
clause, "for as long as the payee lives," and it's all
mine for just a few dollars a month. And that's another
reason why I believe that there is no substitute for
life insurance.

One grand thing about this business of ours is that
we do not have to retire. So many of my friends and
customers are concerned with their retirement date. For
some it will come too soon and for some too late for the
enjoyment of their economic value. And many of them are
concerned with what they are going to do with themselves
after that retirement date. But we don't have to worry.
We can work just as long and as hard and as diligently
as we desire. Oh, I really hope that I never have to
retire. There's too much fun, too many thrills, too many
new ideas, too many challenges in this business to think
of retiring and giving it up altogether. But, if the
time ever comes when I decide—or if I may be forced—to
exchange these working shoes for house slippers or
bedroom slippers, if that time ever comes, all these few
dollars a month that we have put into these policies
will then have accumulated sufficient value so that it
will provide Margaret and me with an income each and
every month for as long as we both shall live.

That phrase sounds familiar.

We've all attended weddings where the marriage charge
was to love, honor and cherish for as long as ye both
shall live. And somehow I feel that life insurance
policies have a part in guaranteeing that marriage vow.
Because it must be difficult to love, and honor and
cherish if you have no income. If your capital's all

gone. If you're just plain broke. But with a financial plan that quarantees a monthly income for as long as a man and a wife shall live—with such a plan, perhaps it will help you and me and any man to be somewhat worthy of love and honor, and worthy of cherished memories.

For these reasons, my friends, it is my conviction that there just is no substitute for life insurance.

Thank you.

THE COOPER INSTITUTE ADDRESS

ABRAHAM LINCOLN

Abraham Lincoln delivered this speech in New York City on February 27, 1860, during his campaign for the Republican presidential nomination. Not only did Lincoln need to become better known in the East, he also needed to prove that his views on slavery provided an acceptable alternative to those of the Democratic favorite, Senator Stephen A. Douglas, and those of Senator William H. Seward, the presumptive Republican nominee. Fortunately, Lincoln was able to take a position between the two that satisfied both his principles and his ambitions. To him Douglas and Seward were extremists; Douglas's concept of popular sovereignty was too soft a line, and Seward's view of the "irrepressible conflict" was too hard. Taking the middle ground, Lincoln stood on a Constitution principle that would restrict the extension of slavery, but would guarantee protection in states where the institution already existed. In May, 1860, he won the Republican nomination.

Factors other than the speech assuredly contributed to Lincoln's success; nevertheless, the Cooper Institute Address was a vital element in his campaign. He worked on the manuscript of the speech for months, and used the text as a campaign document after his nomination. Few speakers prepare with such care because few find themselves in such unusual circumstances. Despite the circumstances, however, and despite the fact that the speech was not extemporaneous, it is instructive for ordinary speakers in ordinary situations. Later, we will comment specifically on such matters as its organization, its evidence, and its stylistic features. As you read the speech, remember that slavery was the most volatile issue of the day—perhaps the most volatile in the history of the nation—and it is interesting to see how Lincoln approaches this highly charged topic.

Mr. President and fellow-citizens of New York: The facts with which I shall deal this evening are mainly old and familiar; nor is there anything new in the general use I shall make of them. If there shall be any novelty, it will be in the mode of presenting the facts, and the inferences and observations following that presentation. In his speech last autumn at Columbus, Ohio, as reported in the *New York Times*, Senator Douglas said:—

Our fathers, when they framed the government under

which we live, understood this question just as well, and even better, than we do now.

I fully endorse this, and I adopt it as a text for this discourse. I so adopt it because it furnishes a precise and an agreed starting-point for a discussion between Republicans and that wing of the Democracy headed by Senator Douglas. It simply leaves the inquiry: What was the understanding those fathers had of the question mentioned?

What is the frame of government under which we live? The answer must be, "The Constitution of the United States." That Constitution consists of the original, framed in 1787, and under which the present government first went into operation, and twelve subsequently framed amendments, the first ten of which were framed in 1789.

Who were our fathers that framed the Constitution? I suppose the "thirty-nine" who signed the original instrument may be fairly called our fathers who framed that part of the present government. It is almost exactly true to say they framed it, and it is altogether true to say they fairly represented the opinion and sentiment of the whole nation at that time. Their names, being familiar to nearly all, and accessible to quite all, need not now be repeated.

I take these "thirty-nine," for the present, as being "our fathers who framed the government under which we live." What is the question which, according to the text, those fathers understood "just as well, and even better, than we do now"?

It is this: Does the proper division of local from Federal authority, or anything in the Constitution, forbid our Federal Government to control as to slavery in our Federal Territories?

Upon this, Senator Douglas holds the affirmative, and Republicans the negative. This affirmation and denial form an issue; and this issue—this question—is precisely what the text declares our fathers understood "better than we." Let us now inquire whether the "thirty-nine," or any of them, ever acted upon this question; and if they did, how they acted upon it—how they expressed that better understanding. In 1784, three years before the Constitution, the United States then owning the Northwestern Territory, and no other, the Congress of the Confederation had before them the question of prohibiting slavery in that Territory, and

four of the "thirty-nine" who afterward framed the
Constitution were in that Congress, and voted on that
question. Of these, Roger Sherman, Thomas Mifflin, and
Hugh Williamson voted for the prohibition, thus showing
that, in their understanding, no line dividing local
from Federal authority, nor anything else, properly
forbade the Federal Government to control as to slavery
in Federal territory. The other of the four, James
McHenry, voted against the prohibition, showing that for
some cause he thought it improper to vote for it.

In 1787, still before the Constitution, but while the
convention was in session framing it, and while the
Northwestern Territory still was the only Territory
owned by the United States, the same question of
prohibiting slavery in the Territory again came before
the Congress of the Confederation; and two more of the
"thirty-nine" who afterward signed the Constitution were
in that Congress, and voted on the question. They were
William Blount and William Few; and they both voted for
the prohibition—thus showing that in their
understanding no line dividing local from Federal
authority, nor anything else, properly forbade the
Federal Government to control as to slavery in Federal
territory. This time the prohibition became a law, being
part of what is now well known as the Ordinance of '87.

The question of Federal control of slavery in the
Territories seems not to have been directly before the
convention which framed the original Constitution; and
hence it is not recorded that the "thirty-nine," or any
of them, while engaged on that instrument, expressed any
opinion on that precise question.

In 1789, by the first Congress which sat under the
Constitution, an act was passed to enforce the Ordinance
of '87, including the prohibition of slavery in the
Northwestern Territory. The bill for this act was
reported by one of the "thirty-nine"—Thomas
Fitzsimmons, then a member of the House of
Representatives from Pennsylvania. It went through all
its stages without a word of opposition, and finally
passed both branches without ayes and nays, which is
equivalent to a unanimous passage. In this Congress
there were sixteen of the thirty-nine fathers who framed
the original Constitution. They were John Langdon,
Nicholas Gilman, Wm. S. Johnson, Roger Sherman, Robert
Morris, Thomas Fitzsimmons, Abraham Baldwin, William
Few, Rufus King, William Patterson, George Clymer,

Richard Bassett, George Read, Pierce Butler, Daniel Carroll, and James Madison.

This shows that, in their understanding, no line dividing local from Federal authority, nor anything in the Constitution, properly forbade Congress to prohibit slavery in the Federal territory; else both their fidelity to correct principle, and their oath to support the Constitution, would have constrained them to oppose the prohibition.

Again, George Washington, another of the "thirty-nine," was then President of the United States, and as such approved and signed the bill, thus completing its validity as a law, and thus showing that, in his understanding, no line dividing local from Federal authority, nor anything in the Constitution, forbade the Federal Government to control as to slavery in Federal territory.

No great while after the adoption of the original Constitution, North Carolina ceded to the Federal Government the country now constituting the State of Tennessee; and a few years later Congress ceded that which now constitutes the States of Mississippi and Alabama. In both deeds of cession it was made a condition by the ceding States that the Federal Government should not prohibit slavery in the ceded country. Besides this, slavery was then actually in the ceded country. Under these circumstances, Congress, on taking charge of these countries, did not absolutely prohibit slavery within them. But they did interfere with it—take control of it—even there, to a certain extent. In 1798 Congress organized the Territory of Mississippi. In the act of organization they prohibited the bringing of slaves into the Territory from any place without the United States, by fine, and giving freedom to slaves so brought. This act passed both branches of Congress without yeas and nays. In that Congress were three of the "thirty-nine" who framed the original Constitution. They were John Langdon, George Read, and Abraham Baldwin. They all probably voted for it. Certainly they would have placed their opposition to it upon record if, in their understanding, any line dividing local from Federal authority, or anything in the Constitution, properly forbade the Federal Government to control as to slavery in Federal Territory.

In 1803, the Federal Government purchased the

Louisiana country. Our former territorial acquisitions came from certain of our own States; but this Louisiana country was acquired from a foreign nation. In 1804, Congress gave a territorial organization to that part of it which now constitutes the State of Louisiana. New Orleans, lying within that part, was an old and comparatively large city. There were other considerable towns and settlements, and slavery was extensively and thoroughly intermingled with the people. Congress did not, in the Territorial Act, prohibit slavery; but they did interfere with it—take control of it—in a more marked and extensive way than they did in the case of Mississippi. The substance of the provision therein made in relation to slaves was:

1st. That no slave should be imported into the Territory from foreign parts.

2d. That no slave should be carried into it who had been imported into the United States since the first day of May, 1798.

3d. That no slave should be carried into it, except by the owner, and for his own use as a settler; the penalty in all cases being a fine upon the violator of the law, and freedom to the slave.

This act also was passed without ayes and nays. In the Congress which passed it there were two of the "thirty-nine." They were Abraham Baldwin and Jonathan Dayton. As stated in the case of Mississippi, it is probable they both voted for it. They would not have allowed it to pass without recording their opposition to it if, in their understanding, it violated either the line properly dividing local from Federal authority, or any provision of the Constitution.

In 1819-20 came and passed the Missouri question. Many votes were taken, by yeas and nays, in both branches of Congress, upon the various phases of the general question. Two of the "thirty-nine"—Rufus King and Charles Pinckney—were members of that Congress. Mr. King steadily voted for slavery prohibition and against all compromises, while Mr. Pinckney as steadily voted against slavery prohibition and against all compromises. By this, Mr. King showed that, in his understanding, no line dividing local from Federal authority, nor anything in the Constitution, was violated by Congress prohibiting slavery in Federal territory; while Mr. Pinckney, by his votes, showed that, in his understanding, there was some sufficient reason for opposing such prohibition in that case.

The cases I have mentioned are the only acts of the "thirty-nine," or of any one of them, upon the direct issue, which I have been able to discover.

To enumerate the persons who thus acted as being four in 1784, two in 1787, seventeen in 1789, three in 1798, two in 1804, and two in 1819-20, there would be thirty of them. But this would be counting John Langdon, Roger Sherman, William Few, Rufus King, and George Read each twice, and Abraham Baldwin three times. The true number of those of the "thirty-nine" whom I have shown to have acted upon the question which, by the text, they understood better than we, is twenty-three, leaving sixteen not shown to have acted upon it in any way.

Here, then, we have twenty-three out of our thirty-nine fathers "who framed the government under which we live," who have, upon their official responsibility and their corporal oaths, acting upon the very question which the text affirms they "understood just as well, and even better, than we do now"; and twenty-one of them—a clear majority of the whole "thirty-nine"—so acting upon it as to make them guilty of gross political impropriety and wilful perjury if, in their understanding, any proper division between local and Federal authority, or anything in the Constitution they had made themselves, and sworn to support, forbade the Federal Government to control as to slavery in the Federal Territories. Thus the twenty-one acted; and, as actions speak louder than words, so actions under such responsibility speak still louder.

Two of the twenty-three voted against Congressional prohibition of slavery in the Federal Territories, in the instances in which they acted upon the question. But for what reasons they so voted is not known. They may have done so because they thought a proper division of local from Federal authority, or some provision or principle of the Constitution, stood in the way; or they may, without any such question, have voted against the prohibition on what appeared to them to be sufficient grounds of expediency. No one who has sworn to support the Constitution can conscientiously vote for what he understands to be an unconstitutional measure, however expedient he may think it; but one may and ought to vote against a measure which he deems constitutional if, at the same time, he deems it

inexpedient. It, therefore, would be unsafe to set down
even the two who voted against the prohibition as
having done so because, in their understanding, any
proper division of local from Federal authority, or
anything in the Constitution, forbade the Federal
Government to control as to slavery in Federal
territory.

The remaining sixteen of the "thirty-nine," so far as
I have discovered, have left no record of their
understanding upon the direct question of Federal
control of slavery in the Federal Territories. But there
is much reason to believe that their understanding upon
that question would not have appeared different from
that of their twenty-three compeers, had it been
manifested at all.

For the purpose of adhering rigidly to the text, I
have purposely omitted whatever understanding may have
been manifested by any person, however distinguished,
other than the thirty-nine fathers who framed the
original Constitution; and, for the same reason, I have
also omitted whatever understanding may have been
manifested by any of the "thirty-nine" even on any
other phase of the general question of slavery. If we
should look into their acts and declarations on those
other phases, as the foreign slave-trade, and the
morality and policy of slavery generally, it would
appear to us that on the direct question of Federal
control of slavery in Federal Territories, the sixteen,
if they had acted at all, would probably have acted
just as the twenty-three did. Among that sixteen were
several of the most noted anti-slavery men of those
times—Dr. Franklin, Alexander Hamilton, and Gouverneur
Morris—while there was not one now known to have been
otherwise, unless it may be John Rutledge, of South
Carolina.

The sum of the whole is that of our thirty-nine
fathers who framed the original Constitution, twenty-
one—a clear majority of the whole—certainly understood
that no proper division of local from Federal
authority, nor any part of the Constitution, forbade
the Federal Government to control slavery in the Federal
Territories; while all the rest had probably the same
understanding. Such, unquestionably, was the
understanding of our fathers who framed the original
Constitution; and the text affirms that they understood
the question "better than we."

But, so far, I have been considering the understanding of the question manifested by the framers of the original Constitution. In and by the original instrument, a mode was provided for amending it; and, as I have already stated, the present frame of "the government under which we live" consists of that original, and twelve amendatory articles framed and adopted since. Those who now insist that Federal control of slavery in Federal Territories violates the Constitution, point us to the provisions which they suppose it thus violates; and, as I understand, they all fix upon provisions in these amendatory articles, and not in the original instrument. The Supreme Court, in the Dred Scott case, plant themselves upon the fifth amendment, which provides that no person shall be deprived of "life, liberty, or property without due process of law"; while Senator Douglas and his peculiar adherents plant themselves upon the tenth amendment, providing that "the powers not delegated to the United States by the Constitution" "are reserved to the States respectively, or to the people."

Now it so happens that these amendments were framed by the first Congress which sat under the Constitution— the identical Congress which passed the act, already mentioned, enforcing the prohibition of slavery in the Northwestern Territory. Not only was it the same Congress, but they were the identical, same individual men who, at the same session, and at the same time within the session, had under consideration, and in progress toward maturity, these constitutional amendments, and this act prohibiting slavery in all the territory the nation then owned. The constitutional amendments were introduced before, and passed after the act enforcing the Ordinance of '87; so that, during the whole pendency of the act to enforce the Ordinance, the constitutional amendments were also pending.

The seventy-six members of that Congress, including sixteen of the framers of the original Constitution, as before stated, were preëminently our fathers who framed that part of "the government under which we live," which is now claimed as forbidding the Federal Government to control slavery in the Federal Territories.

Is it not a little presumptuous in anyone at this day to affirm that the two things which that Congress deliberately framed, and carried to maturity at the same time, are absolutely inconsistent with each other?

And does not such affirmation become impudently absurd when coupled with the other affirmation, from the same mouth, that those who did the two things alleged to be inconsistent, understood whether they really were inconsistent better than we—better than he who affirms that they are inconsistent?

It is surely safe to assume that the thirty-nine framers of the original Constitution, and the seventy-six members of the Congress which framed the amendments thereto, taken together, do certainly include those who may be fairly called "our fathers who framed the government under which we live." And so assuming, I defy any man to show that any one of them ever, in his whole life, declared that, in his understanding, any proper division of local from Federal authority, or any part of the Constitution, forbade the Federal Government to control as to slavery in the Federal Territories. I go a step further. I defy anyone to show that any living man in the world ever did, prior to the beginning of the present century (and I might almost say prior to the beginning of the last half of the present century), declare that, in his understanding, any proper division of local from Federal authority, or any part of the Constitution, forbade the Federal Government to control as to slavery in the Federal Territories. To those who now so declare I give not only "our fathers who framed the government under which we live," but with them all other living men within the century in which it was framed, among whom to search, and they shall not be able to find the evidence of a single man agreeing with them.

Now, and here, let me guard a little against being misunderstood. I do not mean to say we are bound to follow implicitly in whatever our fathers did. To do so would be to discard all the lights of current experience—to reject all progress, all improvement. What I do say is that if we would supplant the opinions and policy of our fathers in any case, we should do so upon evidence so conclusive, and argument so clear, that even their great authority, fairly considered and weighed, cannot stand; and most surely not in a case whereof we ourselves declare they understood the question better than we.

If any man at this day sincerely believes that a proper division of local from Federal authority, or any part of the Constitution, forbids the Federal Government to control as to slavery in the Federal Territories, he is right to say so, and to enforce his position by all truthful evidence and fair argument which he can. But he has no right to mislead others, who have less access to history, and less leisure to study it, into the false belief that "our fathers who framed the government under which we live" were of the same opinion—thus substituting falsehood and deception for truthful evidence and fair argument. If any man at this day sincerely believes "our fathers who framed the government under which we live" used and applied principles, in other cases, which ought to have led them to understand that a proper division of local from Federal authority, or some part of the Constitution, forbids the Federal Government to control as to slavery in the Federal Territories, he is right to say so. But he should, at the same time, brave the responsibility of declaring that, in his opinion, he understands their principles better than they did themselves; and especially should he not shirk that responsibility by asserting that they "understood the question just as well, and even better, than we do now."

But enough! Let all who believe that "our fathers who framed the government under which we live understood this question just as well, and even better, than we do now," speak as they spoke, and act as they acted upon it. This is all Republicans ask—all Republicans desire—in relation to slavery. As those fathers marked it, so let it be again marked, as an evil not to be extended, but to be tolerated and protected only because of and so far as its actual presence amongst us makes that toleration and protection a necessity. Let all the guaranties those fathers gave it be not grudgingly, but fully and fairly maintained. For this Republicans contend, and with this, so far as I know or believe, they will be content.

And now, if they would listen—as I suppose they will not—I would address a few words to the Southern people.

I would say to them: You consider yourselves a reasonable and a just people; and I consider that in the general qualities of reason and justice you are not inferior to any other people. Still, when you speak of us Republicans, you do so only to denounce us as reptiles, or, at the best, as no better than outlaws. You will grant a hearing to pirates or murderers, but

nothing like it to "Black Republicans." In all your
contentions with one another, each of you deems an
unconditional condemnation of "Black Republicanism," as
the first thing to be attended to. Indeed, such
condemnation of us seems to be an indispensable
prerequisite—license, so to speak—among you to be
admitted or permitted to speak at all. Now can you or
not be prevailed upon to pause and to consider
whether this is quite just to us, or even to yourselves?
Bring forward your charges and specifications, and then
be patient long enough to hear us deny or justify.

You say we are sectional. We deny it. That makes an
issue; and the burden of proof is upon you. You produce
your proof; and what is it? Why, that our party has no
existence in your section—gets no votes in your
section. The fact is substantially true; but does it
prove the issue? If it does, then in case we should,
without change of principle, begin to get votes in your
section, we should thereby cease to be sectional. You
cannot escape this conclusion; and yet, are you willing
to abide by it? If you are, you will probably soon find
that we have ceased to be sectional, for we shall get
votes in your section this very year. You will then
begin to discover, as the truth plainly is, that your
proof does not touch the issue. The fact that we get no
votes in your section is a fact of your making, and not of
ours. And if there be fault in that fact, that fault is
primarily yours, and remains so until you show that we
repel you by some wrong principle or practice. If we do
repel you by any wrong principle or practice, the fault
is ours; but this brings you to where you ought to have
started—to a discussion of the right or wrong of our
principle. If our principle, put in practice, would
wrong your section for the benefit of ours, or for any
other object, then our principle, and we with it, are
sectional, and are justly opposed and denounced as such.
Meet us, then, on the question of whether our principle,
put in practice, would wrong your section; and so meet
us as if it were possible that something may be said on
your side. Do you accept the challenge? No! Then you
really believe that the principle which "our fathers
who framed the government under which we live" thought
so clearly right as to adopt it, and indorse it again
and again, upon their official oaths, is in fact so
clearly wrong as to demand your condemnation without a
moment's consideration.

Some of you delight to flaunt in our faces the warning against sectional parties given by Washington in his Farewell Address. Less than eight years before Washington gave that warning, he had, as President of the United States, approved and signed an act of Congress enforcing the prohibition of slavery in the Northwestern Territory, which act embodied the policy of the government upon that subject up to and at the very moment he penned that warning; and about one year after he penned it, he wrote Lafayette that he considered that prohibition a wise measure, expressing in the same connection his hope that we should at some time have a confederacy of free States.

Bearing this in mind, and seeing that sectionalism has since arisen upon this same subject, is that warning a weapon in your hands against us, or in our hands against you? Could Washington himself speak, would he cast the blame of that sectionalism upon us, who sustain his policy, or upon you, who repudiate it? We respect that warning of Washington, and we commend it to you, together with his example pointing to the right application of it.

But you say you are conservative—eminently conservative—while we are revolutionary, destructive, or something of the sort. What is conservatism? Is it not adherence to the old and tried, against the new and untried? We stick to, contend for, the identical old policy on the point in controversy which was adopted by "our fathers who framed the government under which we live"; while you with one accord reject, and scout, and spit upon that old policy, and insist upon substituting something new. True, you disagree among yourselves as to what that substitute shall be. You are divided on new propositions and plans, but you are unanimous in rejecting and denouncing the old policy of the fathers. Some of you are for reviving the foreign slave-trade; some for a Congressional slave code for the Territories; some for Congress forbidding the Territories to prohibit slavery within their limits; some for maintaining slavery in the Territories through the judiciary; some for the "gur-reat pur-rinciple" that "if one man would enslave another, no third man should object," fantastically called "popular sovereignty," but never a man among you is in favor of Federal prohibition of slavery in Federal Territories, according to the practice of "our fathers who framed the government under which we live." Not one of all your various plans can show a precedent or an advocate in the century within which our government originated. Consider, then, whether your claim of conservatism for yourselves, and your charge of destructiveness against us, are based on the most clear and stable foundations.

And again, you say we have made the slavery question more prominent than it formerly was. We deny it. We admit that it is more prominent, but we deny that we made it so. It was not we, but you, who discarded the old policy of the fathers. We resisted, and still resist, your innovation; and thence comes the greater prominence of the question. Would you have that question reduced to its former proportions? Go back to that old policy. What has been will be again, under the same conditions. If you would have the peace of the old times, re-adopt the precepts and policy of the old times.

You charge that we stir up insurrections among your slaves. We deny it; and what is your proof? Harper's Ferry! John Brown!! John Brown was no Republican; and you have failed to implicate a single Republican in his Harper's Ferry enterprise. If any member of our party is guilty in that matter, you know it or you do not know it. If you do know it, you are inexcusable for not designating the man and proving the fact. If you do not know it, you are inexcusable for asserting it, and especially for persisting in the assertion after you have tried and failed to make the proof. You need not be told that persisting in a charge which one does not know to be true is simply malicious slander.

Some of you admit that no Republican designedly aided or encouraged the Harper's Ferry affair, but still insist that our doctrines and declarations necessarily lead to such results. We do not believe it. We know we hold no doctrine, and make no declaration which were not held to and made by "our fathers who framed the government under which we live." You never dealt fairly by us in relation to this affair. When it occurred, some important State elections were near at hand, and you were in evident glee with the belief that, by charging the blame upon us, you could get an advantage of us in those elections. The elections came, and your expectations were not quite fulfilled. Every Republican man knew that, as to himself at least, your charge was a slander, and he was not much inclined by it to cast his vote in your favor. Republican doctrines and declarations are accompanied with a continual protest against any interference whatever with your slaves, or with you about your slaves. Surely this does not encourage them to revolt. True, we do, in common with "our fathers who framed the government under which we live," declare our belief that slavery is wrong; but the slaves do not hear us declare even this. For anything we say or do, the slaves would scarcely know there is a Republican party. I believe they would not, in fact, generally know it but for your misrepresentations of us in their hearing. In your political contests among yourselves each faction charges the other with sympathy with Black Republicanism; and then, to give point to the charge, defines Black Republicanism to simply be insurrection, blood, and thunder among the slaves.

Slave insurrections are no more common now than they were before the Republican party was organized. What induced the Southampton insurrection, twenty-eight years ago, in which at least three times as many lives were lost as at Harper's Ferry? You can scarcely stretch your very elastic fancy to the conclusion that Southampton was "got up by Black Republicanism." In the present state of things in the United States, I do not think a general, or even a very extensive, slave insurrection is possible. The indispensable concert of action cannot be attained. The slaves have no means of rapid communication, nor can incendiary freeman, black or white, supply it. The explosive materials are everywhere in parcels; but there neither are, nor can be supplied, the indispensable connecting trains.

Much is said by Southern people about the affection of slaves for their masters and mistresses; and a part of it, at least, is true. A plot for an uprising could scarcely be devised and communicated to twenty individuals before some one of them, to save the life of a favorite master or mistress, would divulge it. This is the rule; and the slave revolution in Hayti was not an exception to it, but a case occurring under peculiar circumstances. The Gunpowder Plot of British history, though not connected with slaves, was more in point. In that case, only about twenty were admitted to the secret; and yet one of them, in his anxiety to save a friend, betrayed the plot to that friend, and, by consequence, averted the calamity. Occasional poisonings from the kitchen, and open or stealthy assassinations in the field, and local revolts extending to a score or so, will continue to occur as the natural results of slavery; but no general insurrection of slaves, as I think, can happen in this country for a long time. Whoever much fears, or much hopes for, such an event will be alike disappointed.

In the language of Mr. Jefferson, uttered many years ago, "It is still in our power to direct the process of emancipation and deportation peaceably, and in such slow degrees as that the evil will wear off insensibly; and their places be, *pari passu*, filled up by free white laborers. If, on the contrary, it is left to force itself on, human nature must shudder at the prospect held up."

Mr. Jefferson did not mean to say, nor do I, that the power of emancipation is in the Federal Government. He spoke of Virginia; and, as to the power of emancipation, I speak of the slaveholding States only. The Federal Government, however, as we insist, has the power of restraining the extension of the institution— the power to insure that a slave insurrection shall never occur on any American soil which is now free from slavery.

John Brown's effort was peculiar. It was not a slave insurrection. It was an attempt by white men to get up a revolt among slaves, in which the slaves refused to participate. In fact, it was so absurd that the slaves, with all their ignorance, saw plainly enough it could not succeed. That affair, in its philosophy, corresponds with the many attempts, related in history, at the assassination of kings and emperors. An enthusiast broods over the oppression of a people till he fancies himself commissioned by Heaven to liberate them. He ventures the attempt, which ends in little else than his own execution. Orsini's attempt on Louis Napoleon, and John Brown's attempt at Harper's Ferry, were, in their philosophy, precisely the same. The eagerness to cast blame on old England in the one case, and on New England in the other, does not disprove the sameness of the two things.

And how much would it avail you, if you could, by the use of John Brown, Helper's book, and the like, break up the Republican organization? Human action can be modified to some extent, but human nature cannot be changed. There is a judgment and a feeling against slavery in this nation, which cast at least a million and a half of votes. You cannot destroy that judgment and feeling—that sentiment—by breaking up the political organization which rallies around it. You can scarcely scatter and disperse an army which has been formed into order in the face of your heaviest fire; but if you could, how much would you gain by forcing the sentiment which created it out of the peaceful channel of the ballot-box into some other channel? What would that other channel probably be? Would the number of John Browns be lessened or enlarged by the operation?

But you will break up the Union rather than submit to a denial of your constitutional rights.

That has a somewhat reckless sound; but it would be palliated, if not fully justified, were we proposing, by the mere force of numbers, to deprive you of some right plainly written down in the Constitution. But we are proposing no such thing.

When you make these declarations, you have a specific and well-understood allusion to an assumed constitutional right of yours to take slaves into the Federal Territories, and to hold them there as property. But no such right is specially written in the Constitution. That instrument is literally silent about any such right. We, on the contrary, deny that such a right has any existence in the Constitution, even by implication.

Your purpose, then, plainly stated, is that you will destroy the government, unless you be allowed to construe and force the Constitution as you please, on all points in dispute between you and us. You will rule or ruin in all events.

This, plainly stated, is your language. Perhaps you will say the Supreme Court has decided the disputed constitutional question in your favor. Not quite so. But, waiving the lawyer's distinction between dictum and decision, the court has decided the question for you in a sort of way. The court has substantially said, it is your constitutional right to take slaves into the Federal Territories, and to hold them there as property. When I say the decision was made in a sort of way, I mean it was made in a divided court, by a bare majority of the judges, and they not quite agreeing with one another in the reasons for making it; that it is so made as that its avowed supporters disagree with one another about its meaning, and that it was mainly based upon a mistaken statement of fact—the statement in the opinion that "the right of property in a slave is distinctly and expressly affirmed in the Constitution."

An inspection of the Constitution will show that the right of property in a slave is not "distinctly and expressly affirmed" by it. Bear in mind, the judges do not pledge their judicial opinion that such right is impliedly affirmed in the Constitution; but they pledge their veracity that it is "distinctly and expressly" affirmed there—"distinctly," that is, not mingled with anything else—"expressly," that is, in words meaning just that, without the aid of any inference, and susceptible of no other meaning.

If they had only pledged their judicial opinion that such right is affirmed in the instrument by implication, it would be open to others to show that neither the word "slave" nor "slavery" is to be found in the Constitution, nor the word "property" even, in any connection with language alluding to the thing slave or slavery; and that wherever in that instrument the slave is alluded to, he is called a "person"; and wherever his master's legal right in relation to him is alluded to, it is spoken of as "service or labor which may be due"—as a debt payable in service or labor. Also it would be open to show, by contemporaneous history, that this mode of alluding to slaves and slavery, instead of speaking of them, was employed on purpose to exclude from the Constitution the idea that there could be property in man.

To show all this is easy and certain.

When this obvious mistake of the judges shall be brought to their notice, is it not reasonable to expect that they will withdraw the mistaken statement, and reconsider the conclusion based upon it?

And then it is to be remembered that "our fathers who framed the government under which we live"—the men who made the Constitution—decided this same constitutional question in our favor long ago; decided it without division among themselves when making the decision; without division among themselves about the meaning of it after it was made, and, so far as any evidence is left, without basing it upon any mistaken statement of facts.

Under all these circumstances, do you really feel yourselves justified to break up this government unless such a court decision as yours is shall be at once submitted to as a conclusive and final rule of political action? But you will not abide the election of a Republican president! In that supposed event, you say, you will destroy the Union; and then, you say, the great crime of having destroyed it will be upon us! That is cool. A highwayman holds a pistol to my ear, and mutters through his teeth, "Stand and deliver, or I shall kill you, and then you will be a murderer!"

To be sure, what the robber demanded of me—my money—was my own; and I had a clear right to keep it; but it was no more my own than my vote is my own; and the threat of death to me, to extort my money, and the threat of destruction to the Union, to extort my vote, can scarcely be distinguished in principle.

A few words now to Republicans. It is exceedingly desirable that all parts of this great Confederacy shall be at peace, and in harmony one with another. Let us Republicans do our part to have it so. Even though much provoked, let us do nothing through passion and ill temper. Even though the Southern people will not so much as listen to us, let us calmly consider their demands, and yield to them if, in our deliberate view of our duty, we possibly can. Judging by all they say and do, and by the subject and nature of their controversy with us, let us determine, if we can, what will satisfy them.

Will they be satisfied if the Territories be unconditionally surrendered to them? We know they will not. In all their present complaints against us, the Territories are scarcely mentioned. Invasions and insurrections are the rage now. Will it satisfy them if, in the future, we have nothing to do with invasions and insurrections? We know it will not. We so know, because we know we never had anything to do with invasions and insurrections; and yet this total abstaining does not exempt us from the charge and the denunciation.

The question recurs, What will satisfy them? Simply this: we must not only let them alone, but we must somehow convince them that we do let them alone. This, we know by experience, is no easy task. We have been so trying to convince them from the very beginning of our organization, but with no success. In all our platforms and speeches we have constantly protested our purpose to let them alone; but this has had no tendency to convince them. Alike unavailing to convince them is the fact that they have never detected a man of us in any attempt to disturb them.

These natural and apparently adequate means all failing, what will convince them? This, and this only: cease to call slavery wrong, and join them in calling it right. And this must be done thoroughly—done in acts as well as words. Silence will not be tolerated— we must place ourselves avowedly with them. Senator Douglas's new sedition law must be enacted and enforced, suppressing all declarations that slavery is wrong, whether made in politics, in presses, in pulpits, or in private. We must arrest and return their fugitive slaves with greedy pleasure. We must pull down our free State constitutions. The whole atmosphere must be disinfected from all taint of opposition to slavery, before they will cease to believe that all their troubles proceed from us.

I am quite aware they do not state their case precisely in this way. Most of them would probably say to us, "Let us alone; do nothing to us, and say what you please about slavery." But we do let them alone— have never disturbed them—so that, after all, it is what we say which dissatisfies them. They will continue to accuse us of doing, until we cease saying.

I am also aware they have not as yet in terms demanded the overthrow of our free State constitutions. Yet those constitutions declare the wrong of slavery with more solemn emphasis than do all other sayings against it; and when all these other sayings shall have been silenced, the overthrow of these constitutions will be demanded, and nothing be left to resist the demand. It is nothing to the contrary that they do not demand the whole of this just now. Demanding what they do, and for the reason they do, they can voluntarily stop nowhere short of this consummation. Holding, as they do, that slavery is morally right and socially elevating, they cannot cease to demand a full national recognition of it as a legal right and a social blessing.

Nor can we justifiably withhold this on any ground save our conviction that slavery is wrong. If slavery is right, all words, acts, laws, and constitutions against it are themselves wrong, and should be silenced and swept away. If it is right, we cannot justly object to its nationality—its universality; if it is wrong, they cannot justly insist upon its extension—its enlargement. All they ask we could readily grant, if we thought slavery right; all we ask they could as readily grant, if they thought it wrong. Their thinking it right and our thinking it wrong is the precise fact upon which depends the whole controversy. Thinking it right, as they do, they are not to blame for desiring its full recognition as being right; but thinking it wrong, as we do, can we yield to them? Can we cast our votes with their view, and against our own? In view of our moral, social, and political responsibilities, can we do this?

Wrong as we think slavery is, we can yet afford to let it alone where it is, because that much is due to the necessity arising from its actual presence in the nation; but can we, while our votes will prevent it, allow it to spread into the national Territories, and to overrun us here in these free States? If our sense of duty forbids this, then let us stand by our duty fearlessly and effectively. Let us be diverted by none of those sophistical contrivances wherewith we are so industriously plied and belabored—contrivances such as groping for some middle ground between the right and the wrong: vain as the search for a man who should be neither a living man nor a dead man; such as a policy of "don't care" on a question about which all true men do care; such as Union appeals beseeching true Union men to yield to Disunionists, reversing the divine rule, and calling, not the sinners, but the righteous to repentance: such as invocations to Washington, imploring men to unsay what Washington said and undo what Washington did.

Neither let us be slandered from our duty by false accusations against us, nor frightened from it by menaces of destruction to the government, nor of dungeons to ourselves. Let us have faith that right makes might, and in that faith let us to the end dare to do our duty as we understand it.

3 messages

PREVIEW: CHAPTER 5

Chapter 5 is the first of two chapters on the effects that we introduced in Chapter 3. We distinguished there between awareness and willingness, but here, because of the nature of these two effects, we examine them together. Conversely, the compass of understanding is so broad that we divide the discussion into three sections. We also consider the relationships between effects, discuss the selecting and limiting of speech topics, and include a number of exercises and specific suggestions. The topics are:

Speaking for effects
Awareness and willingness
> As terminal effects
> As instrumental effects

Something to talk about
Multiple effects
Understanding
> Comprehension
> Knowing the implications
> Appreciation

Our goals are at one with the very substance of the chapter. Obviously, our aim is your increased awareness and understanding of awareness and understanding, but we have instrumentality and multiple effects in mind, too. When you have completed this chapter, we hope that you will appreciate the significance of these effects as a point of departure and as a controlling feature in speech preparation, and that our specific suggestions will be helpful in your speaking performances.

listener effects

AWARENESS, WILLINGNESS, UNDERSTANDING

5

SPEAKING FOR EFFECTS

The notion that any message ought to be shaped with effects in mind is hardly new. Cicero said, for example, that a speaker tries "to move men to action or to instruct them or deter them, to excite them or to curb them, to fire them or to calm them down." And centuries later, George Campbell wrote: "There is always some end proposed, or some effect which the speaker intends to produce in the hearer." He goes on to say that every speech is "intended to enlighten the understanding, to please the imagination, to move the passions, or to influence the will." Both Cicero and Campbell stress persuasive goals —an emphasis that has captured most attention in the history of communication studies—and they both distinguish between informative and persuasive speaking.

The distinction seems a reasonable and useful one. As we have remarked, we all participate in much communication that affects our images, but that has no significant impact on the way we lead our lives. Reading and listening, we attend to bits of information that may simply expand or refine our images, and we routinely process bits that do not require important changes in them; such communication is primarily a matter of transferring information. But we are also constantly bombarded with messages calculated to make us do something—or not do something, as the case may be—and these messages are clearly persuasive in intent. Marginal and exceptional instances are not difficult to find, however. Informational messages of a descriptive nature can be extremely persuasive, and that's why it is against the law to shout "Fire!" in a crowded theater, unless the building happens to be burning down. Or, as a more common example, a simple statement of the caloric value of some item of food may "persuade" people not to eat it. In short, a message that is informative to one audience may be quite persuasive to another, and vice versa.

But if the categories blur at the edges, the differentiation between informative and persuasive messages has long been useful to students of speech and communication, and it is possible to view the five effects as stages in the transformation of informative to persuasive discourse. However, we feel that this approach to effects represents a refinement because the different stages offer a more precise grasp, a better handle on the tasks faced in speech preparation. On the surface, the five different effects give a somewhat sharper focus on the goal you have in mind as you try to modify the images of your listeners. Since this modification is the objective of all communication, it seems sensible to use these effects as the point of departure for the entire process of speechmaking.

AWARENESS AND WILLINGNESS

In discussing the effects of awareness and willingness in Chapter 3, we said that listeners might not be aware of a subject or an issue that concerns you—that is, their images might not contain anything directly related to your subject. And if they were aware, they might not be interested, might even be unwilling to hear any more about the subject. Here, we will discuss these two effects together, because, though they can be viewed as different stages, they have one important feature in common: they are often *instrumental*—that is, they serve as means—in achieving the other communication effects. Moreover, this instrumentality has more than one dimension. First, however, let's consider awareness and willingness as *terminal* effects in a speech, as ends in themselves.

As terminal effects

Let's imagine that you are interested in the history of welfare legislation, and you decide that this is a subject appropriate for a speech to a particular audience. Awareness could be the desired effect, the goal being to make your listeners more aware of the long and varied history of welfare legislation in Western culture. In this respect, an appropriate focus would be on the laws passed in England during the reign of Queen Elizabeth I. Some degree of understanding would be achieved, no doubt, but a sweep of the historical aspects is most likely to create awareness, and perhaps the willingness to learn more. This speech might have no further goal, no instrumental purpose. You might decide that's all that needs to be or can be done in this instance—some slight expansion of your listeners' image is not, after all, necessarily a goal to be faulted. There are times when it is enough simply to alert listeners to some issue, with the hope they will have the willingness to give it more thought, or even exchange views on the subject.

*

Starting with yourself and your interests find a subject area where you are reasonably confident that your audience has little or no true awareness. The search may not be easy, but you can surely think of some experiences and interests if you give the question close attention. It is a good exercise in audience analysis, because it makes "How much do they know?" a very real question. Can you develop a short speech in which making your listeners aware is the principal goal, and can you present it in such a way that they will be willing to receive more information on the subject?

*

As instrumental effects

In other communication situations, you may adopt awareness and willingness as goals not from choice, but because your analysis leads you to conclude that they are all you can reasonably expect from your listeners at this time in a single speech. The speech on welfare in Elizabethan times might be shaped in such a way as to prepare listeners to receive further information in later messages. Surely it is naive and unrealistic to think that dramatic changes in images are accomplished with a single speech. As we noted in Chapter 2, images and the behavior attaching to them are difficult to alter, and conversion is an extremely rare event for most people, regardless of what they are converting from or to. Erosion rather than conversion is the ordinary thing, and when there is resistance to change, the goals of awareness and willingness can be the bases for a communication campaign that leads to other stages of effect.

Of course there are occasions when awareness alone is enough to influence behavior. Or has it never happened that your speed decreased slightly when you became aware that a highway patrolman was cruising a lane over and a few car-lengths ahead? And when the party begins at 7:30, the question "Do you realize that it's nearly a quarter to eight?" uses awareness to influence behavior rather directly. These examples are simple, but they underline the principle that the effects of understanding, acceptance, and behavior influence usually can't be achieved unless awareness and willingness can be taken for granted or are developed first. That's what we mean when we say that awareness and willingness often have instrumental value in communication. For another and better illustration, let's look at Marilyn Hayashi Rye's introductory remarks:

> In 1883, a man named Hirokichi Hayashi sailed from Fukuoka, Japan, to America. Perhaps he had heard that the opportunities for success were far more abundant in America than in Japan. Perhaps he had heard that the streets were paved with gold or that the Golden Gate was really made of gold. But for some reason, he came. When he arrived in California, he settled in Alameda where he started a little nursery. He grew rose bushes, azaleas, and seasonal plants. By 1905, he was rich enough to afford one of the greatest personal luxuries for a Japanese immigrant—he sent for a picture bride.
>
> In 1910, my father was born. By this time, my grandfather had a nursery in Oakland. In Oakland, my father grew up and went to school. Now this may not seem to be too remarkable a statement, except that in San Francisco, in 1906, a measure was passed by the school board which prohibited all Japanese from attending public schools.

The point is that she used the narrative of family history to create awareness by getting her listeners to share the realities of bigotry and prejudice as they touched her life, and in this way, she prepared for some possible negative responses—the "ho-hum, here comes another speech on prejudice," or the "Do I have to hear again what a bigot I am?" sort of thing. If Rye could build awareness and willingness, these instrumental effects could pave the way for the stages of understanding, acceptance, and behavior. The instrumentality here is further emphasized by the fact that her ultimate concern was, not the Japanese, but the American Indian! In speeches that followed this one she chose to speak about the status of the Indian, and this speech was but one in a series; she intended this personal statement to serve as a bridge to a later speech when she talked specifically about the plight of Indians on reservations.

SOMETHING TO TALK ABOUT

Since awareness and willingness are such important communication effects in most speaking situations, it follows that they are useful notions for you to use in analyzing your audience and choosing a speech topic. No doubt, your expertise and the occasion will sometimes combine to restrict your freedom of choice, but you will find that you have a rather wide latitude most of the time. Ironically, the candidate for elected office sees opportunity in an open speaking situation, but other speakers, including students, frequently find that there is something frightening about the completely open assignment. In either case, the five effects ought to be a preliminary concern in an intelligent choice of topic. We don't mean to imply that the list of effects will solve all your speaking problems, but we do mean to suggest that it is vital to you as a speaker that you consider the ways in which you can relate your image to the images of the audience, that you center on effects from the outset.

Start with yourself. That's advice you probably have heard in connection with writing as well as speaking. It is excellent advice! Nothing is more personal than communication, and the two of us are not so dull-witted as to suppose that you should consider effects in a vacuum, with no reference to any substance. So how do you start with yourself? Well, a piece of paper and a pencil will help, then some memory and some imagination. How have you earned money? Where have you lived? Where have you traveled? What are your hobbies and other interests? What are the subjects you liked in school? What is your attitude to current events? We can't exhaust the possibilities here, and you won't be able to either on the first try, but a personal inventory will help surmount the hurdles of "I don't know what to talk about" or, worse, "I don't have anything to talk about." Your inventory should be regularly expanded and refined, in the same way that intelligent politicians constantly update the list of important people and critical issues in their constituencies. And right from the start it will prevent you from being tempted to turn to others for ideas or even for complete speeches. It happens. Without commenting on the ethics of such behavior—there seems no need to comment—we would raise the question of how much communication skill anyone can gain when riding piggy-back.

In any event some notion of possible subjects is fundamental, but that isn't enough, of course. Do you remember our earlier suggestion that you look at a newspaper for ideas? Chances are that most pages of any newspaper have news and information that you aren't aware of, and even the front page often contains items that don't capture and hold everyone's attention. All of us make a series of snap judgments as we turn the pages of a paper, and listeners engage in a similar process, although a speaker ordinarily commands more attention than do columns of print. Obviously, some concern for audience analysis will help you choose a subject that has the promise of getting your listeners' attention and the potential for sustaining their interest. Although attention and interest are certainly influenced by the way you deliver your speech, they are also affected by your choice of subject matter and your treatment of ideas. The link between attention/interest and awareness/willingness is a close one.

*

Suppose that your assignment called for you to make a trivial, boring speech. How would you select a topic? How would you satisfy yourself that it *was* trivial and boring? How would you develop a speech so that it showed no concern for relating it to the interests and experiences of your listeners? It could be instructive for you to carry out this exercise on paper, even if you never present the speech.

Your completion of this "assignment" would reveal quite a bit about what you think is trivial and boring. It might also help you gain an appreciation of how speech topics can be adapted in order to gain listener awareness and willingness. Certainly this exercise would carry you into the area of audience analysis just as much as if you were required to make a speech on an important, interesting topic. Think about it.

*

Certainly it takes no great imagination to realize that some subjects are inherently more interesting to most people than are others, and it takes no extended effort in audience analysis to discover that some subjects will do for one group and not for another. Members of the Beef Cattle Improvement Association probably won't listen eagerly to a speech on embroidery, but any number of subjects in the area of nutrition will be interesting to them. And it is safe to predict that an audience of college students will find a speech on premarital intercourse somewhat more fascinating than an analysis of the benefits they can expect under Social Security when they are 65.

Suppose, for the moment, that you *have* chosen the topic of premarital sex for a speech to an audience of college students. Certainly you should have some listener awareness and willingness in your favor at the outset. You have a lot of options for dealing with the subject, too, depending on your preferences and your speaking goals. You might, for example, treat your subject from a sociological perspective, or a moral perspective, or a psychological perspective— perhaps even a legal perspective. And once you have made this decision, you may then choose either an instrumental or terminal goal. Whatever treatment you choose, though, and whatever goal you may have in mind, you will find that it is generally useful to ask "Why?" and to ask "How?"

Why should this audience be made aware of this subject? Why should they care? Why should they listen at all? These and other "Why?" questions apply to relatively neutral topics as well as to extremely controversial ones. The exact answers will depend on your subject and on your audience, and though we can't give you the answers here, we can suggest that to ask the questions is to start toward replies that will help you become aware of the way in which your subject can be related to the lives of your listeners. Each question and answer can suggest ways for you to deal with awareness in your speech.

Answers to "How?" can give you insights into the ways of keeping your audience with you as your speech develops. If your analysis suggests that the audience will be fairly receptive, then your task may be comparatively simple. However, if you suspect that your listeners may be uninterested, indifferent, or somewhat resistant, then challenges arise. In the section of the *Rhetoric* from which we quoted the descriptions of the young and the elderly, Aristotle says that "people always think well of speeches adapted to, and reflecting, their own character," and he is concerned as we are—as you should be—with getting and sustaining interest and attention. He is addressing himself to much more, no doubt, and so are we, so let's give further attention to the matter of choosing and developing a subject.

We have implied that you might do well to select from your inventory a subject that touches an important part of your listeners' lives, and we think that generally good advice, but some cautions have to be added. First, the new and the different often attract attention, and so novelty may touch our lives, particularly in regard to our awareness and willingness to listen. Nevertheless, it would be foolhardy for a speaker to strive always for effects predicated on the esoteric and the unusual. Conversely, the subject that truly touches our lives may somehow become worn out. Toward the end of the Vietnam War, for instance, it was most unusual to hear a classroom speech on this topic. Beliefs and attitudes on campuses remained intense and produced some violent and near-violent demonstrations at the time of the invasion of Cambodia and the mining of Haiphong harbor, but for most speech classes, the topic was threadbare. Students may not have thought the subject was exhausted, but they indicated that they found it exhausting.

Pick a topic that you suspect your audience is tired of hearing about. That's something that shouldn't be difficult—just think of those things *you're* tired of hearing about. But then develop a speech on this subject in which you try to renew the interest of your listeners, even try to make them willing to hear more about it. Obviously success will depend mainly on your *treatment* of the topic, and if you are at least partially successful, you will have learned a preparation technique that will serve you well in other situations. What others do, in class and out, with shop-worn materials will also be instructive.

M. Let me add a related example from a class I was teaching in which everyone was required to present a travelog. Many veterans were enrolled, and we heard tall tales of typhoons in the Pacific, hurricanes in the Atlantic, and air travel to faraway places with strange-sounding names. But probably the most successful speech was one given by a student whose "travelog" consisted of a late night walk around the campus, with his impressions of the library, empty office buildings, students alone and together, lights and shadows, and other sights and sounds of the campus at night.

Narrowing the topic

The point we have been making is that you ought not let your hopes for effects necessarily rest in a quick choice of a subject that seems interesting, nor should you overlook the possibilities of a subject that seems less than promising. We'll consider one of the latter here—television—and use it to expand on the inventory process that we suggested you undertake. Television is all about us, and assuredly it touches all our lives. So what can there possibly be to say about it? At its most extensive, the subject may well yield nothing to say, because it probably would be difficult to find an audience that could stifle its boredom at a speech which attempted to survey the subject of television in general. But let's take the time to sort out some of the potential subject areas within the larger heading.

How about the commercials—what do they cost per minute during the Superbowl game? More than most of us will ever earn in ten years. And why are they so expensive? What does the sponsor expect in return for such an outlay? Then there is the technical aspect of television—production, broadcasting, and reception. Or we might consider the various types of programming—entertainment, news, education, and public affairs. Programs remind us of the issue of ratings, and ratings trigger the thought of trends, and trends suggest the future of television, including closed-circuit and cable installations. Certainly everyone in the United States has some awareness and willingness in relation to all these possibilities; as the focus narrows, however, most listeners probably have rather incomplete images, images that can be expanded and modified.

Now let's take a closer look at one of these narrower topics—TV reception, for example. Again, subtopics arise: How many TV sets are there in the country today? How many different kinds? How does an antenna work, anyway? Why are there only twelve channels on the VHF dial? And why no Channel 1 instead of no Channel 13? And what's the difference between VHF and UHF? Will there be a major change in the design of sets soon? All these questions produce still others, but we trust the point is made. As you divide and sub-divide a subject, you'll be getting into new territory for many of your listeners. So it goes with almost any general topic. Just give such topics a few minutes of attention—free-associating or doing some in-dividual brainstorming—and you are likely to arrive at some fresh angles for speech subjects. You might try the same thing with some item in your personal inventory or with some idea that you just pick out of the air. The more you are involved, the more lively your effort is likely to be, a point that suggests something obvious in regard to your attitude toward your subject: if you don't really care, then it is difficult to generate enthusiasm in preparation and presentation, and your lack of enthusiasm is very likely to come through to your lis-teners.

Research

But interested or not, you will find that a spinning out of subtopics will put you right where many listeners are, in a place where your image may be vague and incomplete. This means, quite simply, that you'll have to do some kind of research. To find a subject which touches the lives of your listeners and which deals with something they don't already know—or have never thought about—frequently means either that you will have to explore some relatively new terri-tory or that you will have to dig more deeply in familiar ground. We wish there were an easier route, but there isn't. You could drop the course, and there's always plagiarism, which we've already expressed our opinion of. But it happens to be a fact that research is a price that many successful speakers pay in order to get willing listeners. We can go back to television to illustrate the point. If you choose the subject of commercials for a speech, you will have something that fits into the everyday experience of most audiences. Some kind of "favorite-commercials-I-have-seen" speech won't call for you to do much research, but neither is it likely to hold your audience for very long. Your listeners may not be particularly receptive to a review of a subject with which they are quite familiar—they may want more than a recounting of what they have already experienced.

*

The reference section of your library is a virtual gold mine of ideas for speeches and materials for developing them. If you have some trouble getting started or if you can't find something you are looking for, talk to a reference librarian. It is unfortunate that many students never discover what a tremendous work-saving and anxiety-reducing resource a reference librarian can be. Do yourself a favor. Get to know your library and its reference staff better.

*

"I have a task and that is talking to you.
You have a task of listening to me.
I hope you do not finish before I do."

M. Gordon

Imagination

Though success in public speaking usually requires research, it also requires imagination, and it is in connection with imagination that we turn to another way of bringing about the effects of awareness and willingness. In some respects, the notion is suggested in the travelog example above, because we are thinking here of instances in which the speaker produces a new slant on an otherwise familiar subject. It's rather like using a filter to enhance the values of the clouds in a photograph, or suddenly getting an entirely different perspective on an object or an idea. By its nature, this approach to a subject is difficult to describe, except by metaphor or example. A pleasant illustration appeared in *Time* magazine recently when a writer used this strategy in an examination of television commercials. The essay described commercials as observers from outer space might interpret them in drawing conclusions about our culture. From their observations of the many messages proclaiming that relief is at hand, the travelers from another planet concluded that this culture is vastly troubled by perspiration wetness. Other discoveries include the fact that gasoline keeps automobile engines clean, that certain tablets will change people's moods in a matter of seconds, and that there are people of different colors here, all of whom get along very well with each other.

You might want to consider this kind of treatment of a topic, as it is a good way to make and keep an audience receptive. And in many cases, some additional point can be made, as in the *Time* example, which contains a bit of social commentary as well. Both of us have watched speakers keep their audiences interested with this technique, even though the presentations were neither particularly dynamic nor especially effective stylistically. And, no doubt, you too probably have heard some speakers who were able to keep their listeners interested and receptive because of the creative ways in which they developed their subjects.

Examples of student speeches that come to mind include one by a student who described and explained the extraordinary qualities of a new "miracle drug," and it wasn't until near the conclusion that it turned out she was talking about aspirin. Another student, given the potentially dreary assignment of explaining to fellow students how they could use the *U.S. Statistical Abstracts*, approached the publication from the viewpoint of a man who was carefully planning a crime. In the *Abstracts*, he would find valuable information about the best kind of crime to commit in terms of popularity and simplicity; he would find the best time of year to commit it, the best location, the potential gain, and so forth. Not only did the speaker illustrate the kinds of information the publication contained, he also demonstrated how the information could be used, and, most important for our immediate purpose, he sustained the interest and attention of the audience. Starting out to explain the many uses of a dictionary, another student remarked that "it contains everything from A to Z." Though the pun caused some groans, he used the alphabet throughout in a way that captured and held his audience's interest. As a final instance, we'll cite the speaker whose topic was an historical account of breakfast cereals in this country. Most of the success of this product was tied to organic foods and health fads, impulses which helped create some of the giants in the cereal industry in the nineteenth century. The Food and Drug Administration's findings that many of today's

*

Listen carefully to a fellow student or some other speaker who you think is good. How many signs can you detect that indicate a concern with audience awareness? It may be difficult to ignore delivery, language, and other things that may be relevant, but try to focus on evidence of audience analysis and the ways in which the speaker makes the listeners feel that the speech reflects "their own character." Some clues are easy to find, but others are quite subtle; can you find both?

*

popular cereals contain relatively little nutrition provided the basis for the irony with which the speaker sustained the listeners' attention.

MULTIPLE EFFECTS

In concluding this discussion of awareness and willingness, we want to make sure we don't leave the impression that audience effects always occur in neat, orderly sequences for all listeners. One stage may follow directly on another, but a single message may result in different listener effects, and the Agnew speech is a particularly interesting example. Recall that he began:

> Tonight I want to discuss the importance of the television news medium to the American people. No nation depends more on the intelligent judgment of its citizens. No medium has a more profound influence over public opinion. Nowhere in our system are there fewer checks on vast power. So, nowhere should there be a more conscientious responsibility exercised than by the news media. The question is are we demanding enough of our television news presentations? And are the men of this medium demanding enough of themselves?

And recall that he went on to make some highly critical remarks about the "instant analysis" of Nixon's important speech on the Vietnam situation. Finally, recall that he also spoke about the concentration of power in network television and expressed dissatisfaction with the bias which, he argued, too often emerged from this power base.

If we look at the speech in terms of effects, it becomes clear that many listeners gained a sharper sense of awareness concerning an important issue. All of us have come to expect that politicians and government leaders will be at least somewhat on the defensive with respect to the press, but here was a message making it obvious that the stance was changing from the traditional defensive posture to an offensive one. And while the matter of awareness seems straightforward enough, there is no doubt that the speech met with strong resistance in some quarters and eager acceptance in others. Representatives of the news media began to counterargue immediately and strongly; some began derogating the source (though much of the derogation was not too public) and still others attempted to transcend the issue by appealing to the First Amendment. However, ready acceptance also was evident—thousands of people wrote and wired support of the position Agnew took, but it is worth remarking that some who offered support did not clearly understand all the issues. On the other hand, while the news media changed some of their behavior— for example, commentators are now careful to announce whether a text has been released before a speech is delivered—the changes do not represent a real willingness to accept the accusations, nor was

Agnew's position one the networks happily accepted as part of their value system.

The implications of the speech go far beyond what we can do with it here, because the issues raised have been smoldering since; on several counts a more complete analysis would be interesting. But for the present, it is sufficient to have derived from the speech some indications of how the awareness effect can be bypassed to produce acceptance (and/or to influence listeners' behavior), sometimes without willingness, and sometimes without understanding. As a spokesman for the Nixon Administration, Vice President Agnew unquestionably enjoyed a special status and commanded greater attention than most people do when speaking; nevertheless, similar examples can be found throughout more ordinary communication activities. They may be less dramatic, but they are abundant.

UNDERSTANDING

Comprehension

Understanding is a minimal goal in most of our day-to-day communication—probably in the majority of public-speaking situations—because we usually intend our listeners to reach some level of comprehension. We want our listeners to be attentive and willing, naturally, but we want them to be so because we really want more—we want them to understand. But what does it mean to say that someone understands?

It's clear enough that we regularly recognize situations in which listeners understand or don't understand; we know which by what they say and do, or what they don't say and don't do. But while we deal with this matter constantly, it remains a perplexing and complicated business. If you were asked what you usually mean by "understanding," the definition probably would give you difficulty. A concept like understanding, as well as the word itself, is a truly rich one with a lot of surplus meaning. Troublesome as it is, though, it is well worth exploring some of the facets of a definition, as they will illuminate the speaker's concern with achieving this effect.

At the most elementary level, all of us probably can agree that we use the word in a narrow sense as being synonymous with *comprehending*. In this sense, we say that our dog "understands" what we say to him, or we tell someone that we "understand" their directions. Our hypothetical speech on historical aspects of welfare legislation should take listeners to a more advanced understanding of the subject, to a point where they have a more expanded view. Here, it may seem that understanding is a terminal goal, but it isn't necessarily, because such an understanding can set the stage for further action, for the reception of additional information, for further modification of the listeners' images on the topic.

Generally, then, understanding-as-comprehension means that some listener has gotten the message and has decoded it without any real difficulty; the listener has the information and can most likely carry out any appropriate behavior that might be called for later, such as giving a suitable reply, following directions, recognizing an item on a test, and so forth. Most educators, for example, would state that their ideal goal is to get students to learn their material, to grasp it and understand it in a broad and deep sense. Yet most educational systems have little choice but to settle for an assessment of a student's learning based only on a few limited "measures" (essays, multiple-choice tests) of the student's comprehension. But comprehension can go beyond just recall or recognition of information. It can include *knowing how* to do something. Thus, if you comprehend Spanish, you know what someone is saying to you in Spanish. If you comprehend a set of directions, you know how to get from, say, Manhattan to Brooklyn.

Understanding-as-comprehension, in short, often involves more than knowing isolated bits and pieces of information and storing them in memory. It is an extremely important—even crucial—facet of un-

*

Two possibilities for creating the effect of understanding in the sense of comprehension: You might plan a speech about a process with which you think your audience is unfamiliar, either because they have never considered it closely or because they used to know it but have forgotten. The goal is to explain *how something works*—how it takes place—and the subject might be the internal combustion engine, the manufacture of paper, sickle-cell anemia, an impeachment proceeding, or the Ruy Lopez opening in chess. Whether mechanical, scientific, social, or legal, however, the process is to be made understandable to your listeners.

The second possibility involves explaining *how to do something.* In this instance, it isn't a matter of telling your listeners how something happens; it is a matter of telling them how to do it themselves.

Either of these process explanations can be trivial and boring if you ignore the effects of awareness and willingness, but if you give the topic some reflection, you can bring about a genuine learning experience. In either case, your goal should be to get your audience to comprehend the process. You may want to decide what a superior level of comprehension would be. Think, too, about the level of comprehension you would be willing to settle for. If practical, prepare a short test to give your audience to see what level of comprehension your listeners have achieved.

*

derstanding. From a speaker's point of view, it can be an essential instrumental or terminal communication goal.

Knowing the implications

It is one thing to comprehend information, but it is quite another to grasp the implications of the information comprehended. For some few subjects and issues, a consideration of the implications follows almost habitually from comprehension. Take weather reports. No matter where we are or what we are doing, if we are interested in the weather report we are also interested in the *implications* of the weather report. We read the paper or watch the TV summary, and we understand that a hurricane is boiling up out of the Atlantic and poses a threat to the Florida Keys. If we live in Denver or Chicago or Los Angeles, however, we don't understand the implications of the storm in the way they do in Key Largo, Long Key, and Key West. People who live in the Keys, on the other hand, miss the implications of the weather report that tells of a blizzard howling out of the Northwest to chill the residents of Sioux Falls and Sioux City. Or consider any single area and a forecast of rain. The tourist understands one thing by it; the businessman, another; the farmer, another; and the politician on election day, still another.

In many cases, though, comprehension will not lead to consideration of implications. People are sometimes not interested in implications and at other times they are not capable of considering them. Certainly this situation presents a clear opportunity or a clear challenge for speakers whose goals are to have the audience reach this level of understanding. Indeed, this addition to listeners' images can be an extremely worthwhile instrumental or terminal communication goal.

Not too long ago, for example, most of us were unaware of the fact that our country was facing an energy shortage. First, as some individuals and agencies began to talk about it, we became aware of the problem. Somewhat later, many of us began to comprehend that our consumption of fossil fuels and other kinds of energy was increasing at a rate faster than that energy could be made available and that certain energy sources would ultimately be depleted. Given this information, it is likely that we have only begun to examine the implications. Certainly there are implications in the energy crisis for every aspect of our lives—including our life styles, our work, our education, transportation, leisure, health, and food consumption. If you were preparing a speech on this topic to draw out certain implications, your emphasis would depend on your own preferences for a topic and your communication goal for the speech.

Getting your audience to see the implications of any issue may involve projections into the future or it may involve a here-and-now approach. When you point out implications for your listeners, you add facets of knowledge to their images, or you polish the facets they already have by helping them to contemplate new or further possibilities. You may even lead them, in some instances, to plausible new conclusions, therefore new understanding. In any case, exploring implications or knowing what they are is the second dimension in our definition of understanding, and a very important one.

*

Prepare a speech in which your goal is understanding. Specifically, concentrate on getting your listeners to see the implications of the subject you choose.

*

Appreciation

The concluding appeal in Marilyn Hayashi Rye's "My Grandfather" rests on an understanding that assuredly goes beyond comprehension. Even if no specific implications are immediately evident, it cannot be doubted that some sympathy—some real appreciation of the circumstances—is evoked. As an aspect of understanding, appreciation encompasses an emotional grasp of the subject or issue, and it is almost invariably present when we try to understand imaginative discourse, poetry in particular. An excellent illustration is Milton's famous lament over the loss of his sight, the poem "On His Blindness":

> When I consider how my light is spent
>   Ere half my days in this dark world and wide,
>   And that one talent which is death to hide
>   Lodged with me useless, though my soul more bent
> To serve therewith my Maker, and present
>   My true account, lest he returning chide,
>   "Doth God exact day-labour, light denied?"
>   I fondly ask. But Patience, to prevent
> That murmur, soon replies, "God doth not need
>   Either man's work or his own gifts. Who best
>   Bear his mild yoke, they serve him best. His state
> Is kingly: thousands at his bidding speed,
>   And post o'er land and ocean without rest;
>   They also serve who only stand and wait.

No summary statement or paraphrase can substitute for the "meaning" of any poem, but here, Milton finds a resolution of his blindness in resignation to the will of God. It can be argued that only another devoutly religious person would most appreciate this level of understanding, would gain the fullest and richest emotional meaning from the poem. Atheists would indeed be in fundamental disagreement with Milton's solution, but they would certainly be able to appreciate the beauty with which the solution is phrased.

Understanding-as-appreciation may well be best illustrated by considering some of the problems that can arise in the effort to bring about this level of response in listeners. Certain aspects of one person's existence and experience may be very difficult for another person really to perceive and appreciate. For instance, what do most of us understand about the circumstances either of unlimited wealth or of grinding poverty? We may dream unlikely dreams about the former, but we try never even to think about the latter.

Perhaps you have tasted the flavor of this subtle, complex problem when you were working at a part-time job and you met people of a different age group, or people with a background quite different from your own. Under such circumstances you may well have decided that certain subjects just had to be avoided because there seemed little hope of making any adjustments in either your image or in theirs. Clearly, people encounter difficulties when they find themselves in a place where, quite literally, they don't speak the language —perhaps you've been there when traveling in another country. Then there is the matter of "culture shock," the difference in social norms that may intrude. Some differences can be overcome easily enough; for example, it does not take much time in Great Britain to comprehend, realize the implications of, and appreciate the way in which the people "queue up"—the way in which they form orderly lines while waiting for the bus, for food service, or for theater tickets.

We form judgments or we discover from both formal and informal speaking whether or not an individual understands at this level. When you say that one of your teachers "understands" the younger generation in this sense, you mean that the teacher brings more than comprehension and a grasp of the implications; the "more" is a feeling for the attitudes of frustration and excitement—in short, a genuine appreciation for the special qualities so often found in the young. But this kind of appreciation is not just limited to people and their situations; it concerns events and things as well. In this connection, the two of us know a genetics teacher who has recently changed his teaching goals and his teaching techniques because he has become especially eager to have his students *appreciate* his subject. He wants more than comprehension—he wants an emotional response as well. He wants his students to share his excitement in the elegance of the laws of genetics, to marvel at the mystery of its processes, and to stand somewhat in awe of its complexities.

Awkwardly enough, perhaps, appreciation may be the most difficult to achieve in areas where it is most needed. Blacks, Indians, women, and other groups have been assigned to subservient status for so long that it may be difficult for whites and males to comprehend the problems of these groups, and next to impossible for them to move beyond comprehension and grasp the implications to the fullest measure of understanding. "You can't understand because you weren't there." Even though we all realize that we understand more than we can express about some subjects, that statement does seem to sum it up. We know, then, that appreciation can be the most difficult level of understanding to reach—whether we are sending or receiving the message—but we also know that this level can be the most vital in communication.

*

A speech that takes your listeners to appreciation need not explore prejudice or emotional experience of the highest order. Its subject could be some significant social problem, or it could be some ordinary experience, springing from your personal inventory of life and times. The simplest sort of appreciation can be important because communication invariably requires that we build on metaphorical experience. We all have been happy, excited, frightened, angry, bored— but those words are merely conventional symbols for emotional states, and no repetition will recreate the state. We can, however, come close to sharing them through verbal expression. In fact, an emotional state is an ideal subject for this assignment. Your goal would not be to create fear or anger or jealousy in your listeners, but to make them appreciate one of your own experiences. Your success will depend on your ability to recall your own and others' experiences, and to shape the materials in a way that will elicit a sympathetic reaction from the listeners. Please don't confuse this with a "My Most Embarrassing Moment" speech, an assignment that often is no more than a fraud.

Certainly, the present assignment need not be restricted; it can extend to music and the other arts, to crafts and hobbies, to sports and games, and to the most serious problems in our society. But whatever your tack, you will have to strike sympathetic chords in your listeners, whether you're talking about music or not.

*

As a final example of communication that leaps from comprehension to appreciation, consider the potential impact in the following passage from "Shoes":

> From our storeroom, I have brought you the first pair of shoes that I ever purchased for our family. These shoes, just the way I put them away nineteen years ago, were worn by all three of our children, and during that period of life, you know, where they get into kitchen cupboards and pull out all the canned goods and the pots and the pans and the lids, and which made walking across the kitchen floor quite an occupational hazard for Ma. But these shoes represent a great deal to me and bring back many happy memories, as I'm sure your baby

shoes will bring back memories to you. I'm going to place these at this end of the board to illustrate the beginning of that period called family life. Now I'll show you the last pair of shoes that I bought for my family, wedding slippers. That was a great day in our life when I walked down the aisle with my daughter, and that day brings back happy memories. I place these at this end of the board to represent the end of the period called family life.

Nothing too fancy here and a touch of the sentimental, but remember that Boyd was speaking to people in the insurance business or people who were contemplating careers there. Most had lived through or were living through similar experiences; consequently, his explanation of house, home, and family had great potential for evoking appreciation in listeners. Moreover, when he went on to replace the working shoes with insurance policies beneath the board, his explaining went beyond appreciation to acceptance, thus automatically making his listeners more content with their careers or the careers they were contemplating.

As we said at the outset of our discussion of understanding, the concept is a rich one, loaded with various meanings. We could say a great deal more, but we will be content if you have sharpened your own thinking about the three different processes of comprehension, knowing the implications, and appreciation. Clearly identifying these three levels of understanding can help you to clarify your own speaking goals—whether they are instrumental or terminal—and can also suggest approaches you may want to consider in the preparation or presentation of your speeches.

PREVIEW: CHAPTER 6

Chapter 6 continues and concludes our examination of speaking for effects. The topics are:

Acceptance
    Based on identification
    Based on internalization
    Based on consistency
    Based on reasoning
Behavior: change and continuation
    Based on compliance
    Based on adoption
    Based on continuance
    Based on deterrence
    Based on discontinuance

We simply extend the discussion in Chapter 5, and our purpose here is the same as our purpose there: when you have completed this chapter, we want you to have a more complete understanding of acceptance and behavior change, and we want this understanding to assist you when you are speaking for these effects.

listener effects

ACCEPTANCE, BEHAVIOR

6

ACCEPTANCE

The term "acceptance" is often used synonymously with "understanding." In this sense, we may *accept* many bits of information that do not have much or any influence on our attitudes and actions. Back to the weather example in Chapter 5: watching a television newscast you accept the description presented—that is, you believe that a hurricane is ripping through the Florida Keys—but if you live in Chicago, you do not immediately jump up from your chair to board your windows and doors. In this sense, we all learn to accept the behavior of others. For example, we can understand—even appreciate—the reasons why a political candidate makes certain appeals, appears in certain places, and uses certain forms of political publicity. We accept this behavior, but we may vote for someone else. These two examples illustrate one kind of acceptance, but in this section, we're primarily concerned with acceptance at still another level—the level that involves a change in our behavior.

As we've been remarking all along in discussing effects, much of our communicative effort is aimed at the value component of our listeners' images and, ultimately, at their behavior. Briefly put, unless a message is rejected altogether, listeners *accept* a communication when it seems to be consistent with their existing value images, or else they modify their value images so that they are consistent with the communication. That's basically what happens. But it's *how* it happens that interests us here—how a speaker can bring about some kind of acceptance in others by communicating with them. Psychologists who study this phenomenon usually talk about attitude development and change; others who have studied and written about the subject talk about persuasion, and we could produce a long list of labels—some general, others specific, many of them overlapping—which describe the various approaches to gaining a listener's acceptance. The skinniest pamphlet on how to sell cosmetics door-to-door, a treatise on the art of rhetoric, and a philosophical inquiry into the nature of human values all may share a common concern for many of the same issues, even though they may vary considerably in regard to assumptions made and applications indicated.

Our own approach to the concept of acceptance will be very general and inclusive. As we noted in Chapter 2, images have an important value component: people can share essentially the same image about what a thing is, but will rate that thing quite differently. Thus, using our previous illustration, two people may agree about the physical make-up of their old neighborhood and disagree violently about its valuation. So too with many, many other ideas and issues and states of affairs. The value dimensions of the image involve personal judgments of goodness and badness, liking and disliking, importance and unimportance, approaching and avoiding, favor and disfavor, and so on. For centuries, some of the best minds in the world have addressed themselves to human value systems and their related consequences, but this is hardly the place to delve into the many ramifications of those inquiries. Nevertheless, we would insist that any discussion of values finally catches us up in the study of communication. When one person tries to get another to accept a particular assessment of the world, the attempt has to encompass communication. Indeed, we have remarked that a discrepancy between two value systems may be the very thing that motivates a person or group or organization or society to communicate with another. And, often, these same value systems are the very things that determine whether the communication will be received and, if it is received, how it will be received. So the subject is truly profound and complex, and it is with an awareness of its profundity and complexity that we proceed with our examination of the acceptance stage of communication.

Our examination owes a great deal to the ideas of the social psychologist Herbert C. Kelman. In his widely respected article "Processes of Opinion Change,"* Kelman raises some fundamental issues:

* *Public Opinion Quarterly,* Vol. 25, No. 1 (Spring, 1961), pp. 57-78.

What is the nature of the actions that people who hold a particular opinion are likely to take, and how are they likely to react to various events? How likely are these opinions to persist over time and to generalize to related issues? What are the conditions under which one might expect these opinions to be abandoned and changed? Such predictions can be made only to the extent to which we are informed about the crucial dimensions of the opinions in question, about the motivations that underlie them, and about the cognitive contexts in which they are held.

Kelman has just begun, and we already like what he is saying, because in our view, he is asking questions and pointing up matters that should be of concern to anyone interested in communication. It seems very sensible to conceive of people's value systems as being developed on different bases and for different reasons. It is reasonable, too, to expect that an understanding of how value images are grounded will put the speaker in a better position to know how, or whether, they can be changed. Developing these ideas, Kelman identifies three basic processes of social influence—identification, internalization, and compliance. Each of these processes can be linked to a different aspect of an individual's value system; each suggests that the conditions of the change in the value system will be somewhat different; and each implies that a relatively specific approach is involved in the efforts to bring about change. We will focus first on the concepts of identification and internalization, before discussing compliance in the section that follows.

Based on identification

In general, the process of identification is an individual's acceptance of the influence of another person or group in order to establish a satisfying relationship with that person or group. The assumption here is a compelling one, one we've mentioned in connection with the image and in connection with resistance to persuasion. This is the assumption that, in many situations, people find a social anchor for their beliefs and behavior instead of thinking their way through to conclusions and solutions. People do this by identifying with persons or groups who seem attractive to them. In some respects, it's a matter of keeping up with the Joneses, providing we like the Joneses. For example, you decide to subscribe to a weekly news magazine; you have some friends who read *Newsweek*, some who read *Time*. Other things being equal, you will probably subscribe to the magazine read by the friends who are most attractive to you. Of course, our example is oversimplified because other things seldom *are* equal, but it does illustrate how identification works. You undoubtedly have seen it operating when students vote in elections, when they pick places of recreation—even sometimes when they select their courses—and you have probably also seen it influence your parents and their friends in similar ways.

If you admire the life style of a particular person or group, you will be inclined to adopt as many features of this style as you can. This kind of behavior is what psychologists call "classical identification," and some part of all of us is the result; we all define ourselves at least partially by taking on the values and behavior of others, beginning with our parents. The process may involve either trivial or important matters, and although it can be subtle in its operation, it can also be blatant. We all know people who seem to take all their values and attitudes from some single person or single group of people. Again, magazines provide a good illustration: there are many people who seem to rely almost exclusively on the concept of living that is set forth in *Better Homes and Gardens,* and still others who look to *Playboy* as the main anchor for their beliefs and behavior.

*

As you know, advertisers constantly use identification appeals to gain acceptance for products and services, and a brief examination of some examples can help crystallize the process in your mind. You might look at newspapers, billboards, magazines, and television for instances; it's particularly interesting to look through magazines from twenty or thirty years ago and compare the appeals made then with those being made now, noting both similarities and differences.

*

We mentioned in Chapter 2 that we are habitually active in searching for and sorting messages, and identification is part of this process; for example, this searching and sorting may explain part of the motivation for exposing oneself to a message in the first place. Certainly other factors operate too, but some of the Republicans who listened to Agnew's Des Moines speech were attentive because of their party identification. Furthermore, the prestige associated with the Vice Presidential office nurtured identification for some people. We could refine this analysis, but the conclusion is apparent: be somebody important—gain elective office, pitch a perfect game, walk on the moon, play lead guitar in a famous rock group—so that others find it easy to identify with you. Simple enough, right? Wrong, of course, but we have to realize that some people are more likely than others to have the potential for eliciting identification because of their reputation. At the same time, everyone has some potential in this regard.

Even though superheroes and superheroines may capture and hold attention, may set patterns that others eagerly follow, identification operates in many less dramatic ways; most of us do a great deal of identifying with those we perceive to be similar to us, who appear to share our images. On the surface at least, as a speaker you ought to find it less difficult to gain identification from other college students than from the local Rotary Club. But the superficial advantage can be lost, the superficial disadvantage overcome. The task for the speaker is to analyze the audience and turn its values to advantage. In his Des Moines speech, Agnew skillfully capitalized on the values inherent in the creation of identification by introducing and attacking the television coverage of a speech that Nixon had delivered a week earlier; the links with party and President intensified the existing identification and resulting acceptance for many listeners. Through examples and through direct reference, you can do the same in your speeches, though it may not be on such a grand scale. Both Rye and Boyd used aspects of family life to make for stronger identification, though in different ways. However, your main problem as a speaker in this regard may be to unfold the potential for identification, to develop your materials in ways that permit the process to function and increase the likelihood of acceptance, whether or not your ultimate goal is the alteration of behavior. And remember that speakers sometimes err in regard to the identification. Perhaps you have heard a speaker upholding a cause in which you believed, but at the end you wished he or she was on the other side, because the speaker's arguments, attitudes, and entire performance reversed your initial tendency to identify and accept.

*

Preference surveys, opinion polls, and other samplings of attitudes seem to be flourishing enterprises in our society. As our culture becomes more complex, the use of surveys enables those willing to expend the energy or the money to learn something about individuals and groups. Obviously, this kind of research is effective or we wouldn't see a continued increase in its use. Just as obviously, a significant amount of survey research is designed to obtain a picture of the relevant parts of people's value images—their preferences, their habits, their opinions, their impressions about objects and people and events. They are also frequently used to learn more about people's various bases for identification, whether marketing a new product or promoting a political candidate. The assumption, and surely it is a reasonable one, is that knowledge about value images will facilitate the designing of products, messages, candidates, and the like, with the design tailored to the value images of a given audience. From our point of view, survey research is nothing but a sophisticated and systematic kind of audience analysis. With this in mind, we suggest the following two exercises:

1. Design your own poll for some speaking assignment and see if you can learn some things about your listeners' identification. You might use the poll to help you decide among several possible topics, or you might use it to help you to develop an appeal for acceptance of a topic that you have already chosen.

2. Given the wide use of surveys in our society, it would be instructive for you to learn something more about their operation and about how clients use the findings. To this end, you might study an organization that does survey research or examine an individual example of survey research. The entertainment industry, the communications media, political organizations, advertising agencies, and retail businesses make rather extensive use of surveys, and your particular interests may take you into one of these areas. A thoughtful analysis of this research can be more than just one more report, can offer further insights into the entire process of human communication.

*

Another aspect of identification that is important to the notion of acceptance emerges from what Kelman calls "reciprocal role relationships." In this kind of relationship, identification is a function of shared expectations; among the more obvious examples are the relationships between friends, husband and wife, teacher and student, doctor and patient, parent and child. All of us play many of these roles, and they help determine whether we are willing to accept efforts to influence our thoughts and behavior. Of course they are relative, and a role that makes for acceptance in one situation won't operate in another. Let's use an extreme example to illustrate. You go to get a medical check-up and are shown to an examination room. The doctor arrives and tells you to take off your clothes. You accept. You take off your clothes, because that behavior is part of the doctor-patient role relationship. But if you met the same doctor at a cocktail party, you wouldn't respond in the same way to the same request— at least we hope you wouldn't—and if that request came from a teacher in a large lecture hall, you'd probably head for the nearest exit. The point is that people are inclined to accept an attempt to influence their behavior when they see that certain thoughts, feelings, behaviors are required by the role relationship. (It is worth noting that the humor in many jokes and cartoons rests on a distortion of the expected relationship, leading to inappropriate behavior. That role relationships serve as the basis for jokes indicates the important part that they play in our lives.) And any particularly rewarding role relationship may be so vital to us that we behave in ways consistent with the role even when our role partner isn't around. Loyal friends are loyal, regardless of time or place, and a happily married man behaves like a happily married man even when he is away from his wife on a business trip or at a convention. The nature and development of the role relationship between Huck and Jim make for some of the finest moments in *The Adventures of Huckleberry Finn,* and in *Wind in the Willows,* Toady's conduct is so delightfully outlandish because he won't accept an appropriate role relationship with Rat, Mole, and Badger.

An important thing to note about both kinds of identification is that the influence process has a social basis. Both are rooted, by definition, in social relationships of some kind, and to the extent that a given social relationship gives us a chance to establish or maintain a satisfying definition of self, we are likely to accept efforts to influence our beliefs and actions. So Kelman's approach produces the very reasonable conclusion that the more attractive and satisfying the social anchor is, the greater the likelihood of acceptance. But the social anchor has to be more than attractive. It also has to be salient. That is, the person being influenced must get enough specific cues from the situation to know the correct role and the appropriate behavior. As we have already suggested, we think that Agnew made the social anchors clear and salient to many listeners during the Des Moines speech. On the one hand, he made supporters feel that the press was being unfair in attacking government—he gave the attack a strong political emphasis. And on the other, the television networks, willing or not, recognized and dealt with the behavior he imputed to them. An unusual situation perhaps, but let's look at another, the "Checkers" speech that Richard M. Nixon gave when he was on the 1952 ticket with General Eisenhower and a campaign fund of Nixon's had been questioned. In this one speech, Nixon identified himself and his wife as simple, modestly dressed, dog-loving folks; he attempted to associate himself with the prestige his running mate had earned during World War II; and, at the end, he specifically requested that the audience respond to his appeal and confirm their conviction of his innocence.

*

Select a controversial subject as a topic to develop—the college grading system, welfare, capital punishment, wire-tapping, ecology— anything on which people have markedly divergent views. Then consider developing a speech for listeners who are likely to be on your side, and try to ground all your appeals and arguments in some kind of identification. Then think how you might pursue the same sort of grounding when presenting the same topic to an audience that is likely to be in disagreement. Even if you never give either speech, to think the problem through will help you clarify what we're talking about here.

*

Based on internalization

Identification is based on social cues and social support, but internalization is acceptance emerging from an individual's value system. Now, if what we said earlier about the image has any merit and if you're thinking about that, you might well contend that values result primarily from social and cultural surroundings, that values are socially based too. And if you argued that way, you would be quite right. However, we think Kelman makes a useful distinction when he defines identification as beliefs and behavior based on expectations associated with social roles, and internalization as beliefs and behavior based on a private value system that does not depend on social support. Even though social roles help create our values, some value images finally become internalized, or autonomous. They exist and function even without social support; in fact, they can become so powerfully ingrained that they persist long after social support has disappeared. Old-fashioned habits of custom and courtesy offer a good illustration of internalized value images. Consider, for example, the insignificant but nettlesome question of whether you should pick up your fried chicken when eating it. Well, the Emily Posts of this world vacillated between forks and fingers for years, but they finally gave their stamp of approval to fingers. But at dinners and banquets, you'll still see people trying to strip the meat from a drumstick with a knife and fork. Once upon a time, the activity was based on identification: "polite people never eat chicken with their fingers." Now, identification —and good sense—point to different behavior, but internalization is so strong for some people that they go on glumly battling their way through a plate of fried chicken. At times, behavior reflects neither thought nor choice, but merely old and habitual patterns.

M. When I was growing up, I noticed what seemed to be slightly odd behavior in some of the solid citizens of our small town. A doctor, a pharmacist, and the mortician chewed on cigars, but they never smoked them. One day I asked my father about this. The explanation was simple enough. When these men had started to use tobacco, chewing was the most popular form, considered by many people less objectionable than smoking. So chewing had social support in the community. Times changed, however, and while the local image of the doctor, the pharmacist, and the mortician encompassed smoking, chewing was now out. So these three men had to put aside their Brown Mule, Mail Pouch, and Copenhagen chewing tobacco, but they maintained their internalized values by smuggling in the old habit under the guise of smoking cigars. Too bad all such conflicts can't be as easily resolved!

Some internalized values apply generally but may vary individually, and in these instances the matter of social support blurs a bit. At Des Moines Agnew remarked, "One Federal Communications Commissioner considers the powers of the networks equal to that of local, state and federal governments all combined. Certainly it represents a concentration of power over American public opinion unknown in history." Throughout the speech, he raised questions con-

Drawing by Ton Smits; © 1959 The New Yorker Magazine, Inc.

cerning this unchecked and biased concentration of power, and although subsequent events give some irony to the charge, he argued that "the American people would rightly not tolerate this concentration of power in Government." Here, we think, he touched upon internalized values long associated with democracy—the checks and balances in the American system, and even our free press. He was trying to get his listeners to accept his communication by showing how the ideas presented were consistent with internalized value images. With a different purpose in mind, William Boyd did the same thing when he listed the objects and events associated with family experience in an appeal to values shared by his listeners. Combining identification and internalization, he made his life seem a proper model, and he made that career fit with important elements in the value systems of his listeners.

Boyd's situation would appear to present no real challenges, but it isn't necessarily easy to tell people what they already know and believe, especially when the subject doesn't involve some pressing issue. Certainly the task becomes greater when there is potential for resistance. For example, suppose you are working on a speech in which you advocate more humane treatment for people in prison. Now our society values the dignity and worth of all human beings, but differentiation clearly is possible, with listeners saying to themselves that those who have been sent to prison have forfeited concern for their dignity and worth. Well, you might explore the essence of the resistance and attempt to create a new vigor for the concept of humane treatment. In this way you might give new vitality to private value images, but it might be wise to go further and make some new connections; you might show how prison reforms lead to greater economy and increase the likelihood of lasting rehabilitation, particularly if you feel that these ideas strike at important values among your listeners.

An important thing to note in this discussion is that identification and internalization are two different sources for acceptance, a fact that helps to explain why what some listeners may find persuasive may not be persuasive to others. But as we have suggested, although identification and internalization are distinct, they are not mutually exclusive; to pretend they are when describing human beings and their behavior is to create an oversimplified portrait that misses much in the object being portrayed. Nevertheless, the conceptual distinction we have been using allows us to identify differences which are important for understanding the business of communication. Let's get back to bicycle riding for a final example. Suppose you are trying to persuade a friend to begin bike riding, or to do more of it. If you argue that it's the thing to do because all your mutual friends are doing it, you would be making an identification appeal. But if you argued that the activity is both healthful and economical, you would be relying on internalization. One approach may work best with some people, the other with different people, but it probably is best to combine both appeals because both identification and internalization function when people accept the influence of others. All this points to a need for some thought about the audience to be addressed, and even close audience analysis if possible. The analysis can help you work out the right kinds of appeals and avoid the inappropriate ones.

Based on consistency

Whatever basis you choose for your appeal, you should note that you need to take the concept of *consistency* into account as well, both as it relates to role expectations or relationships and to value systems. A tremendous amount of theory and research in the social sciences has underlined the importance of the consistency notion, especially as it concerns the acceptance process. The findings show that there is a strong tendency for all of us to need a reasonable degree of compatibility and consistency in our images and behavior. We need to feel that our beliefs, attitudes, and actions don't conflict with each other, and (although this topic ranges far beyond the scope of the present discussion), this need has immediate implications for speechmaking. In preparing for a speech, the speaker should be particularly concerned with showing how appeals and arguments for acceptance are consistent with the listeners' role expectations or relationships and their value systems, and there should be a similar concern for making the appeals themselves have that same consistency.

Based on reasoning

When discussing audience analysis, we suggested that it could be useful to approach the task by estimating how much the listeners knew about the topic and how much they cared. In the last few pages, we obviously have been concentrating on the latter—on caring—for we have been stressing attitudes and values. But if we have emphasized psychological aspects, we hope that logic has not drowned in the psycho-logic. Sound reasoning and good evidence can be tremendously important in the communication process. The guilty may hope otherwise, but in a court of law the innocent surely desire a careful weighing of the evidence and a verdict based on as much fact as it is possible to attain. Although Kelman alludes to the rational element, his purposes do not require extended treatment of the subject, but ours do need further comment. Most of our remarks will be reserved for Chapter 9 and our discussion of structure in argument, but we want to point out here that the nature of the knowing may be fundamental in making a speech successful. Always the knowing will be influenced by the caring, and all of us readily accept new information in a variety of circumstances. Furthermore, we learn to accept that reality may not be what we might want it to be, that there are sound reason for altering our perceptions. Some situations, of course, may not lend themselves to a concentration on reasoned discourse.

M. I worked one summer in a tavern at a resort area, and I was behind the bar on a warm Saturday afternoon in July. A new customer came in and made his way to one of the tables, but the way he walked and the difficulty he had in managing the chair suggested that he might not need any more to drink. The waitress checked and came back to confirm my suspicions. He was drunk. So I told her to tell him that we could not serve him. After she relayed the unhappy news, he stood up and rather erratically walked in my direction. The conversation ran like this:
"I want some beer."
"We can't serve you."
"Why not?"
"You've had enough to drink already."
"Just who do you think you are?"
"Friend, when I'm behind this bar, you just pretend I'm God."
I don't suppose he believed me, but fortunately he accepted the situation; he shrugged his shoulders, and shuffled out the door.

There are times in life when reasoning is fruitless, and there are related times in public-speaking situations. We're not referring to the speeches at banquets after a long cocktail party; we're talking about those times when the listeners understand and accept the basic premises of the speaker for reasons other than the reasonableness of those premises. In such circumstances—and we think that "Shoes" fits into this category—reinforcement may not require anything more than an imaginative and resourceful amplification.

On the other hand, it may be that Lincoln helped his cause precisely because he presented the Republican position with such carefully rational attention to the details of the slavery issue. Addressing Republicans, he argued their cause better than they could have for themselves. And other speakers meet with similar opportunities, for our images develop in ways that may not include the rational bases for acceptance. Many values and degrees of valuation may be accepted and acted upon, even though the individual is not aware of all the good reasons for acceptance and action. Consequently, a speaker may be of greatest service to the audience by exploring those good reasons.

By the same token, we may unconsciously accept values and institutions that won't bear close scrutiny. In fact, the need for such close scrutiny generates much public speaking. This undertaking demands that speakers closely examine all the evidence that bears on a specific issue and the controversy that ensues. What a speaker can contribute to the decision-making process is of special significance in our society, and that contribution may rest on the use of reasoned discourse in achieving acceptance.

*

We have been talking about the use of reasoned discourse in connection with accepted values and in connection with controversy. You may have speech assignments that permit or demand that you treat one or the other. But even without such an assignment, you might find it instructive to consider one possibility from each area, a possibility that flows from the interpretation you have of the society and culture around you.

*

BEHAVIOR: CHANGE AND CONTINUATION

Based on compliance

When we began the discussion of acceptance, we said we wanted to delay any consideration of compliance, as the concept is an excellent introduction to our discussion of the behavior effect. By compliance,

Kelman means the behavior that results when people act in spite of the fact that they do not personally accept the influence effort—behavior that seems not to be grounded in any real need or in any sound argument. Perhaps you have bought something from a persistent salesman, not because you wanted or needed the item, but just so the fool would go away. This is a relatively low-level illustration of compliance, but it is accurate. Compliance is involved in situations where we behave in some particular way not because we believe in or accept the full implications of our behavior, but because the behavior will produce some other satisfying effect. So we may agree to take a trial subscription to a neighborhood newspaper when we really have no interest in reading that particular paper; instead we feel sorry for the newsboy and want him to go away and leave us alone. The stakes aren't high in the trial subscription, but when people sign real estate contracts or buy life insurance for reasons of compliance, it's a different story. And compliance doesn't operate only in the realms of selling and buying; someone working in an office may change the filing system simply because the boss made the suggestion, even though the suggestion doesn't seem wise. Students may be convinced that certain assignments are valueless, but go ahead and carry them out anyway. Social pressure may prompt new members of a group to go along with group actions at times when they don't support those actions. In these instances and in countless others, people behave in a given way even though they don't really accept the reason for the behavior. Instead they comply, because compliance may lead to other rewards—to promotion, good grades, or friendships, to parallel the examples above.

At one time or another, most of us influence others through compliance processes. If you have younger brothers or sisters, you probably have achieved goals through compliance. On the other hand, your older sisters and brothers—and certainly your parents—have turned compliance on you. When any speakers have the necessary backing to insure the compliance of their listeners, they really need not worry about communication skills, nor need they be concerned about audience analysis or anything else that we talk about in this book. If you find yourself in that position, people will do your bidding, and you hardly need fret about any insights that may come from a study of the communication process. However, it's a chancy business to rely on behavior effects that stem from compliance. These effects are pretty tenuous and unpredictable. Although appeals based on compliance are not uncommon, history records no instances of individuals or groups who have had consistent or lasting success with only the use of compliance efforts and techniques. Even dictators with absolute power have not been content to rely on compliance. They all have used a wide variety of techniques to influence behavior.

As you might suspect, we aren't particularly concerned here with the implications of compliance. Chances are it operates for you or it doesn't in a given situation. What interests us most—and, we hope, you—is the situations where communication is the primary means of affecting the images and the behavior of other people, but we want to back off a bit further for a moment to note that many communications cannot be expected to elicit immediate behavior responses.

In the first place, as we have remarked throughout this discussion of effects, goals other than influencing behavior may be most suitable in the communication process. As a speaker you will often be quite content if your listeners develop greater awareness or better understanding of your views, or accept them with more enthusiasm. For example, a woman from one of the nearby television stations spoke to a class on our campus about women in broadcast journalism, and she seemed most interested in having her audience understand her perception of the part women play in this activity. Surely she was also interested in creating a favorable attitude toward the station for which she works, but she did not have any specific behavior in mind for her listeners; she was interested almost entirely in achieving increased understanding.

In the second place, many communications prevent any goal beyond acceptance; the behavior desired may not be fitting at the time. Think about how many times you find yourself unable to respond with the action requested. Speakers ask us to write to our senators and congressmen, but our immediate, snide response to these requests may be, "Give me a piece of paper and a pen, also a stamped envelope." And it's safe to assume that temperance lecturers of the nineteenth century didn't address groups who were in the midst of drunken orgies; maybe members of the Anti-Saloon League encountered likely prospects during their activities, but it's also safe to assume that they met considerable resistance when tearing up some of the taverns. The point to note is that communication asking for specific behavior often takes place in circumstances where the behavior called for is impossible or inappropriate at the moment.

Yet, when it really gets down to cases, influencing behavior is the goal toward which the majority of our communication efforts are directed. Though we may be willing to settle for a communication effect that falls short of the behavior stage, we often are concerned ultimately with influencing the behavior of our listeners: we want them to perform or to stop performing some act. Even in the seemingly most trivial situations, we are likely to have action in mind as a goal in communication. David Berlo, in his book *The Process of Communication,* uses the mundane example of getting someone to pass the salt. Suppose you are sitting in a restaurant, and after your first bite of the steak you decide that some salt is required. You can't reach the salt, but the person next to you can, so you ask, "Would you please pass the salt?" In terms of effects on listeners, the entire sequence is here, if in compressed form. The listener becomes *aware* of a need that you have and is *willing* to consider that need. *Understanding* occurs because your message is decoded, the listener attaching appropriate meaning to the request and knowing what the request demands in the way of action. And we assume *acceptance* of your simple plea, a commitment to pass along the needed salt shaker. But what it all boils down to in that moment, the real acid test, is *behavior*— whether the salt is passed along. If the response is "No, I won't," then you go back three effects and lose one turn. Communication of this sort takes place regularly, often in relatively unimportant matters such as asking someone for the time or for directions. In these simple instances, we get a behavioral response at once, but behavior is the standard by which we finally judge the effectiveness of communication in the more significant events of our lives as well. At the same time, it is important to remember that in almost any situation, the effects of communication may stop short of the behavior stage. For the speaker, this may or may not be satisfactory; much depends on what you are willing to settle for, on what you can expect to accomplish with a particular audience.

But let's take a little closer look at behavior effects in communication. After all, there are many different kinds of behavior, and we ought to be able to do better than lump all of them under a single, gross heading. One group in the stands is shouting, "We want a touchdown," another group, "Hold that line!" One group yells, "We want a hit," another, "Strike him out!" Wallace Fotheringham presents some useful ideas by classifying behavior into four general kinds: adoption, continuance, deterrence and discontinuance.[*] These categories are very helpful; they get at those differences expressed by the fans in the stands and get at some others as well.

Based on adoption

Adoption is the kind of behavior that many people think of in association with persuasion. It involves getting the listener to change a behavior or set of behaviors to a new behavior or set of behaviors. Probably the most obvious kind of adoption appeals appear in advertising. Introductory offers are everywhere, the purpose of which is to get us to try something new or different. The hope is that once we've tried it, we'll like it. But adoption appeals are common in many other kinds of communication. A politician running against an incumbent may argue that the office needs new blood and new ideas to replace the old and worn-out performer. And on every side we constantly are being urged to take on new patterns of behavior, whether

[*] Wallace C. Fotheringham, *Perspectives on Persuasion* (Boston, 1966), pp. 32-34.

in our eating habits, voting, leisure activities, or any other facet of our lives.

*

Suppose you are asking for adoption as the ultimate goal in a speech. What kinds of identification and internalization seem the most useful? The answer will be a function of the topic and the audience, but you ought to be able to think of the social anchors and the value hierarchies that will help in making general estimates.

*

Based on continuance

The primary goal in much communication is to get the listeners to continue doing what they're already doing. The speaker doesn't want them to change; the speaker wants them *not* to change, wants them to do more of the same. Again the examples from advertising are numerous, and many commercials are designed to sustain or increase the loyalty of people already buying the product. But continuance appeals are also all around us in other forms of communication. For example, Boyd doesn't ask for any specific kind of behavior, but for people in the insurance business his speech supports continuance, it points to satisfaction with a career. And, if the team is doing well, continuance is the goal in pep-talks—those exhortations to football teams at half-time, to salespersons at sales meetings, or to precinct workers for a political party.

*

Asking for continuation, a speaker may be satisfied if the listeners simply keep doing what they have been doing. On the other hand, the speech may take on some flavor of adoption because the speaker wants the listeners to do even a better job of doing what they have been doing. How can you use the rational dimension to reinforce some value appeal, an appeal that you know will be effective with a particular audience in gaining continuance?

*

Based on deterrence

Many speeches and other forms of communication are aimed at getting audiences not to do something, to deter them from doing something they might otherwise do. In political life, for example, part of an appeal may involve adoption, but part of it relates to deterrence. Many speeches in Congress have these characteristics, with senators and representatives often urging inaction by asking their colleagues to delay passage of a bill until it can be amended. In some respects, of course, continuance has a kinship with deterrence, a kinship that shows in some advertising campaigns for the product market. However, deterrence is even clearer in advertising campaigns mounted in other spheres, such as the campaigns that have been spawned by the ecology movement.

*

In a speech where your goal is deterrence, presumably your listeners are prepared to do something that you want to keep them from doing. If possible, one of the first things that you should try to discover— or at least estimate—is the strength of your listeners' commitment to action. After all, one possibility that you must face is that there is no way to deter them with a single speech. Maybe the best you can hope for in this case is some kind of delay or postponement. Such a realistic strategy is not unusual.

On the other hand, if the commitment to action is not very strong, possibly you can be effective in deterring your listeners. Once again, we trust that you can see how helpful it can be to know some things about your audience.

If you make a speech on some subject where your goal is deterrence, what kinds of appeals for acceptance would seem best in terms of your topic and your listeners?

*

Based on discontinuance

When we want people to stop doing what they're already doing, our communications have goals that fall into the category of discontinuance. Certainly if we stop one kind of behavior, we often engage in other, different patterns of behavior, so discontinuance can go hand-in-hand with adoption; nevertheless it is accurate to consider these goals separately. Thus, non-smoking may be the final goal for a doctor speaking to a group of smokers, but what he wants the smokers to do

*

It would be a worthwhile experience for you to develop a speech aimed at discontinuance. Certainly one of the keys to its effectiveness would be some understanding of *why* the behavior to be stopped has been occurring in the first place. Some audience analysis might yield such an answer. Knowing the basis for your listeners' behavior would be extremely helpful if your goal were to get them to discontinue that behavior; the knowledge could guide you in designing your appeal. If the behavior were based in identification, you might use one approach; if it were based in internalization, you might use another. Of course it is possible that some combination of these appeals might be even more effective.

*

is to stop smoking, to quit doing what they've been doing. In deterrence, the aim is to prevent possible action; in discontinuance, the aim is to stop what is occurring; those who don't use drugs are warned about trying them, and those who do use them are urged to stop.

As you can see, these four categories blur a bit when pressed far enough, but at the same time, they dovetail quite nicely, and they permit some worthwhile distinctions to be made when you are preparing to speak. You may choose to focus on only one of the categories, as we suggested in the last exercise, or on more than one, as we also suggested. Earlier, we mentioned that Boyd's speech implicitly supported continuance, but it also had marked potential for adoption when presented to young people considering a career in the insurance business. And we also mentioned that Agnew's speech was rich in illustrations of behavioral effects. Although he insisted that he had no intention of censoring or passing laws, we have seen that the speech prompted a variety of behavior, the specific behavior depending on the particular segment of the audience. Surely his status was an important element in all this, but we want to ignore that and use the varied effects he achieved as a transition to some concluding observations.

The Des Moines speech had many effects, and so will speeches that occur in situations that do not involve important pronouncements on important issues. We think we have included enough cautionary advice along the way, but we want to emphasize again that communication effects do not happen in a nice, tidy, orderly sequence. And effects cannot always be placed in isolated pigeonholes. So if the reminder is needed, permit us to warn you again about relying completely on the categories and divisions presented in this analysis of listener effects. Pushed to their final extent, these topics blur and overlap; even worse, unthinking acceptance results in a contrived and artificial picture of our humanity, of what it is that makes us human. That, we hope, is strong enough. But let us be equally strong in insisting that the categories and divisions will serve you well if you accept them for what they are and make them subject to your humanity, to what it is that makes you human.

SUGGESTED READINGS

Gary Cronkhite, *Persuasion: Speech and Behavioral Change* (New York, 1969). This book is a clear, thorough survey of persuasion. Included in the treatment are summaries of the major theories of persuasion, an examination of audience characteristics, and a discussion of measuring persuasive effects.

Jonathan L. Freedman, J. Merrill Carlsmith, and David O. Sears, *Social Psychology* (Englewood Cliffs, N. J., 1970). This book is one of several social psychology texts that can provide a useful introduction to the study of social influences on behavior.

William J. McGuire, "The Nature of Attitudes and Attitude Change," in *Handbook of Social Psychology*, 2nd ed. Ed. by Gardner Lindzey and Elliot Aronson (Reading, Mass., 1969), Vol 3, pp. 136-314. This article is an extremely thorough survey of attitude theory and current research. It is recommended for the reader who is interested in a more advanced study of attitudes.

PREVIEW: CHAPTER 7

Chapter 7 deals with the nature of messages and how they operate in communication. The topics are:

About messages
Messages and meaning
Public and private meanings
Meaning and context
Language: a system of symbols
Language and the image

When you have completed this chapter, you will know more about what messages are and how they can influence both speakers and listeners. Communicators share their images and attempt to influence the images of others through the use of messages. By gaining some understanding of how messages come to have meaning for listeners, you will be better prepared to achieve the ends and effects you want as a speaker.

messages

MEANING AND LANGUAGE

7

What is a message? Let's begin with an illustration. You are driving down a freeway, and suddenly you notice that the needle on the fuel gauge is getting uncomfortably close to the empty mark. Fortunately, you soon spot the sign of a major oil company for which you have a credit card, and taking the off-ramp, you drive into the station and stop beside the gas pumps. A young man wearing a shirt with the name "Jack" just above the pocket approaches your car, and you roll down the window in time to hear him ask, "Fill it up?"

You nod in response, saying, "Regular. And would you check under the hood, please?" This triggers a complicated set of actions by the attendant. After inserting the nozzle of the gas hose, he washes the windshield, and then opens the hood. He checks the hose connections and fan belt; he checks the water in the radiator, the battery, and the windshield-washer reservoir; then he checks the oil level in the transmission, crankcase, and hydraulic systems. You may be thinking that you never get such thorough service when stopping for gas, that this kind usually appears only in TV commercials. Well, the two of us don't get such service often, but sometimes we do—and besides, it's our example, and we can make it turn out this way if we want to.

So this particularly diligent attendant completes his rounds, removes the nozzle, notes the dials on the gas pump, and reapproaches your window. "Everything's OK under the hood. That's twelve and a half gallons; six dollars and ninety cents." You hand him your trusty credit card, and after entering gallons and price, he walks to the front of your car to get the license number. Returning, he hands you your credit card and the credit slip for your signature. "Save stamps?"

"Yes" is your reply as you sign your name on the credit slip, and when he gives you your copy of the slip, he also hands you some trading stamps. "Thanks," he says. "Have a nice day," and he heads toward a new customer who has pulled in at the next row of pumps. You add your own "thanks" while you roll up the window, start the car, and move out into the street.

But there's a lot more to it, isn't there? A few weeks pass, and here comes that envelope with the window in it. Those people at the oil company have sent a statement indicating that they want to be paid for the gasoline, as well as for any other goods and services that you may have charged on the credit card during the billing period. You total your duplicate slips for accuracy, and then write a check to cover the bill and mail it to the company. The writing and mailing of the check begins still other complicated chains of behavior, but this book has a limited number of pages, and we'll focus just on the business at the service station. Even there we have left out many details of the transaction, but we have enough substance to proceed, and we will proceed by asking you to go back over the illustration and see how many instances you can identify that involve the *purposive use of some kind of message*. If you can identify at least ten purposive messages you are doing pretty well. If you can spot at least fifteen you should compliment yourself on your alertness. Actually, there are more than fifteen messages in our illustration, but we don't want to be pedantic about it.

Without belaboring the point, it does rather stagger the imagination to contemplate the sheer number of messages involved in such seemingly ordinary and commonplace aspects of life. We ride in a car, and messages are all about us. And if we turn on the radio in the car, how many more become available! The relatively simple act of buying gasoline is exceedingly complex, especially when the credit card makes the U.S. Postal Service, the banking system, and computerized billing processes function as an extension of and a scaffolding for this brief transaction at the service station. Even if you are not at all inclined to reflect on the human condition, this simple example ought to increase your appreciation of how important messages and message systems are to us and our society. As Norbert Wiener says, messages form the cement which binds society together.

ABOUT MESSAGES

"Message" is a quite abstract term, and to define it adequately for the purposes of this chapter we have to draw some finer distinctions than we did in Chapter 2, where we used "message" and "stimulus" almost interchangeably.

Signs and symbols

A *message*, as we will use the term here, is a special kind of stimulus involving the use of symbols and other signs that a sender expresses for the purpose of influencing some receiver. A closer look at some of the components of this definition will be helpful. First, what are symbols and other signs? You should be aware that scholars in a wide range of disciplines have given the subject of symbolic processes a great deal of consideration. While their various approaches have led to some interesting distinctions, there is general agreement that certain kinds of stimuli can be distinguished because they refer to something other than themselves. They stand for something else—or, if you prefer, they call something else to mind.

For example, a pile of rocks along a trail might be a stimulus to a hiker, a stimulus conveying no more than the thought "here is a pile of rocks." However, if these rocks meant something more to the hiker, if they indicated a certain distance or certain direction, then they would belong to the special class of stimuli that we commonly call *signs* or *symbols*. Generally, those who theorize about the functions of symbols and signs use "sign" as the inclusive term and "symbol" as an important type within the general class of signs. Although words will be the symbols that get most of our attention, it is worth noting that many symbols do not consist of words. In terms of the gas station example, symbols may be diagramatic representations, sounds, lights, and varied colors of the lights, or simply numbers or a needle on a gauge. Emblems, insignia, flags, medals, and various kinds of signs —dollar sign, plus sign, arrow, cross, and so forth—are also symbols. Take such a simple thing as bells, of which Langer notes:

> As for bells, the world is mad with their messages. Somebody at the front door, the telephone—toast is ready—typewriter line is ended— school begins, work begins, church begins, church is over—street car starts—cashbox registers—knife grinder passes—time for dinner, time to get up—fire in town![*]

[*] Susanne K. Langer, *Philosophy in a New Key* (New York, 1948), pp. 47-48.

You should be able to add to this list—and don't forget that gestures or movements can be symbolic. Almost anything can serve as a symbol: clothing, marks on paper, sounds, colors, and shapes.

Forms of expression

But whatever the medium, messages require some form of expression. The precise form of expression will depend on many things, including what ideas the sender wants to convey, the best means available, the situation that elicits the communication, and the intended receivers of the message. So a pile of rocks may be the most satisfactory way for a hiker to communicate with someone who will be coming down the trail a bit later. However, rocks don't really have great potential for communicating. Moses may have brought the Law on stone tablets, and decorative uses of stone can be found everywhere, but the comic strip "B.C." surely indicates the limited potential. We noted earlier that sight and hearing provide us with the greatest range for receiving messages, and here there are myriad possibilities for developing rich and flexible forms of expression.

During the Sixties, mass demonstrations became commonplace forms of expression for communicating grievances, first in regard to civil rights, then in connection with the Vietnam War. During the Spanish Civil War, Picasso expressed his revulsion at the bombing of peasant villages in his *Guernica,* a painting that has become one of the most famous works of art of this century. Other situations and experiences have found effective expression in music of all kinds, in symphonies, in operas, in folk songs, in ballads. The ways of making messages are perhaps limited only by our ingenuity—we can send smoke signals, we can blink lights, dance dances, prepare meals, paint paintings, wave flags, join hands, send flowers, exchange gifts, or even make piles of rocks. We should never forget that communication can involve a great deal more than those messages transmitted through human speech. At the same time words are the most common symbols, and we obviously are most concerned with verbal utterances and their delivery by a speaker.

Purpose of the sender

So we have symbols and their expression through speech, but something more is needed before we have a message. We refer to the intent or purpose of the sender: messages are signs or symbols used by the sender *for the purpose of influencing receivers.* The sender must have in mind the idea of at least attempting to affect the receiver and his image. Whether the receiver gets the message and is influenced appropriately by it, or whether there is no increase in awareness, willingness, understanding, or the like, the message is still a message if it was sent with intent.

We readily concede that the notion of intent and purpose makes our definition of a message a bit sticky. After all, it seems impossible for anyone ever to be completely certain about the intentions of another—in fact, sometimes we can't even clarify our intentions for ourselves. But if we presented a neater and more sanitary definition—and we could—such a definition would be less realistic and less useful. Sometimes, the study of human communication is most interesting for the very reason that questions are raised about the intentions of those communicating. The Danish linguist Otto Jespersen is said to have observed that messages serve three functions: one is to convey ideas, another is to conceal ideas, and the third is to conceal the absence of ideas. You have only to think for a moment about these three general functions to know that his account is accurate. We would all have to admit—when being completely candid—that we have used each of these three purposes as communication goals sometime in our lives. If a consideration of these purposes makes the study of communication more exciting, it must be admitted that the same consideration can make the study frustrating at times. That is no reason to ignore the importance of intent, however, and to omit it from the definition would leave out too many important issues.

Giving and giving off

So messages involve signs or symbols that are expressed by a sender who intends to influence a receiver. As a corollary, there are many signs and symbols that may be meaningful to receivers even though a message has not been sent. A messy desk may indicate a busy person, or a disorganized one, or even one who is busy *and* disorganized. And blistered hands may be a sign of hard work—but neither of these is necessarily a message. A discarded candy wrapper along a trail can certainly be a sign to a hiker that other humans have been there previously, but it would not be a message unless it was left there for the purpose of expressing something else. In this connection, the sociologist Erving Goffman makes a useful distinction between the signs and symbols that are "given" and those that are "given off." In terms of our definition, those signs and symbols that are "given off" do not qualify as messages. They are meaningful, nonetheless and they are interesting and important from a communication point of view.

You undoubtedly can recall occasions when there has seemed a conflict between the message given and the one given off, times when you talked with someone whose words indicated comfort and ease in the situation but whose physical actions suggested marked discomfort. Some signs then may not be intentional—they may not be given—but they can be very important to the process of communication. Some of the signs that we give off are much more difficult to control than the messages we give, and, in truth, it often is impossible for us to control what we give off. Yet, as receivers of messages, we often almost habitually check to see if the signs a person gives off are consistent with the messages he gives. If there is any apparent inconsistency, we are inclined to be suspicious. Clearly, this matter is most closely involved with delivery, with the act of presentation, and we'll give greater attention to it when we look at nonverbal communication in Chapter 10.

*

Several years ago in an introductory speech class, a young man presented a speech in which he attacked the evils of smoking, and he was particularly vehement in denouncing the habit both from the individual and the social point of view. The message he was giving was that no one should smoke. Unfortunately, he gave off quite a different message. He was wearing a light, white shirt, and it was obvious to everyone in the room that there was a package of cigarettes in his shirt pocket. Even the brand was evident.

As an exercise for your powers of communicative awareness, observe one particular speaker and see if you can distinguish between the messages which he or she intends to send ("gives") and any meaningful signs which he or she does not intend to send ("gives off"). Would you judge the signs that are given off to be congruent with the message that you are hearing? Sometimes, especially with skilled, experienced speakers, the cues may be subtle—perhaps even nonexistent.

As an examination of yourself as a speaker, think about a speech that you might be planning to give. What are some of the signs that you might give off? Would they be consistent with your purposive message?

*

MESSAGES AND MEANING

In the two chapters that follow, we will focus more specifically on various considerations in the making of the kind of messages we call "speeches," but first we want to amplify upon the notion of messages and to review some fundamental, general ideas about *meaning*—about how messages and other signs and symbols affect their users. Again we are surveying a rich and complicated subject. As with other areas in the study of human behavior, there are many different approaches, and a great deal has been written on the subject. It is possible, though, to sift out some important areas of general agreement on how signs and symbols come to take on meaning. With some awareness of the basic notions of meaning as a backdrop, our later and more specific discussion of your own speech preparation should be more useful.

How things mean

Our approach is essentially a psychological one. The psycholinguist John B. Carroll is among those who maintain persuasively that we can begin to understand meaning by taking our clues from the way that we learn to use language.* Meanings, in Carroll's view, are learned in the way that we learn anything else. We already have seen that messages constitute a special subset of the general class of stimuli; consequently, meaning can be conceived as a conditioned response to a sign stimulus. That's it in a nutshell. Now let's take a more detailed look at this idea. If a young child hears the word "cookie" paired often enough with the actual presence of a cookie, the child will come to associate the word with the object. At the outset, the cookie is the unconditioned stimulus, and the child's reaching, touching, and other reactions are all unconditioned responses. Then the word "cookie" is paired with the object, and the word becomes the conditioned stimulus, with the child beginning to respond to the word alone more or less as if the word were the actual cookie. This behavior is the conditioned response. The residue of the child's experiences with cookies becomes the basis for the meaning of the word "cookie" to that child.

Words and meaning

The foregoing is a highly abbreviated and simplified account of the process by which meaning develops in people, but the essential features have some important implications for any student of communication. First, the meaning of a given sign or symbol is a function of individual experience, both with the sign itself and with the thing or state of affairs the sign stands for. Fortunately, the images we develop out of our experiences tend to have enough similarity that such a word as "cup" permits us to communicate with a reasonable degree of reliability, and the same holds true for most of the symbols we use for the everyday things and events in our lives. Strictly speaking, even these familiar and ordinary symbols have shades of differences for each of us, but the differences seldom become traumatic. But for some things and events, our experiences differ enough so that our meanings for certain symbols may be very different. Examples abound; here is an excellent one from George Orwell's essay "Politics and the English Language":

> The words *democracy, socialism, freedom, patriotic, realistic, justice,* have each of them several different meanings which cannot be reconciled with one another. In the case of a word like *democracy,* not only is there no agreed definition but the attempt to make one is resisted from all sides. It is almost universally felt that when we call a country

* John B. Carroll, *Language and Thought* (Englewood Cliffs, N.J., 1964).

democratic we are praising it: consequently the defenders of every kind of regime claim that it is a democracy, and fear that they might have to stop using the word if it were tied down to any one meaning. Words of this kind are often used in a consciously dishonest way. That is, the person who uses them has his own private definition, but allows his hearer to think he means something quite different.

Or take the word "politics," from the title of the essay. It can be applied to a rather large class of situations and events in ways that are acceptable to our linguistic community, and the meanings for the word are likely to exhibit far greater variety than exist for the word "cup." This is true partly because there are more things in the world to which the word "politics" can apply than there are things in the world to which the word "cup" can apply. While our general experiences with cups and the word "cup" have a relatively high degree of commonality, the same is not true of our experience of politics and the word "politics." There simply is far less commonality. Surely there will be some overlapping of experience, but there also will be more differences.

We trust that the point is clear: the meanings of symbols and other signs have their foundation in experience, but since our experiences and hence our images differ, the meanings we attach to symbols will differ also. We do think it important to emphasize the fact that a given word may contain a wide variety of potential meanings. Although we all are at least intuitively aware of the problem, it deserves underlining because in many communication situations, people behave as though they were ignorant of this insight into meaning—ignorant, or perhaps guilty of the dishonesty cited by Orwell.

One symptom of the problem is what some students of language call the "one word–one meaning fallacy." In this kind of communication error, senders assume that the meaning of a given symbol is the same for all receivers—as if the meaning existed in the word itself. Apparently, these communicators think that a statement or a question or directions that may be clear in their minds should also be equally clear to any receiver. Take, for example, the word "camping." It may mean back-packing in the Northern Cascades, pitching a tent in the Great Smokies, living out of an elaborate recreational vehicle, or a variety of other things. A speaker who chooses this general topic area and assumes that all listeners' definitions will be the same is in trouble. No doubt such assumptions have complicated all our lives from time to time, if only in minor ways, both as senders and as receivers. We all sometimes forget that a symbol is a special kind of stimulus that triggers meanings that are in people, meanings that can be quite different from one person to the next.

We can extend this issue to the "one phrase–one meaning fallacy" as well, as the underlying principle is the same. Consider the sentence "I took this photo" as a fairly simple example of multiple meanings.

The sentence means either "I caused a camera to make this picture" or "I saw this photo and I helped myself to it." Other phrases are certainly richer than this one in their possibilities for interpretation —a fact that can be a source of confusion, embarrassment, or amusement, depending on the stakes that are involved. Many of you have no doubt developed considerable skill in deliberately saying things that can be interpreted in more than one way. In your dealings with members of the opposite sex, perhaps?

This discussion clearly implies that meanings are dynamic, not static. Events are changing about us, and we are all changing ourselves; our experiences and hence our images are changing, with the result that meaning can and often does change, sometimes just a little, but sometimes dramatically.

*

Meanings are in listeners, not in the words you use and the speeches you make. The expressions you use as a speaker simply trigger associations and meanings that are a part of your listeners' existing images. Of course, it is your goal, generally, to share a part of your image with the audience, perhaps changing part of your listeners' images through your messages. These thoughts should certainly reinforce the discussion of audience analysis in Chapter 4.

For now, we want you to see that although you have some options as to the way you choose to express yourself in a speech, they should be governed by the ways in which your listeners are likely to interpret what you say. No matter what *you* may mean as a speaker, *they* are the ones who decide what it means to them. And that's why some basic understanding of messages and meaning is so important.

*

PUBLIC AND PRIVATE MEANINGS

As we have seen, there is some degree of commonality of the general meaning of certain symbols, but at the same time, there are many nuances of meaning. Consequently, symbols may *denote* essentially the same thing for a group or a community, even while they may *connote* different things. The denotative meaning of a symbol is the agreed-on meaning—the meaning that ordinarily finds its way into a dictionary. A denotative meaning reflects our shared, public image. Thus the word "piano" refers to a large stringed percussion instrument which produces sounds when the keys are depressed. All of us have learned to distinguish pianos from hairpins, saxophones, lawn mowers, tricycles, and hamburger stands, and we can all agree that the symbol "piano" denotes an object such as we have described and not something else.

Connotative meaning, on the other hand, involves the more private, subjective aspects of the use of symbols, aspects of meaning that are tied particularly closely to the private dimensions of one's own image. For two different people, the symbol "piano" may well denote the same keyboard instrument, but the symbol may connote pleasure and relaxation for one person and an instrument of torture for the other, depending on the experiences they have had with pianos.

So it is with most symbols; in a very real sense, we can think of symbols as having their meaning grounded in two levels of experience. The denotative level is a more public and objective one where, generally, a thing must meet certain agreed-upon criteria in order to qualify for a given label or symbol. Thus, a rather specific set of symptoms is denoted by the expression "labor pains." The behavior of a football player must meet certain criteria before the linesman will drop his symbolic handkerchief. The score of a piano concerto indicates that certain notes should be played. In contrast there are no specified criteria involved in the connotative meanings aroused in us. They may be as diverse as the varied experiences people have had with the things that the symbols stand for. While many of us can agree on what an expression like "labor pains" denotes, it is certain that connotation will differ a great deal, depending, for one thing, on whether we have experienced labor pains or not. And so it is with the connotative meaning of other symbols as well; the connotations that words and other signs have are based in private experiences which may or may not overlap those of other people.

M. Growing up in a small town at a time when the Fourth of July was still a big thing, I always looked forward to the evening show. To cap the day's activities, the local post of the American Legion staged a sham battle in the local ball park, a battle in which World War I was fought all over again, complete with charging armies, guns, old Fords disguised as tanks, and plenty of noise and fireworks. For me it was not a "sham battle." For me it was a "shambattle," one word, and since "sham" is not a word that we hear often, I grew up with that connotative meaning distorting my perception of the denotation. In fact, "sham" will always give me some trouble in that regard. You can probably think of a word or expression that has behaved in a similarly strange way in your own experience.

MEANING AND CONTEXT

When we string a series of words together, a number of complex processes are involved, but meaning remains a matter of central concern. Most of the time we don't use words in isolation; rather, we

"I see it as an example of his heightened perceptions discerning a conspicuous manifestation unapparent to others, when he says, 'Look, Jane. Look. Look.'"

combine them to form longer utterances—phrases, clauses, and sentences. The *context* or, if you like, the linguistic environment in which a given word occurs adds to its meaning in ways that usually clarify and sharpen it somewhat. Thus we know that the two kinds of "cup" involved in "Cup your hands" and "Pass me the cup" are quite different and it is the context of these words that determines the difference. Context generally serves to restrict the various meanings that a listener might attach to an expression that has the potential for multiple meanings.

But meaning is a function of context in a broader sense of the term as well; here we are talking about the situation in which communication occurs, the communication context. Clearly, our lives are filled with situations in which the context sharply limits, for all practical purposes, the potential for the things we can do or say, appropriately, as communicators. When the service station attendant approaches your car, you might ask for directions, but you aren't likely to ask for a used copy of the textbook for the introductory chemistry course. At a bookstore, you might ask for directions too, but you probably will not ask for regular gasoline. In our illustration about the service station, we saw how easy and natural it was to move through an extremely complex chain of messages without a moment of concentrated effort, or without any misunderstanding. Such familiar and limited events often have the happy effect of preventing alternative and ambiguous meanings from arising.

Public speaking situations also can have significant contextual restraints, a fact for you to keep in mind as you prepare your speeches. Situations often determine at least the nature of what it is that a speaker can say. Certainly there is some latitude here, but most of us have a kind of intuitive set of standards about what is "appropriate" and what seems to be "out of line." In this sense, then, situations and contexts have a general level of meaning, too, by putting some cultural limits to the meanings of the symbols we use.

LANGUAGE: A SYSTEM OF SYMBOLS

As we have noted before, you have a great deal of expertise in the use of your language. We don't mean to imply that you know all there is to know about the language, nor that you can use it with consummate skill in every kind of situation; rather, we mean that you can function from day to day in your linguistic community with a minimum of error, and you probably have been pretty good at it since you first entered kindergarten. Quite remarkable, especially when this accomplishment ordinarily is achieved without any real formal training, though the chances are good that you've had some since. As Marshall McLuhan remarks, "The reason the children learn a language in a year or two is simply because it is an environment." A happy circumstance, but it has a real disadvantage: because we acquire and use our native tongue so readily and naturally, it is often difficult for us to examine our language with real objectivity. Yet throughout history, both ordinary people and scholars in every kind of ivory tower have marveled at language and tried to fathom its depths. We have already cited some opinions to the effect that a highly complex language system is the most distinctively human trait; here is another such observation from Bertrand Russell:

> Language has two interconnected merits: first, that it is social, and second, that it supplies public expression for "thought" which would otherwise remain private. Without language, or some pre-linguistic analogue, our knowledge of the environment is confined to what our own senses have shown us, together with such inferences as our congenital constitution may prompt; but by the help of speech we are able to know what others can relate, and to relate what is no longer sensibly present but only remembered. When we see or hear something which a companion is not seeing or hearing, we can often make him aware of it by the one word "look" or "listen," or even by gestures. But if half an hour ago we saw a fox, it is not possible to make another person aware of this fact without language. This depends upon the fact that the word "fox" applies equally to a fox seen or a fox remembered, so that our memories, which in themselves are private, are represented

to others by uttered sounds, which are public. Without language, only that part of our life which consists of public sensations would be communicable, and that only to those so situated as to be able to share the sensations in question.*

Russell and most scholars of language and communication define the term "language" quite broadly. They generally regard language as being a *system of symbols.* We have noted already that symbols are things that stand for or point to or call to mind something other than themselves. The "system" part of the definition indicates that languages have rules of some kind which govern the ways in which the symbols can be combined and used appropriately within a given community. Ordinarily we think of language as being a system of oral communication, but we all have heard people talk about other kinds of languages—the language of mathematics, the language of dance, the language of film, the language of gesture, and so forth. Mathematics does meet the requirements of our general definition, for the rules governing the proper use of its symbols are very thoroughly and precisely spelled out. Rules for some of the other "languages" may not be as complete or as clear, may leave a great deal of room for individual interpretation and usage, but to conceive of them as symbol systems does no real damage to the concept. Music is an excellent example of such a language. Consequently, your expertise in language probably extends beyond the ordinary sense in that you may well have expertise in more than one language. It is probable that we are more skilled as receivers of such languages than as senders because we can take some meaning away from a musical message, for example, even though we don't know the rules for the proper use of its symbols. But, fortunately, we can learn our native language quite well without mastery of the rules. The rules for the English language are extensively if not completely reflected in the grammar of English, but it is possible for a person to survive without knowing any of them. Nevertheless, Colin Cherry observes that "language makes a hard mistress and we are all her slaves."

You may well agree with Cherry if you have been struggling to learn some foreign language, but at the same time his statement may seem an odd thing to say about one's native tongue. Again, we are all too accustomed to this slavery, and we may not have given it a second thought. Furthermore it does enable us to get by from day to day. But learning a foreign language, or the attempt to do so, will underline the importance of what we already know in the language we have grown up with. Even more dramatic is the trip to a country where we do not speak the language. Without the language or a cooperative interpreter, we become marginal members in the operation of a different social system. It is only with real difficulty that we

* Bertrand Russell, *Human Knowledge: Its Scope and Limits* (New York, 1948), pp. 59-60.

can obtain the information and services that are required for even the basic necessities of daily life, and we find that we are out of touch with anything beyond the most rudimentary thoughts and feelings. Frustrations are on every hand; we don't like to be so dependent and so obtuse, and all this stems from our inability to communicate, our failure in mastering the language.

Difficulties and frustrations are reduced to a minimum only when one becomes completely at ease with the second language, when the person glances at a clock and thinks "Hmmm . . . il est dix heures," rather than invariably thinking "Hummmmm . . . it's ten o'clock." Undoubtedly, one of the most profound ways in which an individual can demonstrate the ability to operate within any culture is through fluency with the language of the culture. The converse is true also, and perhaps it is here that the point should be more apparent to us. Most of us can recall instances when the way that some person used language served as a give-away that he or she was an "outsider." This is most obvious in relation to different people of different nations, but the same holds true between subcultures, between ethnic groups, occupations, generations, and other cultural units.

LANGUAGE AND THE IMAGE

We humans all start out in this world with quite a bit of similarity in the essential experiences of infancy, but we develop in quite different ways, depending on the facets of culture that shape our images as we mature. The verbal environments that we grow up in have tremendous influence on our conception of and our communication about the world. Each culture and subculture sorts out its world in somewhat different ways, some more dramatically so than others, and the language of the culture programs us to carve up our world in basically the same way. The interrelationships between culture and language prompted the psycholinguist Roger Brown to say (very nicely, we think), "Language in the full is nothing less than an inventory of all the ideas, interests, and occupations that take up the attention of the community. In this extended sense, the study of language cannot be distinguished from the general study of culture."*

In this connection, general semanticists regularly use a map analogy to illustrate some of the ways in which a language can influence the thoughts and actions of its users. A map is a collection of signs, symbols, notations, and words which purports to represent some geographical area. To the extent that the map is accurate and complete, users who can read it will be able to find their way around even in a new territory with a minimum of wrong turns and backtracking. And everyone becomes so familiar with some areas that a map is not

* Roger Brown, *Words and Things* (Glencoe, Ill., 1958), p. 260.

needed; the map, in a sense, is carried in the head as part of the image. Perhaps you have picked up an out-of-date highway map at a service station, and were surprised to find that a long stretch of freeway had been opened since the map was published. A pleasant surprise. On the other hand, most of us wouldn't want to navigate on the oceans by some of those charts that we see reprinted from the sixteenth and seventeenth centuries. It would be pretty frustrating trying to find your way with any kind of map where old landmarks had disappeared, or new features had been discovered that were not recorded.

In this metaphorical sense, the language of a society or culture is a map of that culture. If the map is relatively current and reliable, the culture, or institution, or organization, or individual using the language stands a better chance of operating effectively in it. If, however, the map is distorted in some way, the users may encounter considerable difficulty and severe problems. All of us have had the experience of describing the world in some distorted way, or followed some distorted account, and then suffered the consequences of the inaccuracy. An occasional experience of this sort surely is to be expected, but we all observe individuals, groups, and social systems with chronic and extremely distorted maps of reality. Often our inclination is to avoid dealing with them, and sometimes, of necessity, they become enemies. But in this realm, things are relative, and it is difficult to tell in the final analysis who has the best system for describing the world. The assumptions and biases that create the language maps can be quite subtle.

For example, a visitor from another planet could learn something of the importance attached to athletics in this country just by examining the language. Baseball and football in particular have given many words and phrases to this map of our culture, particularly as it characterizes politics. And in our culture, why does it seem that the word "hate" and its synonyms have more force and vitality than the word "love" and its synonyms? And maybe our world would be different if those who grew up in our culture acquired language habits that stressed conservation and preservation rather than those emphasizing using and consuming. Maybe if we had more words for acceptance and inclusion, we would witness less rejection and exclusion. These may seem rather simple-minded notions, but we prefer to think of them as being put simply, and they are worth some thought.

The things, then, that a culture finds interesting and important gain a place in its language, and, in turn, the language habits of the culture reinforce the way the culture deals with its world. The extent to which this linguistic determinism influences all the users of a language is a matter of some debate, but most people agree that there are important ways in which our language can affect our images and have a real impact upon the ways in which we see and deal with our surroundings. We'll illustrate this tendency with what we consider to be some of the more significant manifestations, and at the same time, we'll consider some of the implications that the varied aspects have for you as a speaker.

Abstracting

Given the way the world is and the way language operates, it just is not possible to say all that could be said about anything. Even a stream-of-consciousness novel leaves out far more than it includes, and if we tell a friend about a motion picture we saw, we give only an abstract or summary; most often, we leave out far more than we tell. And so it is with everything else about which we write or speak. Since June 1972, hours and hours of private and public testimony have been taken, and thousands and thousands of pages have been recorded in the attempt to describe the constellation of events known as Watergate, but even in early 1975, not all the facts are known. But the same holds true for much more limited events in our lives, and though we seldom think about how language operates in this way, there is a sense in which communication largely involves a process of deciding what to leave out. Almost invariably it is a selective process. The more general or abstract a statement, the more detail is left out, and in a very strict sense we constantly give each other incomplete information when we communicate. We do this selecting on the spur of the moment in some situations, but the public speaker often has the time to make a more careful decision. And that seems the intelligent route to us, the considered selection of ideas, ways of developing them, and ways of relating to each other and to the particular audience.

*

Given a limited amount of time for their speeches, one very common mistake many speakers make is trying to deal with too much material. Such speeches usually run the risk of being superficial, of course, as the speaker leaves out the detail that can enrich and clarify the subject in order to be able to "cover" the material. We once heard a student speaker give a five-minute speech on the history of Zen Buddhism which was nothing more than an almost meaningless list of names and places.

The preparation of your speeches should be governed by your awareness of the abstracting nature of language and communication. Give some thought not only to what you will be saying, but to what you will be leaving out. One possible outcome of this consideration is that you may choose to limit the range of your subject. It may be a worthwhile exercise for you to think of two or three ways in which you can limit the breadth of your subject and extend its depth.

*

Reification

Some things that words name can be directly perceived by the senses, such as cups, chairs, telephones, and shoes. Other things that words name, however, are not directly perceivable; instead, they are concepts or constructs which are mental images we create for the purpose of integrating or synthesizing ideas or experiences and talking about them. Consequently, none of us has ever seen a libido, a gross national product, a conscience, freedom, or patriotism, but we talk about them. Such concepts are a bit like the wind; we can't see them, but we can observe their impact and we find it useful to have such words and terms in the language. Reification is nothing more than the tendency to attribute the status of reality to a concept simply because it has a name and can be talked about. At some point early in our lives most of us probably lost a little sleep over the Bogey Man or one of his relatives before we learned that even though he had a name he didn't exist. Nor is reification something that misleads only the young and the naive. There are cases in advertising where we are led to believe that two competing products are different simply because they have different names. In a strict sense, there may be some small differences between two brands of gasoline, for example, but the ingredients aren't nearly as distinctive as the exotic labels used by the advertisers would have us believe.

Although reification may not play as large a role in shaping our images as it does in the so-called primitive cultures, it is operative in our lives as well. We can be confused by this feature of our language because there is nothing inherent in words themselves that warns users of the distinction between the reality that is observable and the reality that is conceptual.

Two-valued orientation

Much of our language seems to have a bipolar quality, a tendency to find natural expression in opposites such as love-hate, success-failure, black-white, hot-cold, smart-dumb, good-bad, and so forth. Now there are circumstances in which these extremes may offer the only appropriate alternatives. On the other hand, there are numerous situations in the world that deserve a more accurate indication of *degree* than this polar trait of our language is inclined to give them. Life or death may be relatively clear-cut alternatives, but the circumstances which put us in life-or-death situations are often more arbitrary, as Thomas Hardy notes in his poem "The Man He Killed":

> Had he and I but met
> By some old ancient inn,
> We should have sat us down to wet
> Right many a nipperkin!

> But ranged as infantry,
> And staring face to face,
> I shot at him as he at me,
> And killed him in his place.
>
> I shot him dead because—
> Because he was my foe,
> Just so: my foe of course he was;
> That's clear enough: although
>
> He thought he'd 'list, perhaps,
> Off-hand-like—just as I—
> Was out of work—had sold his traps—
> No other reason why.
>
> Yes; quaint and curious war is!
> You shoot a fellow down
> You'd treat, if met where any bar is,
> Or help to half-a-crown.

Our language habits shape our images and often we unfortunately talk and think in terms of one extreme or the other, even though we may be inaccurate, simply because these convenient labels make it easy to do so. Actually, thinking and talking in terms of degrees would be more appropriate and more accurate, but it also calls for a search for the right expression, which is harder to do. The speaker may find that this route requires more thought, more research, and more care in preparation, but the two of us have never argued that communication is easy, only that it's natural.

Self-fulfilling prophecy

The way something is labeled or described can influence the way it is perceived and treated. For example, political scientists have contended for some time that the number of votes for a candidate can be increased by the release of polling information predicting victory for the candidate. The contention is debated, but if there is an impulse in that direction, it obviously stems from the desire of voters to vote for a winner. And research has shown that if a credible source labels a child "creative" or "intelligent," teachers will look for and quite probably find those traits in the child's behavior. On the other hand, if the labels are "stubborn" or "dull," teachers will probably find those traits. It is likely that you yourself have seen this fact at work in a classroom, and since we do see ourselves as others see us, you may have known students who were thus labeled, and who responded appropriately. When the labels are positive, the results can be extremely pleasant, but when they are negative, the results can be rather frightening. Of course, saying so doesn't always make it so, but it can have that effect often enough to demonstrate this feature of the way we use language—or, perhaps we should say, the way language uses us.

General awareness of this tendency accounts for some uses of euphemism, the process by which innocuous words or phrases are substituted for those that might be distasteful or offensive. We'll come back to euphemism later, but here it is enough to note that it can cut two ways. Euphemism may signal a useful attempt to take the rough edges off reality, or it may signal the attempt to escape reality. In either case, there is some measure of self-fulfilling prophecy, which constrains us to see what we want to see, find what we want to find. Some of this is in all of us as a part of our image, and we can't avoid the filtering that takes place. Nevertheless, we would emphasize that the tendency can prevent a thorough and complete analysis of a problem. If you approach a topic convinced that all the evidence will be on one side or the other, convinced that an existing label really tells it all, then the odds are that you will filter out any discrepant information and ideas. It may seem too elementary a mistake to be mentioned, but it happens often enough that it has to be.

Static language for a dynamic world

The notion that language is somewhat static derives rather directly from the map analogy we discussed earlier. Languages do change, but they have aspects that change more slowly than the world changes, and they exhibit marks of cultural lag. And they may change in unusual ways, as we noted when talking about etymology. For example, "album" originally came from the word *albus* ("white" in Latin); then it was used to refer to a book with blank pages on which one could write or to which one could attach pictures and the like. Next, phonograph records were kept in albums. But now, a single long-playing record constitutes an album all by itself. The latter meaning doesn't cause serious problems for those accustomed to the earlier use, but old labels and old descriptions may mislead us into thinking that the situations and the things they speak of haven't changed, when, in fact, they have. At least a piece of this notion is illustrated every year in colleges and universities in the discussions about changing the grading systems. Both major and minor reforms have been introduced in recent years, but many instructors apparently have difficulty thinking in any terms other than the traditional marks of A, B, C, D, and F. In fairness, we must remark that there are many students who have the same difficulty.

But as the world changes, language has to adapt and adjust if we are to have any influence on that change. As Alfred North Whitehead comments, "The successful adaptation of old symbols to changes of social structure is the final mark of wisdom in sociological statesmanship." The words of the Constitution of the United States haven't changed at all, but the society to which those words refer has changed drastically, and the meaning of the words undergoes continuing reinterpretation. An even more dramatic example exists in the differences between the societies in which the Old Testament was written and the societies in which it is applied today. And hardly a day passes when differing interpretations of one of these documents doesn't produce some kind of argument or conflict. We don't mean to suggest that either the Constitution or the Old Testament can be assigned a precise and exact interpretation, nor do we mean to imply that a newer interpretation of the meaning invariably will be the superior. We simply want to stress that communication can be seriously hampered when people and groups persist in trying to function on the basis of outdated descriptions.

*

Language is so much a part of our social environment that we very often miss some of the ordinary ways in which it can affect or reinforce our images or the images of our listeners. Now that you have been made aware of this phenomenon, see if you can find some instances on your own. Listen carefully to a speech or, better still, read the text of some speech and pay specific attention to ways in which the use of language may be shaping or reinforcing the image of the listener. Can you find language in the speech that reflects a two-valued orientation or a self-fulfilling prophecy? How about instances that suggest reification or static language? We don't expect that you will find abundant use of all these properties of language in any one speech, but we would be surprised if you found none at all.

As you prepare your own speeches, be careful not to let language use you in the ways described above. Thoughtful, well-informed listeners may reject all or part of what you are planning to say.

*

These descriptions conclude most of what we want to say in this chapter, but since they center on the ways in which language uses us in some measure, and since we have talked here and elsewhere about how language affects our environment, we want to end on a different note. We already have suggested ways in which a speaker should be alert to possible problems, but we'd like to close this chapter with some general remarks about the creative potential in language use. And despite any limitations that apply, the creative potential is profound. Although the impact of science and technology in our lives is staggering, we have come to accept it rather calmly. Computers design everything from traffic control systems to tire treads. Jet travel enables us to have breakfast in London, lunch in New York, and dinner in Los Angeles. Space travel puts astronauts' footprints on the moon. Such achievements are monumental, and none could have been accomplished without language.

At a less exotic level, consider the many ways in which the richness and flexibility of language permit us to share and modify our own images and the images of others. Surely there are times when the best advice is "Smile and keep your mouth shut," but all of us have witnessed occasions when even the most change-resistant images have been altered through a sensitive and intelligent use of language. Communication surely reaches its most significant level when the outcome is a sharing or modification in the dimensions of life that are vital to basic attitudes and values. The tremendous range of possibility extends from the passing of the salt to the decision that produced the message beginning "When in the course of human events. . . ."

SUGGESTED READINGS

Roger Brown, *Words and Things* (New York, 1958). A readable and sound introduction to the psychology of language. The treatment ranges from the acquisition of speech to the uses of propaganda.

John B. Carroll, *Language and Thought* (Englewood Cliffs, N.J., 1964). This is a psycholinguistic approach to the study of language, its acquisition, and its use. Carroll gives particular attention to language and cognition.

John C. Condon, Jr., *Semantics and Communication* (New York, 1966). This is a convenient examination of semantics, or the study of meaning in language and language use.

Joseph A. DeVito, *Language: Concepts and Processes* (Englewood Cliffs, N.J., 1973). An anthology of readings, one of the best of the several that are available.

PREVIEW: CHAPTER 8

Chapter 8 deals first with speech organization, then with structure and reasoning. The topics are:

Organizing the speech

Organizational sequences

Chronological sequence
Spatial sequence
Topical sequence
Mixed sequences

Structure and reasoning

Problem and solution
Cause and effect
Deduction
Induction

We emphasize the importance of organizational sequences in general, but beyond that, we hope that our discussion of specific sequences will help you in developing your speeches. The comments on structure and reasoning will help you analyze and limit a topic, and they will introduce additional organizational sequences.

messages

ORGANIZATION, STRUCTURE, REASONING

8

The French language contains a delightful idiom, *l'esprit de l'escalier*, which translates roughly as "the wit of the staircase." The literal meaning suggests the metaphorical meaning: someone has left the room, gotten halfway up the stairs, and suddenly thought of what might have been said, has thought—too late!—of the *bon mot* that would have made the perfect exit line. Writers give such lines to characters in plays, novels, and short stories, but in real life they often come to us on the stairs if they come at all. Somehow it seems to happen this way even when we have mentally rehearsed such a perfect line; somehow the occasion never arises when we can introduce that prepared witticism or that profound observation, because the flow of the conversation or the interview has escaped our control. Control. That's the key, and that's why playwrights and novelists succeed where we fail. They are in complete control of their fictional characters. By the same token, public speakers have relatively complete control, at least when compared with a casual conversation or a committee meeting with a set agenda. Important political figures get heckled and the possibility of being interrupted exists in almost all public-speaking situations. But as we have noted, audiences usually don't participate verbally unless asked to do so, however much they might like to. Consequently, public speakers have many choices that allow them to control their message and the response to it.

ORGANIZING THE SPEECH

We already have talked about some of the available methods of control—about the choice of a topic, and about limiting it, and about your desired effects in terms of what the audience knows and how much it cares about your subject. Now we will talk about making messages in ways that are even more immediately applicable to the matter of speech preparation. Our initial concern will be with organization, structure, arrangement—more or less synonymous terms for the control that you can produce by attention to the overall pattern of your speech. Speech preparation, as we've noted, seldom works out in a neat and orderly fashion, but that doesn't mean that the process should be chaotic. It does mean that most speakers find it helpful to make matters of structure a part of their habitual approach. Any pattern you select should be a function of the topic, the audience, your own customizing inclinations, and the other choices that you have made.

Assuming that you have settled on a topic and have decided on the effect to be achieved, some thought about organization can invigorate the entire undertaking. When you attend to the larger structural elements, you will find that your thinking is clarified. Consideration of these elements may trigger further thought and investigation, may force new and different relationships to the surface. As a result, you will be in a better position to know how to proceed, know how to revise, know what should be eliminated and what should be added. But attention to organizational patterns does more than assist in the creation of your speech. It helps at the moment of presentation. Circular as it sounds, one of your biggest problems as an inexperienced speaker is your lack of experience. You have developed considerable expertise in communication, but until you gain some familiarity in the realm of public speaking, this lack of experience means that you, like most people, will encounter some difficulty in adjusting to this different situation. Again there is no magic formula, and many factors are involved in the adjustment, but a speech that has a coherent pattern of organization will be easier for you to recall, producing an additional pay-off at the time of delivery.

Strictly speaking, the purposes above are not merely selfish, nor should they be. In the long run, they serve the general ends of communication because they make the process more effective. The tendency to group phenomena together and to pattern our experiences is common to us all, and this tendency extends to communication, whatever our role in the process. Obviously we all can err when preparing a speech, but if it seems to develop in coherent fashion for the speaker, the chances are good that it will make a similar impression on the audience. That's a most important goal. Think of your own response as a listener; when you attend a lecture or some other public speech, don't you find it easier to stay with the speaker when the speech progresses in a systematic manner? As listeners, we expect speakers to take the time and trouble to structure their ideas in a way that makes them easy to follow. Furthermore, we generally respond more positively to speakers who appear to be in command of the speaking situation, and so there are broader implications in the fact that attention to structure can assist in the act of presentation: if the organizational pattern helps with delivery, then it can lead directly to more effective communication. We'll give more attention to this matter in later chapters, but at this point we want to consider some specific patterns that can be used in organizing speeches.

Since some textbooks include rather extensive lists, you may well have met with some or all of the sequential patterns we will discuss. For the moment we will look at only three—the chronological sequence, the spatial sequence, and the topical sequence. They frequently overlap, and the last is something of a catch-all, but we think they are the most important and the most useful patterns. Certainly they are the most natural, for they arise from our fundamental perceptions of the most important aspects of our images.

ORGANIZATIONAL SEQUENCES

Chronological sequence

As we remarked when exploring Boulding's concept of the image, a sense of time is important to us all. It's a part of our cultural inheritance, and although some cultures do not have our fascination with time, we who live in a highly industrialized society find that our perception of the past, the present, and the future is basic to the lives we live. We observe temporal patterns everywhere. If we didn't, the *Guiness Book of Records* probably would be reduced by half. But even more importantly, we would have trouble giving any semblance of order to our experiences. To underline the basic character of the chronological sequence, we'll quote the introductory sentence from Edgar Allan Poe's *The Fall of the House of Usher:*

> During the whole of a dull, dark, and soundless day in the autumn of the year, when the clouds hung oppressively low in the heavens, I had been passing alone, on horseback, through a singularly dreary tract of country; and at length found myself, as the shades of evening drew on, within view of the melancholy House of Usher.

Few writers have been more concerned than Poe with the union of form and substance in communication, but it does him no injustice to claim that this long sentence really says, "Once upon a time. . . ." For most of us, the "once upon a time" may stir memories of Little Red Riding Hood and other stories from childhood, but the phrase merely prepares us for something taking place at a certain time. This temporal pattern can be seen in short stories, novels, plays, biographies, histories, and other genres of writing. The frequency of this pattern gives it a special familiarity, and speeches developed around a chronological sequence can be most comfortable for many listeners because the pattern is so much a part of our lives.

*

You have agreed to make a speech about the school you are attending. How can chronology serve your purposes? For entering students, a typical day might do the trick. Older alumni might best be reached through events that took place when they were in school. What chronological approach might be most satisfactory when talking to potential benefactors?

*

Comfortable because it is so natural, the chronological approach can be comforting in another way; that is, it can help a speaker circumvent potential resistance from the listeners. Undoubtedly you own books that are not based on a chronological sequence, but it is almost impossible to find a subject that cannot be discussed with reference to historical developments, and the temporal pattern may offer a solution when marked resistance seems likely. Whether the subject be pension programs, campaign spending, regulation of firearms, drugs, women's lib, or any of countless others, you may decide that your ultimate goals will find few converts in the audience, that some awareness, willingness, or understanding is the most that you can hope for. Whether these effects are instrumental or terminal, a historical survey of earlier views and attitudes could be a relatively neutral way of treating the subject. Our example of the Elizabethan welfare laws applies here, and a speech on firearms control could focus on the background that led to the Second Amendment in our constitutional Bill of Rights.

Now we don't mean to imply that the chronological sequence cannot be effective in an attempt to achieve instrumental effects, nor that it is inappropriate when a speaker wants the listeners to accept or act on the message. To the contrary. Historical interpretation may be integral to a speech in which listeners are urged to continue doing what they've been doing or in one in which they are asked to change their behaviors. If the Second Amendment does become an issue in relation to the control of firearms today, it assuredly is necessary to know what was meant in the eighteenth century by the words, "A well-regulated militia, being necessary to the security of a free State, the right of the people to keep and bear arms shall not be infringed." Whether the speaker wants to apply the meaning today or to reject it, the different purposes both require a sense of time.

We did not select our four speeches for the purpose of illustrating this pattern, but Agnew, Boyd, Rye, and Lincoln all make use of various kinds of temporal sequences. Boyd, for example, gives much of his attention to what he terms "the family life period"; Lincoln understandably analyzes votes on the various legislative acts in chronological order; Agnew uses a temporal pattern from the second through the fifth paragraphs; and chronology is at the heart of Rye's presentation. And all these examples reinforce our point that a temporal sequence can be effective in influencing behavior. Later, we'll talk about other patterns in these same speeches, but the regular incidence of the chronological sequence also reinforces our claim that it is a most ordinary and natural pattern for structuring communication.

Spatial sequence

If it is natural for us to think about the "when," it is every bit as natural to be concerned about the "where." The where may loom most significantly when we have misplaced something we need or when we don't know which exit to take from a freeway, but our sense of location and general spatial orientation are vital to the equilibrium we try to maintain in our lives. Space is another matter that we discussed in connection with the image, and it's another matter that plays such a natural part in our lives that we accept it as quite ordinary. We have to learn about space and its function. All animals do, not just humans.

V. Returning from a fishing trip off the northern California coast, we tied up at a small wooden float at the mouth of the harbor, a float so small that it lacked real stability. As we prepared to go ashore, another returning boat tied up at the same float, and a brown male dachshund leaped out and headed for the piling to which the float was secured. He lifted his leg, but just as he did, the float tilted, completely disorienting the dog's sense of the target range and bearing. Disconcerted, the dog lowered his leg. Then he raised it again, but this time the float tilted to the other extreme and hurled the dog squarely against the piling. Uttering a startled "yip," he scurried across the float and hurried up the wooden steps that led to land, to the place where fire hydrants, parked cars, and trees do not move about in such erratic fashion.

So space and spatial relationships are important in our lives. Think of games. What would happen to chess if the number of squares was doubled? To football if the field were two hundred yards long? To Monopoly if the blue avenues were all mixed up with the yellow? In other ways, our sense of space and location is much more fundamental in that we all develop a sense of personal space, a sense that the immediate area around us should not ordinarily be violated by other people. Games, then, would be good topics in terms of spatial treatment. So would any subject in the fields of geography, geology, or cartography. Furthermore, the concepts of place and space lend themselves naturally to a discussion of city planning, architecture, astronomy, recreation, and any number of other topics.

Like chronology, space may provide a pattern that is especially useful for explanatory purposes, when the speaker is not immediately concerned with influencing behavior. For instance, locations, distances, and geographical elements might be ideal for developing a speech on a national park or on a system of state parks, and the spatial pattern could be equally useful for a discussion of mass transportation, city zoning, the Cathedral at Salisbury, or the internal combustion engine. And all baseball fans know that size and shape of the ball parks were brought up in connection with the number of home runs hit by Babe Ruth and Hank Aaron. However, this last example has contained some controversy, as do others we have cited, and a spatial orientation also may be an excellent framework for speeches intended to gain acceptance or influence behavior.

*

Returning to the example of the speech about your school, what features of space might you use as your main idea? Its architecture, of course, and any of its physical areas that serve a particular instructional purpose. Perhaps there are apparent and important differences between the old buildings and the new. Does it seem that learning is easier in one classroom or building because of some special physical features?

*

The allusion to spatial implications in the relationships between old buildings and new takes us back to the overlapping between categories. We mentioned earlier that there was some overlapping between the three organizational sequences we are discussing. Often both time and place may function together as an organizational framework. "Had we but world enough and time," is the line that begins and controls the ideas in Andrew Marvell's poem "To His Coy Mistress," and our usual conception of fiction involves adventures through both time and space. In *The Adventures of Huckleberry Finn, The Hobbit,* and *The Lord of the Flies,* Huck, Bilbo Baggins, Piggy and

Ralph, and all the other characters are caught up in time and place. Chronology is more dominant in "My Grandfather," but notice how often that basis overlaps with spatial elements. Notice also in how many different ways space enters into "Shoes," with his use of the board and pairs of shoes perhaps the most obvious example. At times, then, communication will rely on both temporal and spatial patterns, but there is another pattern—the topical sequence—that almost invariably appears in most communication.

Topical sequence

Interestingly enough, the word "topic" originally meant "place," another illustration of the tendency to give spatial location to ideas. For centuries, when rhetorical theorists wrote of "topics," they meant "places of argument," stock ideas to which a speaker could turn when developing materials for a speech. Some of the flavor remains, for if you start research in a card catalog or in the index of a book or journal, you are starting your investigation in a particular place. But in addition to any assistance it may lend to the gathering of material, the concept of topic suggests strategies. We don't mean strategy in the sense of cunning trickery; we mean the selecting and emphasizing of materials that seem most important. Again our initial exploration of the image is pertinent.

As we noted in Chapter 2, we all learn to be selective in responding to the world about us, a process that involves hierarchies of valuation. Its opposite—a complete lack of selectivity—can be seen in the infant babbling in vocal play, but even the infant learns quickly enough. The valuing and the ordering based on it become unconscious parts of our lives, and they influence our communication whether we are sending or receiving messages. Not only do we learn that there is a time to speak and a time to keep silent, we also learn what ought to be spoken about. Now we're back to the notion of abstracting and the fact that it is simply impossible to say everything that might be said about anything. What is selected depends on many variables, including the personality of the individual, but in truth, we seldom speak or write without making a conscious or unconscious judgment about what to put in and what to leave out, and this is true even when the subject is trivial. Consequently, it seems fair to say that most speeches should reveal topical elements worth noting.

Other patterns appear in Agnew's speech, but we think that the topical element—bias in television news—is especially illuminating. And consider the speeches by Boyd and Rye. In "Shoes," the family-life period extends over time, but instead of examining it from a basis of chronology, Boyd divides the period into the subtopics of food, medical care, recreation, and advancement. Although spatial elements appear, "My Grandfather" rests on a time sequence, but Rye's selectivity centers attention on prejudicial acts, and the ultimate impact of the message owes much to this topical character.

Clearly, we're arguing that all speeches have important topical features but we are not suggesting that you abandon the temporal or spatial pattern. What we are suggesting is that any pattern you choose should eventually lead to choices based on a selection that responds to the demands of the speaking situation, that responds to the demands of your subject, your audience, and the effects you desire.

*

Let's return to the speech about your school once more. If you tried either of the earlier exercises, you probably demonstrated for yourself the point we have been making about selectivity. And if the assignment were entirely unrestricted, what features would you select? And what are the elements that would govern your selection?

*

Mixed sequences

Prepared originally for a section of an introductory speech course, Marilyn Rye's speech is relatively short, and it tends to follow a chronological pattern. Nevertheless, we noted other patterns in her speech, and we have seen mixed features in the longer speeches as well. This fact is something to remember. A single pattern may predominate in short speeches, but as speeches become longer, their individual units may take on characteristics that differ from the pattern of the speech as a whole.

As an illustration of this mixed approach to structure, let's consider some examples from the subject of language. Any language has its historical aspects, and the history of the English language offers many topics that demand chronological treatment. Changes in pronunciation, developments in grammar, and the influence of other languages are only three of the possibilities. But dialect study may invite spatial analysis in terms of the three broad dialect areas in the United States—Eastern, Southern, and General American. And what about the study of place names—the study of how rivers, cities, mountains, and other topographical entities got their names? As with dialects, place is the origin of selectivity. Nevertheless, the study of place names inevitably involves social and cultural dimensions, so a topical selectivity is required. The same is true of an examination of the history of the language or dialect study too. Some aspects, however, do not lend themselves to mixed treatment. Meaning, for example, demands the topical approach. We have already noted such matters as semantics and context, but many other subjects could be included in a complete analysis of meaning, so a speaker would have no choice but to make selections on a topical basis.

Of course, the ultimate basis for your decision is to be found, as we've suggested, in the interrelationships that exist among the various components of the entire speaking situation. You, your subject, your purpose, and your audience combine to influence your choice about the overall pattern of organization, and there are times when the choice will be easy for you to make. Other times may require considerable thought. At still other times, there may be alternatives of seemingly equal value, and you can do no more than decide on what seems best to you. Certainly your chief criterion should always be what seems best for the particular audience.

STRUCTURE AND REASONING

Discussing the nature of structure and argumentation, Monroe Beardsley remarked, "Whether or not an argument is a good one depends ultimately on its structure." In this usage, "good" means that the argument is structurally solid, that is, sound in terms of traditional logic. Later in this chapter, we'll give attention to both inductive and deductive reasoning, but the analysis will be far from exhaustive. We think that we can profitably examine the structural character of argument in terms of everyday activities, and we will try to show how common a thing it is that reasoned inquiry shapes our images.

Problem and solution

Consequently, we prefer to begin by turning to John Dewey's description of reflective thought as an "active, persistent, and careful consideration of any belief or supposed form of knowledge in the light of the grounds that support it, and the further conclusions to which it tends." Amplifying this definition, Dewey traces a movement from problem to solution, saying that this kind of thinking reveals

> five logically distinct steps: (*i*) a felt difficulty; (*ii*) its location and definition; (*iii*) suggestion of possible solution; (*iv*) development by reasoning of the bearings of the suggestion; (*v*) further observation and experiment leading to its acceptance or rejection; that is, the conclusion of belief or disbelief.[*]

It is possible that you have met this fivefold reflective-thinking process somewhere in your education. Since it offers a format for finding solutions to problems and since it is readily adaptable to group problem-solving, Dewey's program has been widely adopted in textbooks on group discussion. And with good reason. If you have ever used this format in a problem-solving discussion, you know that the structural sequence can be helpful in both controlling and stimulat-

[*] John Dewey, *How We Think* (Boston, 1910), p. 72.

ing the entire process. Nevertheless, Dewey is describing individual thought, and the reflective-thinking concept is appropriate to various levels of the public-speaking situation.

Before we move directly into any of those levels, we want to point out a general characteristic of the various structural elements we'll be considering. Most are either macroscopic or microscopic. That is, they apply either to the broad overall pattern a speaker uses or to individual units within the larger pattern. Our examples will illustrate both these possibilities, but we wanted to call the matter to your attention here so that we won't have to repeat it constantly.

Returning to the reflective-thinking process, we think it could be argued that Dewey's pattern is applicable to any public speech. We won't pursue the notion very far, but it seems to us that any speaker who gives any thought to speech preparation necessarily gets involved in the movement from problem to solution. You may not have thought about it that way, but the prospect of making a speech is surely a "felt difficulty," whether it comes as an assignment in a speech class or as the result of accepting an invitation from some organization. The other steps can apply, too, without forcing them, and it might be worth your while to give those other elements some thought in connection with your efforts to improve as a speaker. If you do, you will un-doubtedly find both macroscopic and microscopic implications.

Both appear when we turn to the immediate task of speech preparation. If you choose a controversial area, the reflective-thinking scheme can guide your analysis. No scheme in the world can prevent some people from reaching predetermined conclusions, but the very structure of Dewey's format invites a consideration of alternatives. For example, suppose the topic is marijuana legislation. The possibilities are myriad. The law can be left unchanged, made more severe, removed entirely, or modified in any of several different ways. The choice should be made on the basis of thinking about "the bearings of the suggestion" and "further observation and experiment." Let's qualify that last in a hurry. We aren't suggesting that you buy some marijuana and have a party but that you think, do the necessary research, and think some more. For another topic, the same advice.

Whatever the topic, whatever the problem, the reflective-thinking process may offer a complete pattern for the speech being developed. The situation may seem to require that the speech develop in the full logical sequence that Dewey suggests for reflective thought. It is more likely, however, that your audience analysis will suggest using only a part of the entire sequence in any given speech. A speaker may perceive a problem, think it through carefully, do monumental research, and come up with an exquisite solution. But it may be that the audience will merely yawn, will not be concerned about the problem at all. So the real job is to create awareness, to make the listeners feel the difficulty (Dewey's steps 1 and 2). On the other hand, the audience may be all too aware of the problem, and time spent there would be wasted. Time would be better spent working toward understanding or acceptance of a particular solution (Dewey's steps 3 and 4).

*

Time will always be a factor in any speech, but it becomes particularly critical in a speech course. You may overcome some of the limitations, with your instructor's permission, by combining speeches on the same topic under the problem-solution umbrella. You might, for example, do one speech in which your goal is to create awareness of a problem, then follow it in the next assignment with an argument for a particular solution.

Even if you cannot pursue this suggestion, a problem-solution analysis can clarify a general topic and isolate subjects for different speeches to different audiences. Consider, for example, all that is encompassed in the question of amnesty for those who avoided the draft or deserted during the Vietnam War. Now? Never? Conditional? Unconditional? To different people, the problem may not appear to be the same, so their solutions will differ. That should be reason enough to consider the problem-solution analysis. It can help you locate your audience with reference to the topic.

*

Cause and effect

In describing reflective thinking, Dewey rejects traditional categories, but some customary topics remain useful, and we will examine causal reasoning, deduction, and induction. Strictly speaking, cause-and-effect relationships are not susceptible to precise formal analysis, but these relationships do exhibit characteristics that lend themselves to structural considerations. In fact, the apparent structure can be misleading because cause and effect are so ubiquitous in the images we develop. Tap the patella and the knee jerks; ice on mud puddles means it's cold; a badly worn needle will damage phonograph records. The business of going from cause to effect or effect to cause is so much a part of our lives that we just live with it naturally, much of it being quite out of our control. But the relationships may point to resulting problems and decisions. The freezing of water, for example. Depending on the location, we may keep anti-freeze in the car radiator all year round, drain the radiator on those few nights when the weather is really cold or trust to the warmth of the garage, or just sympathize with people who live in cold climates. These don't exhaust the possibilities, but they suggest ways in which causal relationships affect our lives constantly and at times lead to a consideration of implications. But we become so accustomed to dealing with them that they can be, as we've said, misleading, and they may take on a one-to-one relationship that is invalid. Obviously any problems will be compounded when we move from physics and chemistry to the general area of public controversy. These are the areas where the structure of causal relationships are of special significance to any speaker. Initial analysis demands care, and so does the selection of materials for a particular speech.

Consider the Volstead Act. It could be argued that an all-out enforcement effort would have made Prohibition a success, but what did happen, as opposed to what might have happened, is that the effects were not at all what the proponents of Prohibition had expected. Of course, the argument for Prohibition included many causal elements, and consisted of an elaborate structure. Here are some arguments from another more current debate, each claim asserting a cause-to-effect sequence. "General availability of birth-control pills promotes sexual promiscuity." "Relaxation of abortion laws will increase sexual promiscuity." Presumably, each of these claims could be proved or disproved, depending on the evidence that was found. Each might be the subject for a speech, or a number of speeches. On the other hand, each might be but a small unit in a larger argument. We will move on to other patterns now, reminding you only of the need to examine carefully any causal claims. They seldom are simple.

*

Select some local and limited controversy, something from the campus or the surrounding community. Think about it, talk to people, and read whatever is available. Try to isolate causal factors. The effort will demonstrate rather quickly that causal relationships are almost invariably complex. You will find that "causes and effects" is ordinarily more accurate than "cause and effect." As you proceed, try to assess the role of the communication process, asking yourself how the communication about the controversy seems to alleviate or aggravate any difficulties.

*

Deduction

Once upon a time in ancient Athens, some citizens were discussing the fate of Socrates. Although they agreed with the court that Socrates had corrupted the youth of the city by telling them to question their elders, one of the group lamented the verdict, saying, "Too bad he will have to drink that cup of hemlock." Another immediately retorted, "What difference does it make? He has to die sometime." The first asked, "Why do you say that?" The reply:

All men are mortal.

Socrates is a man.

Socrates is mortal.

We indulge in poetic license, but this example is the most familiar one used to illustrate the syllogistic form in deductive arguments, in which the conclusion follows *necessarily* from the premises. If we accept the premises (the reasons), we must also accept the conclusion. We make a statement that is true for all people and locate Socrates within that class, so that anything invariably applying to the larger class must apply to him.

Frequently, however, a deductive argument does not move from general to specific, but from specific to specific. For example:

Paul's bicycle is newer than Brian's.

Regina's bicycle is newer than Paul's.

Regina's bicycle is newer than Brian's.

Structurally, this illustration meets the requirements of the syllogism and must be accepted as valid. Consequently, we must accept the conclusion. Suppose, however, that one of the premises is not accurate, that Brian's bicycle is newer than Paul's. That fact would destroy the conclusion, despite any formal validity, and it happens that deductive forms often rest on debatable premises. For purposes of illustration, we'll turn to a poem, Andrew Marvell's "To His Coy Mistress":

> Had we but world enough, and time,
> This coyness, Lady, were no crime.
> We would sit down and think which way
> To walk and pass our long love's day.

Thou by the Indian Ganges' side
Shouldst rubies find: I by the tide
Of Humber would complain. I would
Love you ten years before the Flood,
And you should, if you please, refuse
Till the conversion of the Jews.
My vegetable love should grow
Vaster than empires, and more slow;
An hundred years should go to praise
Thine eyes and on thy forehead gaze;
Two hundred to adore each breast,
But thirty thousand to the rest;
An age at least to every part,
And the last age should show your heart;
For, Lady, you deserve this state,
Nor would I love at lower rate.
  But at my back I always hear
Time's wingèd chariot hurrying near;
And yonder all before us lie
Deserts of vast eternity.
Thy beauty shall no more be found,
Nor, in thy marble vault, shall sound
My echoing song; then worms shall try
That long preserved virginity,
And your quaint honour turn to dust,
And into ashes all my lust.
The grave's a fine and private place,
But none, I think, do there embrace.
  Now therefore, while the youthful hue
Sits on thy skin like morning dew
And while thy willing soul transpires
At every pore with instant fires,
Now let us sport us while we may,
And now, like amorous birds of prey,
Rather at once our time devour
Than languish in his slow-chapt power.
Let us roll all our strength and all
Our sweetness up into one ball,
And tear our pleasures with rough strife
Through the iron gates of life:
Thus, though we cannot make our sun
Stand still, yet we will make him run.

Whatever you may think of Marvell's argument, it can be neatly cast into a syllogistic mold, and this is part of the artistic excellence of the poem. The structure is clear at the beginning because Marvell is very straightforward in saying that the coyness would be no crime *if* they had "world enough and time." Becoming less direct in the second section, he still makes it clear that they do not have time enough. That the coyness is a crime is not stated explicitly, but it is obviously implied, so we can put the argument in the form of a hypothetical syllogism:

If our time is limited, then coyness is a crime.

Our time is limited.

Therefore, coyness is a crime.

Not a very seductive argument in such bald terms, but an old one —older far than Marvell's poem—and still used today, if perhaps more indirectly. It is worth noting that deductive claims abound in poetry, a fact that underlines our point that reasoning is everywhere in our lives. Most poems don't illustrate the deductive process as neatly as "To His Coy Mistress." Many do, however, and often they reveal the more ordinary uses of deductive reasoning, the uses that lack those necessary connections between classes. If, for example, we were to accept Marvell's argument at face value—as a literal attempt at seduction—we would have to recognize that form is not enough. The fact is that many deductive modes contain debatable premises. To the contention that there is not enough time, the response could be, "Wrong!" To the contention that coyness is a crime, the response could be, "Wrong!" So it goes in most important questions, whether they are matters of private or public debate.

For a more mundane illustration, here's an argument that was made by a state official in California when he contended that special gasoline allocations should be given to tourists because tourism is California's third largest industry. His argument can be put like this:

Important industries must receive special gasoline allocations.

Tourism is an important industry.

Tourism must receive a special gasoline allocation.

The form is valid, but the official's hierarchy of values in his definition of "important" is debatable, third most important industry or not.

Or look at this one:

Anything that promotes sexual promiscuity is undesirable.

Relaxing abortion laws [is something that] will promote sexual promiscuity.

Relaxing abortion laws is undesirable.

Again we encounter a matter of definition because what constitutes "sexual promiscuity" can't be all that precisely defined. In addition, many would extend this matter of definition into an attack on sexual mores in our society, aggressively challenging the values in the first premise. The second premise, of course, takes us back to cause and effect, because that is where the claim must stand or fall. But there is more. There are implicit considerations as well: people might accept the value expressed in the first premise, conclude that the weight of evidence was on the side of the second, and still argue that abortion laws should be relaxed. They might contend that a slight increase in sexual promiscuity was the lesser evil. Worse, for them, would be the physical and psychological hazards that both married and unmarried women face when seeking illegal abortions.

We are not pointing out these complexities merely for their own sake. Let's go back to the start of this chapter and the notion of structure. A mind both quick and trained may be easily able to see all the ramifications of an argument, but for most of us good argument is no easy matter. Consequently, it may be helpful to sketch out an argumentative structure on paper. This procedure helps most of us quite literally *see* an argument, and this seeing can reveal the points where an issue is open to debate, and what needs to be investigated and researched for the debate. Most important, a concern for argumentative structure can coalesce with audience analysis, helping the speaker discover where time and effort should be expended.

*

Here is an advertisement for a dairy located in the Sacramento Valley:

> Quality is spelled freshness. Freshness is spelled local! And local means lower prices. It just stands to reason. The closer the cows are to the consumers, the fresher the dairy products. The fresher the dairy products, the higher the quality. And premium quality, after all, is what you're looking for. Well, Crystal fine dairy products are processed locally. By local people. From local milk. That gives you a pleasant bonus: non-premium price.
>
> Other brands are shipped to the Valley from all over California. They can't be as fresh after spending all that time on a truck. And guess who's paying the freight. You are.
>
> That's today's easy lesson: "Quality is freshness . . . freshness is local . . . local means lower prices. Crystal is the local dairy." So, with Crystal you get premium quality at a non-premium price.

Can you cast parts of this advertisement in deductive form? It shouldn't be difficult, because more than one syllogism lurks in the copy. Remember, however, to test the degree of debatableness of each premise, regardless of its formal validity.

*

When analyzing deductive arguments, you will often find that something appears to be missing, that a premise seems to have been lost along the way. But the premise is not missing—it is implied. Look at these versions of earlier examples: "Tourism must have a special gasoline allocation because tourism is an important industry (*and important industries must receive special gasoline allocations*)." "Abortion laws must not be relaxed because that would promote sexual promiscuity (*and anything that promotes sexual promiscuity is undesirable*)." Part of the argument—the italicized words in parentheses —is suppressed, but it is suppressed on the assumption that the listener will provide the necessary link. This is the rhetorical syllogism, the *enthymeme*. The term may not be familiar, but the mode of reasoning is. It is one that we all use regularly. In his Des Moines speech, for example, Agnew asks his audience to supply parts of various arguments in a number of places, though the missing elements are particularly evident in the final paragraph when he says, "Now, my friends, we'd never trust such power as I've described over public opinion in the hands of an elected government. It's time we questioned it in the hands of a small and unelected elite."

It is possible that enthymemes are potent because they require the listener to participate rather directly in the very development of the argument. This means, of course, that the enthymeme must develop out of audience analysis, so that the speaker can be sure the audience will cooperate. We all use enthymemes without any conscious effort all the time. Two baseball fans are discussing the coming season, and one says, "The Giants can't win the pennant because they just don't have the pitching." The other may disagree about the strength of the Giants' pitching staff, but real fans can be counted on to accept the fact that pitching is tremendously important in professional baseball. That's taken for granted. And any speaker should be alert to whatever is taken for granted in a speaking situation. An inaccurate estimate of how much the audience knows may produce nothing more serious than inattention and boredom, but when controversy arises, the poor estimate may result in effects contrary to the speaker's intentions. Bored listeners may only daydream, but listeners who find their beliefs and values challenged may become active resisters. Let us qualify again: we are certainly not saying that a speaker must dwell minutely and exhaustively on every potential enthymematic statement, but it seems reasonable to suggest that the important aspects be charted. And unless a speaker wants to be a deceiver of receivers, both altruistic and selfish purposes support the charting.

As receivers, we ought to demand good arguments. Whether the counterargument remains internalized or becomes part of public debate, the right to disagree is one of our inalienable rights. Moreover, our society is predicated on the notion that this right becomes a responsibility. Any time that any of us is part of the decision-making process in a group or organization where dictatorial control does not exist, we fail as individuals if we fail to demand sound argument. The blade cuts the other way in a situation where group goals may transcend those of the individual. In the long run, most of us would like to believe that individual and societal goals can move ahead together, without doing great damage to either, but even the most selfish purpose should support the use of good argument in the public-speaking situation. The speaker who uses weak arguments is easily countered, and what can we, as listeners, conclude about sloppy argumentation? That the investigation has not been thorough? That there hasn't been enough reflection about the evidence? That the investigation and reflection lack any semblance of objectivity? Or that the speaker is deliberately trying to mislead us? The application of all this to your own efforts is too obvious to require further comment.

Induction

Lincoln opened his speech at the Cooper Union with an inductive argument. That is, he examined a number of specific instances, and then he made a generalization (or *inference*) based on those specific instances. In Lincoln's speech, the specific instances were the thirty-nine men who had framed the Constitution, and their votes concerning slavery in the federal territories. With a majority of those votes on his side, Lincoln went on to infer that those who left no records *probably* would have voted in the same way. The "probably" is important, for induction always demands an inferential leap. Consequently, the conclusion is always probable and is never certain. The confidence with which we can make the inductive leap and the force it has in argument depend on the sampling of the population and the characteristic being discussed.

Hasty generalization. That's the most common of the weak links in the inductive chain, and it defines itself. A hasty generalization rests on a distorted sample, a collection of too few or too untypical instances.

M. This anecdote is so appropriate that you may think I made it up, but, unhappily, I did not. It happened back at the time when the civil rights movement was blooming. A part of the movement was the vigorous denunciation of racist terms, and a student in one of my classes touched on this matter in a speech about race relations in the South. Racist terminology was a subtopic, and he dismissed it rather casually with the assertion that, as far as he knew, "Negroes really didn't mind being called 'niggers.'" But he didn't leave that assertion entirely unsupported. He marshalled inductive evidence. That evidence consisted of a poll he had taken two weeks before on the streets of Atlanta. His sample: "I was waiting for this bus, and there was this old colored man standing there, and I asked him if he minded being called a 'nigger.' Well, he told me that he didn't mind at all."

Lincoln, of course, could limit and define his sample rather precisely, and similar restrictions may be easily imposed in many circumstances. Enrollment at the University of California at Davis is pushing toward 17,000, and the campus police report that nearly 15,000 bicycles appear on campus during class days. Some faculty and staff ride bicycles, but most belong to the students, so it is safe to generalize that a student at Davis probably rides a bicycle to class. But note that complications can arise: someone coming to Davis directly from high school might conclude that most college students ride bicycles to class on campuses all over the country.

Obviously, the sample—the class of instances being examined—must be defined as precisely as possible, the characteristic under consideration must be restricted, and the sample must be recognized for what it is. As we have seen, a too limited sample may produce the hasty generalization, but there are other problems too: the sampling may skew or distort results. A famous case of skewing was the 1936 election survey made by *The Literary Digest* when Alfred M. Landon was running for president against Franklin D. Roosevelt. The *Digest* conducted its poll by telephone. In those Depression days, millions of voters could not afford telephones, a fact the *Digest* people overlooked when they predicted a landslide victory for Landon. To their surprise the vast majority voted for Roosevelt.

This poll did not account for a most significant variable—the proportion of voters who did not own telephones—and variables must be accounted for in any inductive conclusion. Not long ago, newspapers regularly carried stories about students being arrested for the possession of marijuana, but one reads far fewer of these stories today. It is possible to conclude that fewer students are using pot, but people close to the college scene might have some questions to raise about that generalization. On some campuses at least, the police adopt a live-and-let-live policy toward the use of marijuana, and they arrest only the most blatant offenders. Consequently, any induction about the incidence of marijuana smoking that is based on newspaper stories may not be all that accurate.

Making generalizations from samples is one of the chief ways in which basic research is carried out, so that control of variables and precise sampling is at the heart of much of the information-gathering in a variety of fields today. The results are reported to us in connection with population growth, crime, gasoline mileage, homosexuality, grade-point averages, smoking, and almost any other subject you can list. Sometimes, of course, we receive no more than a mathematical computation, a numerical total, but often we find that the most interesting evidence is much more than merely statistical in nature. It is most interesting in interpreting and predicting human behavior, and we can't help being fascinated by such information. Fascinated or not by the increasing uses of statistical analyses, we have come to rely more and more on the inductions that arise from them. If, as a speaker, you address any social problem—even a seemingly simple one—your research will take you to reports that are quantitative in nature. As a result, it can be argued that the well-educated person of today—whether a sender or receiver of messages—should have a good understanding of statistical procedures and their uses. Before you can be a competent sender, you must be a competent receiver if you are to use such evidence in your speeches. And conflicting experimental results demonstrate over and over again that mathematical formulas cannot guarantee the investigator's skill or the lack of all bias in the reporting. In the long run, then, the best way for you to evaluate the generalizations produced is to have an acquaintance with the methods involved. It may even be that you might even want to devote an entire speech to the defending or the challenging of a study or studies of the type being discussed here.

*

Annually, we read in the newspapers about the incidence of crime in the United States, usually about the increase in major crime. What is the source of these reports? How are they assembled? What is a major crime, and who draws the distinction? You may discover that smaller communities only appear to have less crime. What reporting methods bring about this apparent discrepancy?

*

As we have suggested throughout this chapter, your speeches can be improved if you give some attention to their general structure and to the structure of your arguments, customizing both in terms of your topic and your audience. In one situation, your topic-audience analysis may make you decide that the question demands a systematic rundown of the pros and the cons. In another, you may conclude that the effect you seek can be achieved by slighting formal argument and centering on other modes of acceptance. In still another, some careful blending may appear the best course.

We have come back to the question of how much your listeners know and how much they care, but we would remind you again that these dimensions are not separate. Lincoln suggested a distinction between judgments arising from hot passion and cold reason when he remarked, "That is cool!" Nevertheless, his own performance emphasizes our point. Concentrating exclusively on the most volatile issue of the day, he relied exclusively on reasoned argument, but it was far from being a *coldly* reasoned discourse. In this and the other speeches we have included, the logically valid segments seem anything but cold and distant. They demonstrate the integral relationship between knowing and caring, and it is the nature of this relationship that you should keep in mind throughout your speech preparation.

SUGGESTED READINGS

Monroe C. Beardsley, *Thinking Straight*, 3rd ed. (Englewood Cliffs, N.J., 1966). An excellent treatment of the applied uses of traditional logic. The applications always are pertinent and frequently witty.

John Dewey, *How We Think* (Boston, 1910). There is much more here than the familiar problem-solving sequence cited in this chapter. The book is well worth a reading for its many original insights into the cognitive process.

Douglas Ehninger and Wayne Brockriede, *Decision by Debate* (New York, 1963). Primarily concerned with formal argumentation, this book departs from formal logic in its reliance on the theories of Stephen Toulmin, which the authors adapt for their own purposes in Part III.

PREVIEW: CHAPTER 9

Chapter 9 begins with a discussion of euphemism, which sets the stage for detailed comments on many considerations involved in developing the substance of a speech. We first give attention to structural aspects, and then we turn to some ways of amplifying ideas in your speeches. The topics are:

Euphemism
Outlining
Conclusions
Introductions
The body of the speech
    Some general patterns
    Familiarity and novelty
    Comparisons and contrasts
    Examples and illustrations
    Quotations and testimony
    Visual aids
    Humor
Further aspects of style

When you have completed this chapter, you will realize the importance of starting well and stopping well, and the importance of all that goes between. Furthermore, you will learn some specific ways in which you can build a speech that starts well, stops well, and goes well in between.

messages

DEVELOPING IDEAS

EUPHEMISM

In order to provide a basis for discussion here, we want to begin with a further reference to George Orwell's essay "Politics and the English Language" and to his statement that political utterances are often used to support the insupportable. He argues that this tactic regularly forces the speaker to rely on euphemism, which he illustrates thus: "Defenceless villages are bombarded from the air, the inhabitants driven out into the countryside, the cattle machine-gunned, the huts set on fire with incendiary bullets: this is called *pacification*." Pacification! The word not only avoids reality, it distorts reality. At the least all euphemism permits, as a dictionary tells us, "the substitution of an inoffensive or mild expression for one that may offend." However, euphemism has another dimension—the desire to create a higher status for oneself through language. The two dimensions overlap and merge, as we'll see, but we'll look at the avoidance dimension first.

Orwell was writing in 1943, but the three decades that have passed do not appear to have diminished the tendency for governments to indulge in euphemism when it comes to war. In fact, all bureaucracies, public and private, seem to thrive on such expressions. But the most obvious and familiar examples of avoidance involve linguistic taboos, and in our culture these are most common where sex or some other biological function is concerned. For instance, in *To Kill a Mockingbird,* a young girl is told that rape means "to have carnal knowledge." Great explanation, right? But while we all like to believe that we are liberated and while there has been considerable relaxation in recent years, what do you do when a television newscaster talks about "call girls" or a "red-light district," and your five-year-old sister wants to know what the words mean?

The Victorians were among the worst in this regard. The era invented countless ways to avoid calling a spade a spade, and although many of their usages have lost most of their force, we still commonly say "light meat" and "dark meat" when asking our guests which part of the chicken they would prefer. Those are Victorian coinages, to avoid the unmentionable "thighs" or "breasts." In those days, people didn't even have legs, let alone thighs. They had "limbs." And even today, you won't hear many people asking where they can find a toilet; we have "bathrooms, restrooms, men's rooms, women's rooms," or just the signs *Men* or *Women.*

But if our bodies require euphemism when they are functioning, they also demand it when they have ceased to function. Who dies? Everyone, but how people struggle to say something else! Here is but a partial listing from *Roget's Thesaurus:* "breathe one's last, decease, depart, expire, give up the ghost, go to the happy hunting grounds, join one's ancestors, pass away, pass on, perish, succumb." And does death result in a corpse? No. It results in "the last remains." The possibilities here and elsewhere are almost limitless, but it happens that these last examples of avoidance lead directly into the second dimension of euphemism, into the vainglory that marks the search for status in language.

Those last remains will be "interred," not buried. But where? Not in a graveyard, certainly. Maybe a "cemetery." Or maybe in a "lawn," such as East Lawn or Memorial Lawn. And if you let your fingers do the walking through the Yellow Pages, they won't trip over undertakers and morticians these days. They'll meet with "funeral directors" who operate "chapels." No doubt there is some avoidance here, but there is more. In *The American Language,* writing about occupational titles, H. L. Mencken remarked sardonically:

> An American, probably more than any other man, is prone to be apologetic about the trade he follows. He seldom believes that it is quite worthy of his virtues and talents; almost always he thinks that he would have adorned something far gaudier. Unfortunately, it is not always possible for him to escape, or even for him to dream plausibly of escaping, so he soothes himself by assuring himself that he belongs to a superior section of his craft, and very often he invents a sonorous name to set himself off from the herd.

Let's be honest. We all get a thrill from a sonorous title, whether it sets us off from the herd or not; that's why you'll find some college teachers who prefer to be addressed as "Doctor" or "Professor." So it is hardly surprising that we have come from undertaker through mortician to "funeral director." And you won't find many janitors around these days because most of them are "custodians," and real estate agents are "realtors," and hairdressers are "stylists," and beauty operators are "beauticians," and a bartender may even be a "mixologist"!

We human beings certainly don't restrict this search for glory to occupations; we spread it around everywhere. Where, for example, do beauticians learn their trade? Possibly at a school, but more likely at a "college," just as barbers do. Why not? Normal schools became teachers' colleges became state colleges became universities. At colleges and universities, departments and other units move to new designations; the old Department of Irrigation now is the "Department of Water Science," while the people who used to work for Drafting and Duplicating suddenly find that they are employed in "Reprographics."

And so it goes. A great deal more could be said about euphemism, but for now the purpose of the discussion has been accomplished if you have a better understanding of the process, if you have a better grasp of its two emphases of avoidance and status-seeking, which sometimes are hard to distinguish. Some of the examples appear to reveal human frailty, but it is hazardous to label any linguistic phenomenon as all bad or all good—and, besides, that really is a different subject. Here it is enough to conclude that euphemism is in our language, in our culture, in all of us.

Stop! Stop and look back at the last eight paragraphs. What we have done in those paragraphs is to create a self-contained message. It is approximately a thousand words long, and when delivered at a normal speaking rate, it would take about five minutes to present. What it amounts to is the kind of short speech that is regularly part of the introductory class. We might have warned you but we thought it would be fun to indulge in a bit of chicanery, even if it prevents us from ever going to our reward in the Big Classroom in the Sky.

OUTLINING

We don't present this discussion of euphemism as a model of excellence, but in fact it does more than illustrate what might happen in the introductory class. For example, the same general organizational pattern could be considerably refined and amplified; the pattern once actually served as the basis for a two-hour report in a seminar on the English language. Certainly its organization and other aspects cannot be applied to every speech, but we have tried to introduce a number of elements that are common in spoken discourse—elements that function regardless of the length of the speech or the effect being sought.

Consequently, this example gives us a point of entry in examining further details of speech preparation. In that examination, we will first take a closer look at structural details, then at units within the structure, and finally at stylistic matters. We begin with a slightly oversimplified outline:

Euphemism

General effect: Understanding
Specific effect: Understanding two aspects of euphemism
 I. Introduction
  A. Use Orwell quotation.
  B. Distinguish between avoidance and status-seeking.
 II. Body
  A. Avoidance is most obvious in connection with sex and other biological functions.
   1. Examples from sex:
    a. Rape
    b. Prostitution
     i. The women
     ii. The places
   2. Examples from biology:
    a. Victorians and chicken
    b. The bathroom
    c. Death
  B. Status-seeking appears in job titles and other labels.
   1. Examples from job titles:
    a. Teachers
    b. Funeral directors
   2. General examples:
    a. Schools
    b. Units within schools
 III. Conclusion
  A. Restate two aspects of euphemism.
  B. Comment on the process.

First a word on mechanics. As we noted above, this outline is simplified in that it doesn't include all the examples mentioned in the "speech" itself. On the other hand, we have included five levels of outlining, more than are usually necessary for a short presentation. We should also note that the outline is composed of mixed entities. That is, although some of the headings consist of phrases or single words, we have used complete sentences for all items at the second level. These too could have been words or phrases, and the words or phrases could have been complete sentences. We have been consistent within our mixing, but your instructor may ask for outlines that are consistent in form throughout. Whatever the method, the important thing is that the outline ultimately contribute to the creation of an effective message.

*

We have been talking about various facets of structure for some time, and now we ask you to consider how you could reorder Part II of the outline. Can you restructure the section in a way that would not make for substantial alterations in the basic message?

*

If you attempted the exercise above, you should have found it easy enough. Clearly our outline reflects a topical pattern, and the two main units could be reversed, status-seeking coming before avoidance. And within the categories, the examples could appear in different order without making any radical change in content. We don't mean to suggest that the materials can be tumbled about willy-nilly; obviously, transposing the major units would demand a reordering of the internal elements. So one choice will influence others.

Our sample outline is typical and traditional in having three parts: introduction, body, and conclusion. The formal analysis of discourse is the oldest mode in our civilization, and earlier rhetorical treatises contain exhaustive discussions of the various parts of an oration. Much of the detail seems tedious now, but theorists have long been raising the same questions that speakers ask today: What is the best way to get started? Is there a best time to use this argument? How can I make the conclusion most effective? Hugh Blair's *Lectures on Rhetoric and Belles Lettres,* an extremely detailed examination from the eighteenth century, is a good example. Blair examines the various parts of a speech at length, but while he bows to tradition, he does not scrape. He notes the various functions that an introduction can perform, but he also says that there are excellent speeches in which the speaker "uses no introduction, but enters directly on his subject; where he has no occasion either to decide or explain; but simply reasons on one side of the question, and then finishes." "My Grandfather" is an example of a speech that lacks an introduction in the formal sense, and note that while Lincoln does include some introductory remarks, they are very brief.

Like a novice driver, you as a novice speaker will be most interested in starting and stopping, so we will discuss introductions and conclusions first. And we will start with the stopping, because as we will point out there are times when the introduction will be the last thing you should worry about.

CONCLUSIONS

Assume that you have sketched out the main ideas for your speech. You have some idea of where you are going and some idea of where you will take your audience. We have some cautionary advice that is based on sad experience—much of it coming, incidentally, from outside the classroom. Far too often the two of us hear speeches that do not have an integrated conclusion, and we think that there are two principal reasons why. The first is simply a lack of thoughtful concern for the speaking situation, a carelessness, a failure to make a real effort at integrating the entire message. And the second is the predetermined conclusion: the speaker sets out to prove a point and is so caught up in the conclusion that the development of ideas becomes subsidiary. To get off the freeway at the right place may be more difficult than getting on.

The last words a speaker says may be the most important, but they should not be the most important because the audience just may be thankful that they *are* the last words. To help you avoid that possibility, we offer some concepts for your consideration—a recipe, if you will. Its ingredients are summary, climax, and control.

Summary

No doubt you've heard the stock advice for the speaker: Tell 'em what you're gonna tell 'em; tell 'em; tell 'em what you've told 'em. In many situations, that is sound advice. After all, a speech is ephemeral. Once given, it's gone. Some people get their speeches taped and printed, of course, but most of us don't. So the effect desired may dictate that a speech close with a rather direct summation, or recapitulation, of what has gone before—no more than a restatement of the main points in a speech. That was how we concluded our discussion of euphemism.

There our conclusion aimed at understanding, but restatement may function well in other effects. A speech on anti-busing legislation, the oil-depletion allowance, affirmative action programs, or the United Nations might well terminate in a review of the main ideas. That review, however, may become more than a simple listing; it may include reference to the main ideas, but it may also amplify and reinforce all that has gone before. Some speeches, of course, do not need or lend themselves to a formal summary as such. The four speeches we included are all examples of this type.

Agnew's speech, however, can be said to summarize by refining. In the closing paragraphs, he repeats issues he has raised in the speech, but he goes beyond a mere repetition, particularly in the final paragraph, where he issues a challenge. We would argue, also, that Lincoln summarizes. Or is it fair to argue that his echoing of all that he has said is a form of summary? Maybe we extend the notion too far, but what we are trying to suggest is that the notion of summary is both flexible and adaptable. It may be obvious and direct, or indirect and subtle, and it may work in any speech, whatever the effect you want. On the other hand, don't forget that a summary statement may not be the most useful conclusion to some speeches.

*

As a general rule, the longer your speech, or the more difficult its subject matter, the more some kind of summary is needed. If your speech is relatively short, and deals with a relatively uncomplicated subject, a full-blown summary isn't needed. In fact, for relatively simple, brief speeches, a summary would be redundant—it might even insult your listeners. If a summary-type conclusion is a part of your strategy, ask yourself this important question: *how much* summary do I need?

*

Climax

If you have decided to give a speech about how caviar is processed, assuming that you had once worked in a caviar factory, the process of separating and salting the eggs might not lend itself to summary. And it probably would not lend itself to climax. The Greek word is *klimax*, meaning "ladder," and the rungs on a ladder suggest the heightening of emotional intensity that we associate with climax. There is a climbing, a building to a higher level of force.

Clearly, this is what Rye does in "My Grandfather" when she moves from a series of specific examples to a wider and more challenging view of prejudice and bigotry. She hardly summarizes. On the other hand, there is both summary and climax in "Shoes," for Boyd pursues the personal element, specifying it in terms of his working shoes and of his family life, and he brings it all back to the thesis with which he began, to the contention that "there is no substitute for life insurance." We have suggested, too, that Lincoln may be doing some summarizing, but we were a bit tentative about that. We are not tentative, however, about his use of climax. We will not take the time to trace the manner in which Lincoln builds emotional intensity, but a close reading of the speech reveals a stronger and more demanding tone at the end of each of the three main segments. Furthermore, when Lincoln moves from the attack on Douglas, through the debate with the South, to his words for the Republican party, he creates another climactic order.

*

There is an element of climax in three of our speeches. What of the fourth? Does Agnew seem to build toward greater impact as the speech moves along? Furthermore, is there anything that seems to be typical of climactic order—any characteristic or characteristics that cut across two or more of the speeches?

*

Control

In some respects the notion of control is redundant here because it encompasses what we have been saying about summary and climax. Clearly, a speaker should strive to make the most of terminal remarks. Whatever form a conclusion may take, it should be a suitable culmination of what has preceded, and its ultimate goal should be to assist in controlling the response of the listeners.

The idea of control applies in another way, in relation to the mastery that the speaker exerts over the materials of the speech. We mentioned this in connection with our first remarks about organization, and we repeat it here. Other things being equal, an organic conclusion— one that is integrated with the rest of the speech—will be more satisfying to both speaker and listener because the integration will increase the likelihood that the speaker is in command of the materials and situation. And even if the conclusion doesn't summarize neatly or build to a strong climax, control of the closing words is important. It is better for all concerned when the speaker truly concludes rather than simply stopping, or, worse, just running down weakly like the alarm on a clock.

*

Perhaps you considered some of these things in connection with the conclusion to your last speech. Be sure to do so for those that follow. Topic, purpose, and other choices will influence what you will be able to do, but consciously plan to make the conclusion work in the ways we have been talking about here.

*

INTRODUCTIONS

Hugh Blair, whom we quoted earlier, states that the starting should be the last thing developed, that the introduction "should not be planned, till after one has meditated in his own mind the substance of his discourse." He warns that when the order is reversed, the speaker is likely to be caught in one of two traps. On the one hand, the speaker who plans the introduction first may find that "he is led to lay hold of some common-place topic." On the other, he may discover that "instead of the introduction being to accommodate to the discourse, he is obliged to accommodate the whole discourse to the introduction." Dwell on the substance first, he argues, for after "close meditation on the subject, materials for the preface will then suggest themselves much more readily."

And some close meditation may be necessary. Rhetorical theorists have traditionally stated that an introduction is useful in establishing rapport between speaker and audience, in forecasting the lines of inquiry, and in blunting any negative attitudes. Most of this advice centers on controversial and highly charged emotional situations, but it can be worthwhile to give some thought to what you might make your introduction do for the rest of your message. There will be times, certainly, when the introduction emerges full-blown and will require no special attention, but even a relatively neutral topic may profit from a careful planning of the introduction. The ingredients of our recipe for planning are attention, direction, and control.

Attention

As we suggested earlier, and as common sense tells us all, a message will be lost or distorted if it does not gain and hold attention. Without attention, there is no meaning. This applies to the entire message, but it is something to be particularly concerned about at the very start of a speech. Now, the physical arrangements of the public-speaking situation usually insure that speakers have an initial advantage in this regard. They are the focus of attention because they are separated by a desk or a podium, by standing rather than sitting. It is important to capitalize on this initial advantage, particularly because listeners are making up their minds right from the outset about the entire message. Their opinion probably will be an unconscious one, but it is an opinion that will profoundly influence their comprehension of the message.

The most obvious extension of this initial physical attention is to be found in the delivery itself. We're not talking about intense, dramatic activity. We're talking about movement and gestures directed to all the listeners, about a voice that is adjusted appropriately to the circumstances, about eye contact with people in the audience. Such things are important in establishing and maintaining attention. But the initial, physical attention exists because the listeners expect that something will be said, and what is said offers a tremendous range for factors of attention.

Although "My Grandfather" has no distinct introduction, the approach is suggestive. The "once upon a time" flavor and the implied promise of a story dealing with family experience are likley to invite an identification from the listener. "Shoes" also uses and emphasizes the personal aspect, but note that Boyd immediately ties this personal dimension to the careers of his listeners. We quoted Orwell in our "speech" (hoping that you have read *Animal Farm* or *1984*), because we thought his words might give a bit more prestige to the analysis of euphemism. Lincoln uses quotation in quite a different way. Taking the "text" from Douglas, he centers on the topic, but at the same time, he implicitly invites fellow Republicans to share his attitudes towards the Democrats. But the possibilities are myriad. Perhaps your introduction will gain most attention if you begin with a simple and direct statement of where you are going. In a different situation, you may feel it necessary to cultivate the good will of your audience, trying to find common ground that will sustain their willingness to listen throughout the speech.

We have only scratched the surface with these examples and hypothetical illustrations, and what you choose to do will depend on all the varied elements in the specific situation. We do hope that the discussion has alerted you to the rich potential from which you might choose. Other possibilities will become evident later in this chapter, in the sections devoted to the body of the speech.

Direction

In some respects, direction may be a function of attention. Consider the road map. With a long trip in the offing, we attend to the map, but we are satisfied with the most general sense of direction. It is enough to know that Interstate 5 or 19 or 20 or 70 goes in the direction we want to go. Our needs become much more specific, however, once we approach the destination. And this is so often true in a speech. The goals of gaining and holding attention may indicate a sense of direction, but that sense may not be clearly focused. In "My Grandfather," this sense emerges as the narrative progresses. Agnew is much more explicit. He does not anticipate all the subdivisions of his topic, but he clearly indicates that he will raise questions about the news media. Lincoln, of course, systematically dissects the "text," and although he does not say specifically that he will attack Douglas's position, the audience doesn't need to hear that. They know!

In none of these speeches is there a complete overview statement; our euphemism "speech" is the only example that includes one. This is partially explained, perhaps, by the fact that the other four speeches are intended to go beyond the effect of understanding. But whatever the explanation, these few examples and a great deal of research suggest that it may not be useful to clutter an introduction with an elaborate sketch of what is to come. As Blair notes, the speaker may help the listeners most merely "by giving them some hints of the importance, dignity, or novelty of the subject." In this regard, we suggest you turn back to the exercise on page 207. Our comments there apply to the introduction as well as to the conclusion.

Control

In some respects, the notion of control is even more redundant here than it is in connection with conclusions. Control surely is implied in what we've said about attention and direction, and it is obvious that control of the message is most important in the early stages. A final shaping of response may be attempted in the conclusion, but that attempt cannot count for much if the listeners haven't been with the speaker most of the time. But even if the fact is obvious, we still think it deserves some thought.

Furthermore, there is a related aspect of control that merits comment—control of self in the speaking situation. Psychologically, the first part of the speech ordinarily produces the biggest problems in adjusting to the speaking situation. Consequently, control will lead to control. That is, the more carefully you work out your introduction, the easier your presentation will be. And as we've already noted, the audience will respond more favorably to a speaker who appears to be in command of self and materials. That's quite important, and the initial impression of competence you make can serve the ultimate goals of communication from the point of view of both listener and speaker.

*

In preparing the introduction for your next speech, develop two or more possibilities and select the one that seems most appropriate. Again the choice will be influenced by other choices, but it should reflect the conscious decision that *this* introduction will work best. Once you have made the decision, you might reflect upon the reasons for it.

*

THE BODY OF THE SPEECH

For the remainder of this chapter, we'll be taking a closer look at some ways of giving substance to your speech, some ways of giving full expression to your ideas. As the heading indicates, we will concentrate on the body of the speech, but most of what we have to say applies to conclusions and introductions, if your speech happens to have those distinct elements. In general, we think it useful to approach the development of speech substance with reference to *amplification, clarification,* and *emphasis,* three interrelated and overlapping concepts.

Clearly, the first thing a speaker has to do when creating the substance of the speech is to amplify, to decide the best ways to add detail to the ideas being developed. Clarity is a further goal; in Aristotle's words, "Style to be good must be clear, as is proved by the fact that speech which fails to convey a plain meaning will fail to do just what speech has to do." Comprehension, then, is the ultimate test. And as we have noted earlier, there are times when this seemingly more preliminary effect will follow acceptance. The volunteer worker who arrives at party headquarters during a political campaign reveals acceptance and is behaving in a way that needs only to be directed through understanding. On the other hand, it often is necessary to think of emphasis, to think of an impact that goes beyond clarity. Listeners may understand before the speaker begins, and it takes a forceful, vigorous development of ideas to move them to accept or to change their behavior.

Some general patterns

In addition to structural sequences, discourse can be described in terms of other patterns, such as narration, description, explanation, or definition, which you undoubtedly have encountered before. These are not pure categories; for example, it may be difficult to decide when an explanation can be distinguished from a definition or from a description. Furthermore, a single discourse will exhibit varied elements and patterns within patterns. In our euphemism illustration, for instance, specific examples provide the staple, but we include a limited dictionary definition—and definition, in a much broader sense, is the intent of the entire message. Notice, too, the materials that constitute the narrative in "My Grandfather"; Rye explains and describes a series of incidents, and she does some general defining, as well. And after his first remarks, Agnew relates the responses to Nixon's earlier speech in narrative form.

So any discourse may have a dominant pattern made up of differing individual units. Recognition of that fact is not guaranteed to work magic for a speaker, but awareness of the method or methods being used can be of assistance. Awareness should lead to greater precision in selectivity. In emphasizing selectivity, we simply refer to the making of decisions concerning what to say and what not to say, what to put in and what to leave out. Unfortunately, a finished speech may be difficult to assess completely on this basis because we only know what the speaker chose to put in, not what may have been left out. Nevertheless, some judgments can be made. After listening to a particular speech, we might feel that the complexities in one section seemed to have demanded an internal summary that was lacking. In another instance, we might conclude that a speaker spent too much or too little time with the details in one part of the speech. At another level, we might conclude that something should have been said about what was not said. For example, suppose you are describing the operation of a nuclear power plant and decide to say nothing about pollution. Failure to explain the decision could prevent understanding for many audiences; the issue receives so much attention that they would expect something to be said.

All this echoes some of the things we said about abstracting, about how we can never tell everything we know. It may seem a chore to construct the substance of a speech, but in the long run, the real chore may be in deciding what *not* to say. What you do say necessarily will be a form of amplification, but as we remarked, amplification should be at the service of clarity and emphasis. These two concepts will be controlling elements throughout the rest of the chapter, though the distinction between them must not be pressed too far.

Sometimes, clarity and emphasis are impossible to separate, but it seems sensible to accept that one or the other may be the most important consideration in a given instance. At the same time, we will have occasion to comment on their interrelationships as we move through other matters relating to the development of speech substance.

Familiarity and novelty

"Go from the known to the unknown" is advice often given to writers and speakers, and we introduced it in connection with your selection of topics, suggesting that you start with your own interests and knowledge. That decision should be tempered by what the audience knows and how much it cares, but as the discussion also indicated, a concept such as familiarity has both cognitive and emotive characteristics. We think that the significance of these characteristics is delineated well enough in our earlier discussion of the image, but there are some related ideas that deserve consideration.

Given the listener's image, it is all too obvious that its make-up must be the point of departure for any communication, but the speaker can make use of that make-up in more than one way. Clearly, it should function when listeners are being taken to understanding or some other effect, but it has more limited applications. At its most limited, we could talk about language and vocabulary because communication necessarily requires a common store of experience at this level. But such things as examples, metaphors, extended comparisons, and even visual aids may be most functional when they are tied to the familiar. Thus, a discussion of camping in France, whatever the intended effect, may profit by being compared with camping experiences in this country, the known helping to explain the unknown.

V. Talking to a class once about the impression that a young man had made during a speech, I remarked, "Well, didn't he strike most of us as being sort of a Jack Armstrong?" The response? Blank faces. I grew up with radio and Jack Armstrong, the All-American Boy, but my audience had grown up with television, and my reference was a complete wash-out.

We're not suggesting that every example and every allusion be familiar to everyone in the audience—you just won't find audiences of such homogeneity. And it may even be that you have decided to challenge your listeners a bit. Familiarity is something to think about as you develop a speech, though, because familiarity may do more than make ideas clear; it may work toward emphasis.

Familiarity may breed contempt, but there are many times when familiarity also breeds comfort. Again we remind you that every

"You're always quoting from Aristotle, Plato, Socrates, Juvenal, Cicero—when are you going to quote something from your own head?"

human being has an image, and every one of us needs to have some sense of who, where, and what we are. As a result, ideas that strike close to home ordinarily will have greater impact than those from afar. Both generally and specifically, the Everglades are more pertinent to the residents of Fort Myers, Florida, than to people who live in Rapid City, South Dakota. As an example where familiarity works, we need look no further than Boyd's speech with its lists from family experience. In these lists, he surely achieves clarity, and most of his listeners probably found real comfort in the familiarity. By the same token, the general ideas and specific references in "My Grandfather" had greater meaning for people in California than they would have had for residents of New Hampshire.

Familiarity is a point that ought not be pressed too far, however, because we all know that the coin can be turned, that the new and the novel may have inherent attractions. All of us realize that aspects of the unknown are terrifying, but most of us like to think that we are a bit adventuresome. Despite our need for stability and familiarity, we all like a little spice in our lives from time to time. Appeals to the new and exciting commonly appear in advertising, with an appeal for us to escape from our ordinary, humdrum existence. That may be an effective motive appeal in a speech, too, but we're thinking here of novelty in slightly different senses.

One was suggested in Chapter 5 when we talked about taking a fresh look at seemingly tired topics. The new perspective may, of itself, create interest and hold the attention of listeners. In a more limited sense, novelty can be very important for creating and sustaining interest throughout a speech. Examples, anecdotes, quotations, or other forms of amplifying an idea may have something new or unusual that will catch the listeners' fancy. We think that Lincoln does this when he presents his mock debate with the South to his New York audience. And although New York long has been accused of provincialism, Agnew gives a new twist to the charge when attacking the news commentators and producers who live in the New York-Washington orbit. We also think that Boyd supplies an interesting example when he says, in summing up food costs, "But evidently it takes that much to raise 23 pounds of brand-new babies into 495 pounds of grown-up kids." What we're trying to get at here, then, is not novelty born of forced and contrived concern, but novelty that emerges naturally from a bit of thought and a bit of imagination. The effort may apply to varied elements in the development of a speech, and the effort is just one more thing that should become a part of your habitual preparation.

Comparisons and contrasts

Like familiarity and novelty, comparisons and contrasts are encompassing ideas, concepts that involve more specific modes, such as figures of speech, examples, or testimony. It happens, too, that contrasts may feed on comparisons, whether implicit or explicit, but comparisons do not present alternatives as frequently as contrasts do. Rather, a comparison may transfer the qualities of one object or phenomenon to another, as a metaphor does. Comparison, in fact, is responsible for all the dead metaphors in the language, for the words or phrases that remain in use long after their origins have been forgotten. An example is "bunk," in the statement "What he said was a lot of bunk." Other figurative expressions apply here, even when they are clichés: the politician "joined the team" or the baseball player "hit the ball into orbit," for example. An extended example may also serve as the essence of comparison; that was Conwell's technique in the success stories that dot "Acres of Diamonds." Naturally a greater impact results from the number of cases he cites, but each of his stories carries the message, "You could and should do the same."

An extended version of examples or instances can produce an *analogy*, the kind of comparison in which elements are directly juxtaposed. For example, suppose the topic is coeducational dormitories on a college campus. Surely the best sources of information are campuses that have had experience with these dormitories, and a speaker might want to make the comparison the basis for an entire speech.

Used for the purposes of explaining, the comparison could produce understanding, but a different approach could turn the comparison into an argument from analogy. Thus, a speaker would argue that coed dorms work in such and such a college and they will work in ours. The logical use of the device of the analogy demands careful attention to the details. Are the situations truly comparable? Are there, despite similarities, significant differences? What does other evidence say about the validity of the speaker's claim that what happened there will happen here? But an analogy may be quite forceful, even though the comparison is highly figurative. Lincoln's highwayman metaphor is a brief, figurative analogy, and in spite of his moving from the threat of the gunman to the threats from the South, few of his listeners were likely to examine the logical adequacy of his association.

A comparison, then, may be expressed in a single word, or it may be spelled out in great detail, depending on the uses that the speaker expects it will serve. Whether limited in scope or expressed in amplified form, the comparison contains a wide range of possibilities. It may clarify ideas, and it may also give them greater intensity for listeners.

*

For your next speech, choose and develop a comparison that will clarify and/or intensify your topic.

*

While a comparison may sometimes emphasize variation, a contrast is, by definition, something that concentrates on dissimilar elements. For a commonplace illustration, think how often a contrast emerges when you talk with your friends about different places in this country. Similarities will crop up, of course, but a discussion about Chicago versus San Francisco, or Boston versus New Orleans, will almost certainly be in terms of the *differences* between them—the contrasts. Using contrasts is so much a part of the way we establish quality or valuation that it forms the basis for any number of old jokes. Here's one of them: "Let me tell you about the speaker I heard last night. His delivery was just terrible, but what he had to say was incomprehensible." In real life, on the other hand, contrasts frequently ask us to make a sometimes difficult choice between two genuine alternatives. Then, of course, there are the advertisers. What would they do if contrasts were taken away from them? In newspapers and magazines and on radio and television, we constantly are bombarded with the "differences" between various brands of razor blades, deodorants, detergents, and pain-killers. However, if you are suspicious of advertising, remember that the impartial testing in *Consumer Reports* invariably and legitimately relies on contrast, and comparison too to a lesser degree.

*

You will find a number of contrasts in our "speech" on euphemism. Actually, once you think about it, contrast is essential to the very notion of euphemism. If you look for them, you will also discover an abundance of contrasts in the four sample speeches, and a consideration of them—both the obvious and subtle instances—will make you more alert to possible applications in your own speech preparation.

*

As we've suggested, while contrasts may clarify, they often move toward emphasis. The contrast in Lincoln's debate with the South is a case in point. He clarifies the position he thinks Republicans should take, but at the same time, he argues with vigor. In this instance, Lincoln's contrast was calculated to take his listeners beyond understanding. He hoped they would accept his message, and that he could influence their behavior. As we have suggested, a speaker may have similar goals when using comparison, particularly in the form of analogy. Analogy frequently becomes the springboard for argumentation, and it appears in numerous disputes. Before the advent of Medicare, opponents cited the problems that Great Britain has had with its government-financed medical system and contended that ours would suffer the same difficulties. Currently, the National Rifle Association and others who oppose legislative restrictions on handguns draw analogies with similar legislation in Europe; you undoubtedly can come up with other examples from your own experience. And whether fleshed out as a full-blown analogy or not, comparisons and contrasts are very much a part of ordinary experience when people try to make other people understand or try to give greater life to that understanding. Need we draw the obvious moral for the speaker?

Examples and illustrations

Have you any idea how many times you have read in this book "for example," "for instance," or "to illustrate"? And even without these verbal cues (as in the paragraph above), we have used examples and illustrations again and again. They may well be the most common form of developing ideas, and one of the most natural ways for us to make ourselves understood in day-to-day communication. Think how often you use them discussing people you know; this example or that event tends to illuminate facets of their characters. And how often in conversations do we regularly spend time exchanging similar brief experiences that bear on the same general point? Examples from personal experience often are especially useful because the speaker feels comfortable with them. There is a hazard, however, because the comfortable memory may lead to more detail than is needed, with a loss of focus on the point being illustrated.

Again selectivity should operate. Illustrations, examples, or anecdotes should serve some broader purpose. That is, they should clarify or emphasize. When they do so, it is because their specific nature invites attention and creates a vividness that the more general idea does not have. Some topics, such as our treatment of euphemism, demand the use of examples. We can hardly imagine a discussion of language that did not include examples of usage. No doubt one could talk about the general functions of slang without using illustrations, but chances are it would be a very dull talk.

The appropriateness of the examples used always should be a consideration, just as it should be in relation to all facets of style, from the broadest to the most narrow. Here we are not thinking merely about good taste. We're thinking about what the examples have to contribute to clarity and overall effectiveness. Do you remember our description of the speaker who cited examples of insurance coverage to the parents of children going camping? That was not appropriate to his purposes, unless he really intended to upset his audience. So examples and illustrations should focus on and give life to the main ideas—not distract from them or blur them. Certainly they are used skillfully in several of the speeches we have included. Rye constructs her introductory narrative by means of a series of examples, and Agnew centers and directs attention with the example of Nixon's speech and network analysis of it.

*

It's possible to put together a speech that *doesn't* contain any examples or illustrations, but it is fairly unusual. If the reports we hear from our students are an accurate measure, the lack of concrete examples is probably the main reason why certain teachers are considered to be boring lecturers. Very often their lectures are said to be "too abstract."

As a test of your own inclinations concerning speech development and style, try constructing a speech that doesn't use either examples or illustrations. How does it look to you? If you are able to give the speech, how was it received?

We hope you can see that it's often not so much a question of whether but *how* to illustrate or exemplify.

*

Lincoln's speech invites special mention here because of its extended inductive sequence. The series of examples emphasizes the argument because the examples create logical force for it. We have already alluded to another series of examples—the one in Conwell's "Acres of Diamonds." In the midst of reciting the many stories of success, Conwell says, "I want to illustrate again, for the best way to teach is always by illustration." Assuredly the illustrating worked for him, and although his claims lack the logical validity of Lincoln's, they have the potential for great psychological impact. In both these speeches, emphasis owes something to the clarity that arises from the repetition. In the introductory class, you will not always have the time to make such an extensive use of examples during a speech, but your time limit is, after all, one of the variables you must consider in making your judgment as to what is appropriate.

Quotations and testimony

Besides examples, we've also used quotations throughout the book in the hope of both clarifying and emphasizing various ideas. As we said at the very beginning, we have taken materials from whatever sources seemed appropriate, and we have found many quotations that were in that category. Some were chosen primarily for clarification, others for emphasizing; if we have chosen well, however, all the quotations—including the poetry—probably serve both purposes. Many short passages or single lines from literature get quoted so often that their original context is often forgotten. That is because of their power to clarify. They have this power because their authors have expressed a thought so felicitously, have said something so particular in such a special way that people admire these lines for having been expressed in just that way. On the other hand, you may encounter a phrase, sentence, or longer passage that strikes you as being a succinct statement of your own ideas, and you may feel that the borrowed statement will clarify your thought better than you could in your own words. Then there is Lincoln quoting Douglas. We can't overlook the political associations and attendant emotions, but the brief quotation at least begins as a clarifying element. Later, Lincoln uses his "text" to satirize Douglas's reasoning, and he extends it into his attack on Southern arguments, but the emphasis he achieves derives from the initial clarity. The same, we think, can be said of Boyd's quotation from the insurance policy near the end of his speech. He has already built his case, and it is largely for the purpose of reinforcement when he quotes the fact that "the proceeds of this policy shall be payable in monthly installments, for years certain and as long thereafter as the payee lives."

Aside from the direct reinforcement, the use of quotations can emphasize in an indirect way. They can contribute to the impression that the speaker is competent. Without a doubt there are speakers who are qualified to rely entirely on their own resources, people who are real experts in some field. Their knowledge and experience, in fact, generate speaking situations. Few of us, however, find ourselves in such circumstances when we speak. Usually, we have to do some homework, and listeners unquestionably have the right to expect that the homework has been done. There are many ways to demonstrate that you have given thought and attention to your subject, and quotations can be one of them. Appropriate uses may indicate to the audience that you have invested time and imagination in creating your speech. Not a bad impression to create, other things being equal.

The same impression can result when testimony is utilized, but it may perform a special function. Quotation and testimony may be synonymous, but testimony usually refers to someone's opinion on a matter, whether it is quoted directly or just made a part of the analysis. Testimony may clarify, as it does in the courts, but it often becomes a part of a deliberate attempt to add emphasis to a position, and that may happen in the courts too, depending on the witness. But one doesn't have to attend a trial to observe the use of testimony. Just glance at a newspaper, listen to people talking, or turn on the TV, where the commercials afflict us with the entire range of possibility, every sort of testimony from the average housewife to the well-known personality to the report from some impartial investigating agency. Some of this testimony does no more than create an awareness of the product, and maybe that is the objective.

But, ordinarily, good testimony should do more. It may help clarify, but as we noted, it is important that it should have some weight. Otherwise, why bother? And the weight assigned to any testimony will vary along several dimensions. Clearly, we shouldn't put much store in the opinion of some formerly popular actor or actress on the merits of coffee, soap, or any other consumer product. Nor should we immediately accept the word of some established expert, even when the testimony relates to that expert's area of expertise. Whether sending or receiving, we have to protect ourselves. Surely you have read conflicting accounts of the same phenomenon too often to believe that every expert is free from bias. Does the testimony fit in with the individual's expertise? Any reason to suspect bias? What do other people have to say on the same topic? These are some of the questions we should ask. And it may be necessary to qualify the testimony introduced in a speech. It may be necessary to anticipate that some listeners will respond, "Who?"

The quotations from Orwell and Mencken in our euphemism sample have a testimonial flavor to them, and it could be argued, incidentally, that we should have established the credentials of both men. Some of the other speeches include no testimony at all, but notice that Lincoln has occasion to make use of Washington's comments on sectionalism and that he relies on Jefferson's opinion. And Agnew makes considerable use of testimony, both direct and indirect.

Visual aids

Perhaps this section should be called "Audio-Visual Aids" because of the prevalence of records, tapes, and cassettes in our lives, and because both of us have seen audio and visual materials used effectively in classroom speeches. Often, however, it is extremely difficult to use records or cassettes in short speeches. We will only point out that these possibilities do exist, and we will emphasize that they should be used with the utmost care and planning. Electronics should not triumph over the speech.

Certainly the same can be said of any visual materials employed —pictures, charts, graphs, maps, or whatever. But when they are used well, visuals can aid your presentation. For example, they can attract and hold attention. Do you remember the first time you saw the periodic table displayed in a chemistry class? We'll come back to the attention factor momentarily, but let's turn to clarification, the real purpose behind that periodic table and other visual aids.

Clarity, whatever the effect being sought, is a purpose that should prompt you to think about using visual aids in a speech. They will not be appropriate all the time, but in some instances they can be extremely useful. Remember all the maps, graphs, and pictures in your geography textbooks? Perhaps the maps helped you understand what the text said about climatic zones or population distribution; the graphs with the references to agricultural or manufactured products; the pictures with cultural differences in the various countries. And haven't you often followed diagramed instructions when putting together a toy, building a model, or assembling a piece of equipment? You can readily transfer any of these devices into the speaking situation, and instructors use them with their lectures constantly. But if visual aids help clarify, they can also emphasize.

An apparently simple diagram or graph may add great emphasis because it enables the speaker to take listeners quickly beyond minimal understanding. Look at a newspaper or watch television for a wide variety of visual examples that emphasize and reinforce the verbal presentations. Some of the examples on television are extremely expensive productions that have no parallel in public speaking, but many devices are those that any speaker might employ when arguing that a certain course of action should be followed. The old saw about a picture being worth a thousand words doesn't apply all the time, but it does often enough to be worth repeating.

"Shoes" comes immediately to mind in this regard. It is our only speech with visual aids, but we think that we would have difficulty finding a better illustration. The board, the shoes, the insurance policies, and the other objects all contribute to clarity, but they do much more, for they become an integral part of Boyd's thesis about life insurance.

Integration is the key, and that's why we said we'd return to attention. The visuals should aid in a speech, not call attention to themselves. Sadly, however, they frequently become distractions. For example, it really happened once that a young man taped half a dozen center-fold pictures from *Playboy* on the blackboard and then talked for eight minutes about photography. He had some pretty fierce competition with his message! But visual aids can distract the speaker as well as the audience. The problems of adjusting to the speaking situation can cause the novice speaker to escape into a visual aid, it being all too easy to concentrate on the map or deliver a speech to the graph on the blackboard. In these circumstances, we should talk of visual hindrances rather than visual aids. To make them truly aids requires some care in planning. A little care will produce aids that are large enough to see, in a format that can be handled easily by the speaker, and appropriate to their purpose—aids that will *aid* and not get in the way of the message.

*

If you are planning to use some kind of object or device to help enhance your presentation, be sure that you can really *use* it. We have seen too many speakers turn to the map they brought along and then not be able to find the place they were looking for; we have seen too many speakers turn to the gadget they had in front of them only to have it fail to work properly; we have seen too many speakers bring charts and graphs that they couldn't interpret or that the audience couldn't see clearly. The list of such situations—embarrassing to the speaker and distracting to the audience—is potentially endless.

Know your visual aid and rehearse with it enough so that you know how to use it. No one needs any obstacles to communication!

*

Humor

Almost everyone agrees that a sense of humor is a pleasant characteristic. It is simply normal and ordinary to appreciate people who can laugh at their humanity and who can appreciate some of the funny sounds in our "blooming, buzzing confusion." The witty turn of a phrase, a short anecdote, sometimes even a bad pun can function in a speech just as they do in our day-to-day living. Humor can give some variety and relief and it can point up an idea being presented, but we urge you to keep your humorous touches easy and natural. Don't force them. When people admire a sense of humor they are not thinking, ordinarily, about professional comedians or the satire of Swift's *A Modest Proposal*. Interestingly enough, studies of communication have yet to establish the impact that humor can have, maybe because it's so terribly hard even to define what it is. In any event, humor unquestionably can leave a favorable impression of the speaker's personality, but any humor in a speech should be there only if the situation and the materials call for it. The tired joke and forced devices can detract from the speaker's purposes. And a negative response can constitute negative feedback for the speaker. What is more dismaying than an uneasy silence instead of the obviously expected laughter?

FURTHER ASPECTS OF STYLE

Throughout our discussion in this chapter, we have attempted to tie our comments to the problems that speakers face, but there are some aspects of style that deserve special attention in the speaking situation. They are not matters foreign to writing, but some of them take on added significance when the expression is oral.

Summary and repetition

We have already had some things to say about the summary statement that may form part of the conclusion, but we want to expand on what we said. We want to point out that our remarks on summarization may apply to the entire speech, even a relatively short one. Speech is ephemeral. Consequently, the audience may need internal summaries along the way. A summary is a form of repetition, but the repeating may certainly take other forms. You probably have had a teacher who said, "Underline that in your notes," or "Remember that, if you remember nothing else," or "Let me repeat that because I want you to remember it." And a summary statement need not be a listing of ideas, but any expression that emphasizes the point that has been made. Because the listener cannot reread, the speaker may find it useful to repeat, restate, and summarize in ways that would seem too repetitious in a written essay.

A speaker also may find it useful to repeat ideas in a way that extends them throughout the speech. Notice, for example, how Lincoln uses the understanding of the Founding Fathers as a refrain. And notice how, just before she concludes, Rye echoes her introductory sentences about the optimism of her grandfather.

Questions and exclamations

At least one rhetorical question appears in each of the speeches included, and question marks appear regularly in those of Agnew and Lincoln. Rhetorical questions are those to which we customarily do not expect a reply, and they are very common in ordinary language. At political rallies and on some other occasions, a speaker may intend questions to elicit a vocal response from the audience, but these cheerleading tactics are atypical. It is more customary to expect that there will be no answer, even when the answer is all too obvious. And when the answer is that obvious, the purpose may be equally evident; if the listener knows how to respond, the chances are good that the question is adding reinforcement. Questions with not so obvious answers may prompt the audience to think about them; thus they also invite participation in the communication act by adding impact to the speaker's meaning. Some questions, on the other hand, may serve simply as signposts, as devices to give a sense of direction or limit the scope of discussion. Agnew uses questions in these ways when he addresses himself to the role of the news media. Lincoln does the same, but in a much more specific fashion, when he dissects the "text" at the start of his speech. Clarity might be the primary concern of these two examples, but they also have the potential for creating greater emphasis. Surely Lincoln is emphatic in the questions he hurls at the South.

As for exclamations, they usually have a markedly emphatic character. They may consist of a single sound or word, a phrase or some other sentence fragment, or a whole short sentence. No doubt they may serve some directional function, as they do when Boyd includes the sequence "So what? . . . Well, here's what. . . . That's what." But most often they represent attempts to add vigor to the meaning. There is an example in Boyd's speech that simply cannot be done justice to in print. It occurs in the "Well" that comes right at the end of the long list of health factors. That "Well" serves as a summary of all the lists that came before, and one has to hear the recording to appreciate the single word. Boyd surrounds the word with long pauses, and, half sighing, he prolongs the pronunciation and uses a falling inflection. If a single word can be eloquent, this is an example. Further examples of exclamatory elements appear in Lincoln's speech: "But enough!" and "John Brown! Harpers Ferry!" and "That is cool." When Lincoln used "cool" in this context, his audience knew that he was alluding to the difference between cool reason and hot passion, and the implied contrast can be seen in some current slang usages of "cool." For Lincoln, it was not slang, but it is worth noting that slang and other informal expressions may function as effective exclamations. When used with discretion and imagination, they may accomplish more than can be accomplished with some conventional words or phrases.

Interestingly, Agnew employs almost no exclamations in his speech, despite his reputation as an aggressive spokesman against the news media. Such expressions do crop up in some of his other speeches, but in the Des Moines speech he tends to seek effect in the cleverly turned phrase or in vivid adjectives—in "instant analysis," "querulous criticism," "gaggle of commentators," "normality has become the nemesis," or "small and unelected elite." Most of these phrases are used to underline his argument, to add emphasis. That may be the primary function of colorful language, but it can also clarify, if used imaginatively.

Metaphor

Language is a symbol system, and the function of metaphor is to take the process a step further, because metaphor transfers symbolic associations to new contexts. Consider the complexities, for example, in Winston Churchill's famous sentence "An Iron Curtain has come down across the face of Europe." Curtains in the theater are not made of iron, nor did such a curtain actually drop in Europe, but the potential associations helped establish a regular usage for the term "Iron Curtain." This potential for saying what something is in terms of something else is tremendous, and it is everywhere in our language. Unfortunately, too many speakers seem to feel that figurative expressions are the sole property of those who write poetry or imaginative literature. You can prove to yourself that this is erroneous by simply concentrating on almost any conversation. Slang and other informal uses of language regularly demonstrate the use of metaphor, and if some of the examples you discover seem trite, many will be lively and fresh. No reason why such life and vitality should not be used consciously in your speech preparation.

The comparison that exists in a metaphor is usually most effective in adding emphasis, but surely a good metaphor must also clarify. Consider the following few lines from the poem "Freshmen," by Barry Spacks. Reflecting on the classroom situation, Spacks divides students into two groups:

> The best look like the swinging door
> to the Opera just before
> the Marx Brothers break through.
> The worst—debased,
> on the back row,
>
> as far as one can go
> from speech—
> are walls where childish scribbling's been erased;
> are stones
> to teach.

These lines clarify the poet's perception in that there must be an understanding, if only unconscious, of what elements are being compared before a metaphor can be effective. Nevertheless, in these lines emphasis remains the dominant consideration.

Imaginative figures of speech may attract and sustain attention by giving a fresh view of an object or an idea; they may reflect favorably on the speaker who creates them; and they can surely strengthen the expression of the message. Lincoln's metaphor of the highwayman is a good example; so is the barbed wire at the conclusion of "My Grandfather." And then there is the appropriately homy flavor in Boyd's notion that "having a child is just like having a twenty-year non-taxable mortgage, with little bitty payments to begin with and great big payments the last six years." And even a single word in Agnew's "gaggle of commentators" evokes the hissing and honking of geese.

But whether you search for the suggestive symbolism that resides in a single word, or whether you employ more extended figurative expressions, you should think about the vitality and vigor that metaphors can add to your speaking style. They work for others, and they will work for you.

Oral style

We conclude this chapter with some brief comments on the use of the spoken language. The main point we will emphasize is that all of us accept greater informality in speech than in writing. In this regard, the ephemeral character of a speech is an advantage. Errors in grammar and pronunciation may stand out, but we really don't notice that a speaker may go on and on and on, using "and" or some other word to connect what ordinarily would be separate sentences in print. Because of your familiarity with this greater formality in written discourse, we edited "Shoes" to the extent of using periods in places where commas might have appeared. See if you can find some of these places. On the other hand, we set off the word "well" in the printed version, and we deliberately included sentence fragments in the euphemism example. However, we have also used fragments here and there in the text of this book, to emphasize the fact that oral-written distinctions are not all that hard and fast.

We are not trying to suggest that your natural speaking style is one with which you should be completely content. No matter how big your vocabulary is, for example, you can enlarge it, creating a richer potential for precise expression. And the preparation and presentation of extemporaneous speeches can further enrich that potential by giving you the opportunity to work at larger units of expression— from phrases and sentences to the kinds of development we have been talking about throughout this chapter. Almost all speakers can discover both flaws and virtues in their style, and the practice speeches will help you to suppress the flaws and enhance the virtues. But as we have indicated, we do not mean that you should take refuge in the more formal patterns of written usage. Your skill in the spoken language—your expertise—has already carried you far, and even if it could stand improvement, it should be your starting point. It has to be: you will progress most rapidly as a speaker when you start with yourself as a speaker rather than as a writer.

SUGGESTED READINGS

Jacques Barzun, *On Writing, Editing, and Publishing* (Chicago, 1971). Although not intended for an introductory class, the book is far from being as awesome as the title suggests. Filled with Barzun's wit and wisdom, this collection of essays is worth consulting.

Mary McEdwards, *Introduction to Style* (Belmont, Cal., 1968). A straightforward and readable treatment, this discussion includes an excellent variety of illustrative materials, some of it from speeches.

Ralph H. Singleton, *Style* (San Francisco, 1966). Singleton is a bit too eager to fault the informality of spoken style. With that exception, however, his discussion is easily adaptable to speech composition.

4

speakers

PREVIEW: CHAPTER 10

Chapter 10 centers on the impression that speakers make as individuals. In the first part, we emphasize personal traits, and then we turn to nonverbal aspects of communication. The topics are:

Some important traits of speakers
> Competence
> Familiarity
> Trustworthiness
> Dynamism
> Attractiveness
> Power

Nonverbal aspects of communication
> General aspects
> Five specific aspects

When you have completed this chapter, you will have a keener appreciation of the ways listeners respond to a message on the basis of the speaker's personality, and the ways you, as the speaker, can cultivate a favorable response. The sections on the nonverbal (silent) aspects of communication are intended to help you become more aware of this part of the process, and we hope this awareness will assist you in your own delivery.

speakers

WHO THEY ARE

10

In the framework of our rather broad conception of communication, it becomes immediately apparent that there are many kinds of message-senders. We know, certainly, that every time an individual talks or writes or gestures, the talking or writing or gesturing makes the individual a message-sender. But nations can be senders, too, and so can all kinds of groups, organizations, agencies, and other collective units. Sometimes, a single person may speak for one of these units in such a way that it becomes clear to the audience that the person is not speaking as an individual. At other times, as in the case of many written publications, it may not be possible to identify any single individual as the sender; the sender is the entire unit.

In a television commercial, for example, you may find that a show-business personality has discovered the wonders in some brand of coffee, deodorant, or household cleaner. We all receive the message, but who is it exactly that is sending the information about the glories of the coffee, the deodorant, or the household cleaner? Is it the show-business personality? The television network? Company X? Company X's advertising agency? All of them? Any or all of them might be correct, depending on how you choose to define the word "sender." In the study of communication, the definition will depend on the focus of interest, and that focus will mean that one apparent source or the other will get primary attention. That is, it makes a difference who or what the sender is and how that sender carries out the sending of the message. We will be commenting on the importance of this point in the present chapter, and, naturally, we will concentrate on the sender in the public speaking situation.

The very act of speaking is, as we have noted, a part of our being human. Nevertheless, it is a rather incredible phenomenon. Charlton Laird nicely captures both the marvel and the complexity of the process in his book *The Miracle of Language:*

> The miracle of language does not grow less if we examine it. Let us consider what happens. At first let us take the simplest sort of instance, in which one person speaks a word and another hears it. Any word would do, but let us use the word *wrist*.
>
> What has the speaker done when he utters this word? By gentle pressure of the diaphragm and contraction of the intercostal muscles he has emitted a little air, scrupulously controlled, although the muscles which expelled the air are so strong they could shake his whole body if they were used vigorously. He has slightly tightened some membranes in his throat so that the column of air has forced the membranes to vibrate. Meanwhile a number of minute movements, especially of the tongue, have caused the center of vibration to spread sideways across the tongue, move suddenly forward, concentrate just back of the upper teeth, and then cease. With the cessation of this voiced sound, the column of air hisses against the upper teeth, and gums, and is suddenly and momentarily stopped by a flip of the tongue. The tongue strikes the roof of the mouth with the portion just back from the tip, and spreads so that the whole column of air is suddenly dammed up and then released. All this must be done with the muscles of the throat relatively relaxed, and when the little explosion has taken place, everything must stop at once.
>
> Now the word *wrist* has been spoken, only a word, but the whole operation is so complex and delicately timed that nobody could do this by thinking about it. It can be done successfully, in the main, only when it is done unconsciously.*

It is through this largely unconscious, complicated series of physical actions, then, that our most common vehicle for thought is provided. The speaker's message-forming apparatus, by generating and manipulating a column of air, translates cognitions, beliefs, values, and attitudes into symbols which are intended to affect the images and behavior of listeners. But a speaker is a great deal more than lungs, larynx, and vocal cords. The speaker is a person, another human being, and we interpret messages on the basis of the human being who is the sender.

* Charlton Laird, *The Miracle of Language* (Greenwich, Conn., 1962), pp. 13-14.

SOME IMPORTANT TRAITS OF SPEAKERS

For centuries, serious students of speech communication have tried to discover and describe the proper traits that speakers should have in order to increase their effectiveness as communicators. You can imagine why this knowledge could be useful. If it were possible to identify some specific, desirable properties that speakers should have in the typical speaking situation, the teachers and scholars of communication would have acquired some important information to be used in understanding this business and in giving advice to others. Certainly one of the earliest and most influential students of the qualities of the speaker was Aristotle. For him, these important traits came under the heading of the Greek word *ethos*, which involved three somewhat more specific characteristics:

> As for the speakers themselves, the sources of our trust in them are three, for apart from the arguments there are three things that gain our belief, namely, intelligence, character, and good will. Speakers are untrustworthy in what they say or advise from one or more of the following causes. Either through want of intelligence they form wrong opinions; or, while they form correct opinions, their rascality leads them to say what they do not think; or, while intelligent and honest enough, they are not well disposed, and so perchance will fail to advise the best course, though they see it. That is a complete list of the possibilities. It necessarily follows that the speaker who is thought to have all these qualities has the confidence of his hearers.

So Aristotle believed that a speaker who showed intelligence, character, and good will would win the confidence of the audience, and his discussion of *ethos* forms the basis of advice that teachers continue to give students. And no wonder—it is excellent advice, advice supported by current research. Much of this research has centered in source credibility, and new dimensions have been discovered, but the findings tend to support Aristotle's original formulation of *ethos* and its effect. In discussing the influence that a sender exerts as a sender, we will rely on that formulation, but we will add some items to Aristotle's original list of intelligence, character, and good will.

From our communication point of view, our concern is not so much with the ways in which speakers may differ; rather, we want to talk about the ways in which audiences *see* differences in speakers. This may seem like a trivial distinction, but when it comes to communication, it is almost always the judgment of the audience that counts. In a very objective sense, for example, speakers may be honest and in their hearts they may know that they are honest. But, as unfair as it seems at times, the crucial question in terms of communication is whether the audience *sees* them as being honest. We can probably all think of times as communicators when we knew we were being perfectly honest, but we weren't able to convince our listeners of that fact. It can be pretty frustrating, even though there is some comfort in our own knowledge that we are honest. At any rate, our concern here will be with some of the important ways that speakers can differ, from the point of view of their audience. In a sense, people who seek to improve their abilities as speakers are trying to develop a better means for controlling the ways in which their listeners perceive these traits. Let's look at some of these traits, and then we will have more to say about how these qualities can influence a communication situation and what you might do to make the most of these traits as a speaker yourself.

Competence

Some speakers know what they are talking about and some don't. And some speakers *know* that they know what they are talking about and some speakers don't know that they *don't* know what they are talking about. And so on—we'll refrain from spelling out the other combinations which involve speakers' knowledge of their subject and their awareness of their knowledge. Listeners, too, almost habitually make their own judgments about the competence of speakers in the subject under discussion. There is, of course, no reasonable way to estimate how often audiences are correct in their assessment of the competence of speakers and how often they are incorrect. Speakers who have made some effort to analyze the audience, however, can often make some intelligent estimates of the listeners' ability to judge their competence. In general, to the extent that audiences perceive speakers as having knowledge or skills or experience in the subject being discussed, they will be inclined to make a favorable assessment of the speakers' competence.

*

As a speaker, you have some choice as to subject and as to the manner in which you develop it. Clearly, you will have difficulty making listeners feel that you are competent if you don't know much about the topic and if you are not in control of the materials. This means that research, preparation, and rehearsal are important components in the finished speech. This may sound like moralizing, but, if so, the moralizing is on the side of wisdom.

*

Familiarity

Speakers differ in the extent to which they are known to their audiences. Obviously, professors from whom students have taken one or more courses become familiar figures for them, so much so that the students can often tell a great deal about the biases and the moods of these professors, even from a few subtle cues that would go unnoticed by students who were listening to them for the first time. On the other hand, an audience of Rotary Club members may hardly know what to expect when an unknown man gets up to address them after dinner. Certainly they may be able to make a few guesses as to the nature of their speaker based on the way he is introduced or the title of his speech, but for the most part they are in the dark. For such a speaker, whether it is advantageous for him to be well known or to be a stranger to the listeners depends on what they know of him in general and what they know about his past—his "record" in a sense —as it pertains to him generally and as it relates to his speech topic. If the audience knows of the record and has a positive regard for it, the speaker can at least be assured of some receptive listeners; in this case the audience's familiarity is an advantage. On the other hand, you can see how a speaker's past record can be a disadvantage. If the audience has a negative view of the record, then the speaker may be in a situation where familiarity breeds contempt or some other attitude that detracts from the message.

*

If the speaker's record is too negative, we are likely to avoid the message entirely. But you might try to recall how a favorite teacher built a positive record with most students, and you might keep track of records, including your own, that develop during a speech class. It hardly needs to be said that familiarity and its impact become a function of the other elements we are talking about here and elsewhere in the book, and it follows that careful application is more likely to produce the right kind of record.

*

Trustworthiness

Our consideration here involves the private motives of the speaker and the audience's perception of the speaker's motives. You probably know from your own experience that there are times when speakers are concerned only with their own best interests when they communicate with others. In the extreme case, their motives would be very self-centered and little or no thought would be given to the interests of the listener. It is fairly common, too, for a speaker not to have the welfare of the audience at heart but, rather, to be loyal to some group or cause external to that particular speaker-listener relationship. Now we also know that, given these self-centered or external loyalties, some speakers are honest and open—they freely and frankly tell us what their motives are. But most of us have been mildly or dramatically deceived often enough, and we are inclined to be a little cautious in accepting at face value the word of many speakers. When we suspect that speakers have an ulterior motive, we will tend to be suspicious of their efforts to influence our images and our behavior. This suspicion is one of the reasons why we might make use of some of the resistance tactics discussed in Chapter 4.

No doubt you can appreciate how the concept of familiarity often applies here; we know the past record, and that record makes us trust or distrust the motives and purposes of a speaker. Even when we are not familiar with the speaker, we may feel we have detected something in the speech that makes us a bit cautious. Perhaps it is something in the very delivery, a nonverbal element; or maybe it is a description, a definition, or some statement of a "fact" that seems contrary to our experience. Actually, there has been a great deal of research on the ways that listeners perceive the objectivity, the intentions, and the trustworthiness of speakers, but the results are not as clear-cut as we might hope. There are times, it seems, when audiences accept speakers' appeals, or part of them, even when they have doubts about the trustworthiness of the speakers. That this is true appears to be the result of a high evaluation in one or more of the other traits we're discussing here.

*

All of us have had the experience of having an immediately favorable or unfavorable reaction to someone who reminded us of someone else and whom we either liked or disliked. And all of us have altered such judgments as time passed and the record became fuller. As senders, one can do little or nothing about such initial responses. In developing the message, however, there are many things you can do, and we have mentioned most of them more than once. Things that will help you clarify your own communication goals. Things that will help give you control of self and materials in the speaking situation. Things that have to do with your attitude toward the speech situation. Things that can reflect your awareness of the listeners' needs and interests. Of course you can slight your responsibilities in this regard—you can even deliberately dissemble or mislead your listeners—but that seems a risky business when it comes to establishing trustworthiness.

*

Dynamism

Even as a speaker is delivering a speech, the listeners begin to form judgments that are based on the way in which the speech is presented. Does the speaker seem interested in the subject? What about the subject and the audience—does the speaker seem to care, seem willing, seem even enthusiastic about conveying the material to the listeners? It is this evidence, the evidence of caring and enthusiasm, that constitutes dynamism for an audience. Most of a speaker's perceived dynamism derives not so much from what is said, but rather from the way it is said—that is, the speaker's vocal qualities, posture, facial expression, and physical gestures.

Part of our expertise in communication is the habitual judgment we make concerning the nonverbal cues of a speaker. On that basis, we evaluate the speaker's attitude toward the subject and toward us, as listeners. Most of us probably share similar stereotypes in regard to the extreme boundaries of dynamism in speaking. On the too dynamic side, we may think of the wild-eyed extremist who assaults the audience with a kind of nonverbal overkill. The enthusiasm is overdone, the movements too frequent and exaggerated, the voice too loud and too emotional. At the other extreme, you may think of an instructor who was, or is, all too monotonous; the material seems of little consequence, whatever the instructor's credentials, and the students don't seem to be a very important audience. Fortunately, most speakers fall between these extremes, and it is also fortunate that dynamism, by itself, is not enough, is not the controlling element in effective speaking. Nevertheless, a speaker will profit from any evidence that exhibits a genuine interest in the subject and some enthusiasm for communicating that subject to the audience. At a minimum, this evidence will make listeners more attentive and more willing to continue listening.

*

Once more, earlier advice applies. It simply is more difficult to care about, to be enthusiastic about a stray or borrowed subject. To select a topic that interests and stimulates you is not the whole answer, but it is a big first step. Then you might want to experiment with your delivery of the speech. What can you do to inject more enthusiasm and interest into your presentation? It is often good advice to *give something of yourself* in a speech. We don't mean that you should act unnatural, but we would urge you to try extending yourself a bit.

*

Attractiveness

A speaker may be attractive to the audience for any number of reasons. First, a speaker may be physically attractive, particularly to members of the opposite sex. But there are other kinds of attractiveness. People may be attractive because they have qualities that we would like to have, or because they have done or can do things that we would like to do. Thus, a star of the National Football League might speak with a special voice to a group of intercollegiate athletes, might even speak with a special voice to all frustrated athletes. And Kate Millett or Gloria Steinem might be particularly attractive to young people who wish to free themselves from sex-role stereotyping, because of the role these women have played in the feminist movement. This leads to another consideration—the sharing of attitudes, which often is enough to make a speaker attractive. The doing may not be important, if the listener perceives agreement in attitudes and goals.

Finally, a speaker may be attractive as the result of a role relationship, something we talked about in Chapter 6. A family physician, a priest, or someone you work with: any established relationship may make the speaker persuasive on that basis alone. Persuasiveness may be produced by any of the kinds of attractiveness we have been discussing, a fact you can demonstrate for yourself any evening by watching television commercials. We have only to turn to advertising to find examples of the effective uses of attractiveness and of attractive speakers.

*

As you listen to speakers, in the classroom and elsewhere, you might find it both interesting and instructive to make note of the various types of attractiveness that they have for you. Have you heard speakers who are attractive because they express attitudes and goals similar to yours? Have you heard speakers who are attractive because of their role or position, or perhaps because of certain things that they have accomplished? Can you describe speakers whose appearance has been attractive to you?

Think about some things that you might do to increase your attractiveness as a speaker.

*

Power

Another trait which audiences commonly assess is the speaker's power. Obviously, listeners will respond, will pay attention, and will even act in direct proportion to their perception of the speaker's power over them; you can undoubtedly think of situations in which the factor of power was crucial to your reception of a message. Just as obvious is the fact that most of us do not often find ourselves in situations where the audience concedes to us the power to administer rewards and punishments. This kind of power is what the psychologist William McGuire calls "perceived control."[*] That is, in this case, the speaker is seen by the listeners as having some kind of power base that is important to them. That kind of control does not exist in most situations, but McGuire also talks about "perceived concern" and "per-

---

[*] William J. McGuire, "The Nature of Attitudes and Attitude Change," *Handbook of Social Psychology*, 2nd ed., Vol. 3. Ed. by Gardner Lindzey and Elliot Aronson (Reading, Mass., 1969), pp. 194-196. Our treatment of power in this section comes from McGuire's three power components.

*"I just love your voice. It's incredibly warm and sincere—
honest-sounding. I'll bet you could make
a pile doing commercials."*

ceived scrutiny," types of power that do exist generally, types that can be found more commonly in day-to-day speaking situations.

Certainly a speaker will be less influential if the audience comes to feel that this is all a charade and that the speaker doesn't really care about the subject of the speech. It may be, of course, that the speaker *does* care, but cannot project this concern about the topic, and listeners may reach the wrong conclusion. Surely there is no absolute rule, and we can only suggest that you find topics that seem, for whatever reason, interesting and worth discussing. Such topics are the most likely ones to be a source of power—the power that emerges from perceived concern.

The last component of power is what McGuire calls "perceived scrutiny." If an audience has reason to believe that a speaker will be in a position to observe whether a speech has had any impact, the audience is more inclined to grant a certain amount of power to the speaker. Suppose, for instance, that your instructor discusses an important lecture that is coming up in your area of interest and urges you to attend. Chances are that you are more likely to attend if you know that your instructor will be there also, and will be able to note your presence or absence. In short, when listeners know that a speaker can "check up" on them, they tend to grant more power to the speaker.

The notion of power as it relates to communication is a significant one. Even though it may not often relate very directly to your own classroom training in speaking, it is a common element frequently found in our daily, real-world communication transactions. You may be surprised how much power certain audiences will grant to you in some speaking situations. Generally, the more control, the more concern, and the more scrutiny that speakers are able to demonstrate, the more influence they will have on their listeners.

*

Think of someone who is a good speaker and rate that speaker on the traits we have been discussing. Where it seems appropriate, use the criteria we've been discussing here *and* whatever other qualities you want to add in describing your speaker more specifically. In your rating, you should consider which traits are most important and why. If you haven't listened to a good speaker recently, think of one who misses the mark. Then, by making a comparison or contrast, try to understand the varying weights you assign to the traits above.

*

We could add to our list of the characteristics that listeners perceive in speakers, but we've mentioned all the crucial points. If speakers measure up to them for their audiences, their chances of achieving their objectives are greatly increased. Unfortunately, there is no universal formula or short cut on which the speaker can rely. There is little doubt that the optimum standard will vary with almost each and every situation; once again, this is one of the reasons we have been emphasizing the importance of the speaker's analyzing the audience and examining the range of choices in preparing and presenting the speech. There are some indications, however, that the traits we have been considering can have a cumulative, positive effect.

Although these variables have not enjoyed an equal amount of attention from communication researchers, there has been a great deal of study aimed at trying to learn which of these perceived characteristics of speakers, or which combination of them, is most important. The results have not been very clear in this regard, but the trait of competence seems to have emerged clearly and consistently as the most important speaker variable. And, of course, this is not surprising —it means that listeners respond particularly well, other things being equal, to speakers who appear to know what they are talking about. So Aristotle had something in his analysis. There is also some general support of trustworthiness, as well there might be. Additionally, the research perhaps most consistently shows that none of these variables operates independently of any other; indeed, one might outweigh another considerably in any given communication situation, sometimes to the advantage, sometimes to the detriment of the speaker.

*

In your next speaking assignment, rate yourself as a speaker by estimating how you think your audience would evaluate you on our list of
traits in terms of the speech you are planning to give. What trait(s) do
you think the audience will regard as being most important? If this
analysis suggests that you have some shortcomings, you may be able
to do something to minimize them, changing your subject, perhaps, or
your treatment of the subject. Can you think of some ways to strengthen
a couple of already strong traits to minimize your limitations in other
areas?

*

So what can we conclude, generally speaking, from our review
and summary of some of the important traits that audiences perceive
in speakers? For the moment, we have two related pieces of advice
for you as a speaker. First, do what you can to maximize those traits
you suspect will be important to your audience. Most speakers on
most occasions have a surprising amount of flexibility if only they have
the awareness and the interest in making use of it. They can often
choose subjects in which they have some competence or they can frequently acquire some, when they must speak on subjects where they
lack it. If they have doubts about their perceived trustworthiness, they
can use additional sources that are trusted by their listeners to enhance their own trustworthiness. And so on. The simple fact that
speakers should be aware of their strengths and limitations in the eyes
of their audience is, in our experience, an extremely important and
often underestimated one.

Our second bit of general advice follows from the first. If you
want to improve in effectiveness as a speaker, you must be willing to
face the fact that there may be no easy way to bring it off execpt by
working at it. Almost everyone who faces a speaking situation cares
about doing well, but many speakers seem to be unwilling to make
changes or to follow advice for improvement except on their own
terms. In contrast, if what we have been talking about makes any
sense to you, it should be clear that improvement, effectiveness, and
communication success must be defined largely *in terms of your audience*. We will talk in greater detail about some of your specific options in the next chapter. But first, by way of background, we want
to turn to some general considerations about nonverbal communication.

NONVERBAL ASPECTS OF COMMUNICATION

There is no doubt about how much we rely on nonverbal elements
in making meaning in the world about us. That we do it so constantly

M. Once upon a time, the Far West Baseball League operated in Nevada, Northern California, and Southern Oregon, and once upon a time, I spent a summer umpiring in the league. One hot Sunday afternoon in August, I was working behind home plate in Klamath Falls, Oregon. It was late in the game, with the local team thoroughly drubbing the visitors from Medford, and on what seemed a rather routine play, I called a Medford runner out when he slid in at home. Consequently, I was somewhat surprised to see Frank Lucchessi, the Medford manager, charging from the dugout. He bounced around me like a bantam rooster, pointed a forefinger at the plate, then shook it accusingly. His physical actions indicated a complaint, but his verbal behavior went something like this: "Good call, Jerry, but it's been a pretty dull game. Mind if I put on a little show for the fans?" I turned and walked away, saying, "Go ahead, Frank, but don't make it too long." So we put on our show, our postures and gestures telling the fans that this was a heated argument. Finally, he kicked dirt over the plate, and as I bent down to sweep it off, he bent down, too, and asked, "Enough?" I agreed, and he went back to the dugout, accompanied by the boos of the fans.

The impact of nonverbal communication is the main point here, but the incident deserves a further comment because it involves intelligent audience analysis. Frank Lucchessi never would have put on a show at Medford. At home, the fans would have booed me; in Klamath Falls, they booed him. When Frank complained at Medford, he meant it.

indicates how tremendously significant these elements can be, even when words may seem to be the most important part of the message. And once more we have an aspect of communication that people have been aware of for a long time. Though there has been a surge of interest in nonverbal communication in recent years, it is far from new. In Ecclesiastes we read, "A naughty person, a wicked man, walketh with a forward mouth. He winketh with his eyes, he speaketh with his feet, he teacheth with his fingers." In his *Passionate Pilgrim*, Shakespeare has the speaker lament, "Did not the heavenly rhetoric of thine eye, 'gainst whom the world could not hold argument, persuade my heart to this false perjury?" Shakespeare makes much of the nonverbal element throughout his plays, as in the particularly interesting series of examples when Cassius is tempting Brutus in *Julius Caesar* (Act I, Scene 2).

General aspects

Rhetorical theorists understandably have had things to say about the importance of presentation in speaking. Discussing the emotions, Aristotle observed that speakers "who heighten the effect of their words with suitable gestures, tones, dress, and dramatic action generally, are especially successful in exciting pity," and we have to assume that the comment applies generally. Somewhat later, Cicero said that "delivery is a sort of language of the body," and Quintilian devoted almost an entire book of his *Institutio Oratoria* to the subject. About two hundred years ago, the study of delivery became the study of elocution, and many books appeared that concentrated exclusively on the tones, looks, and gestures of the public speaker. While the elocutionists and earlier writers thought in terms of platform performance, much of the current inquiry has centered on more intimate personal relationships, but the ultimate goals are the same: a better understanding and a better use of nonverbal dimensions in communication.

Current writers differ somewhat as to where the precise boundaries are, but most are in general agreement that nonverbal communication involves all behavior, apart from a person's language, that is meaningful in some way. For example, Albert Mehrabian would distinguish nonverbal communication as *implicit* communication; it differs from language, or *explicit* communication, in that there are no formal rules and no comprehensive dictionaries that control and define how we communicate without words.* Nevertheless, our expertise extends to this aspect as well, and most of us have a pretty good grasp of the nonverbal communicative meanings in the social system that has nourished our skill as communicators. Meaning may not ordinarily be as sharp or clear as with conventional language, but sometimes it is unmistakable. Certainly we all know that nonverbal messages are important, and we all know that, in many cases, there is a consensus as to their meanings. Of course there are times when, much to our embarrassment, we read nonverbal behavior incorrectly —when we read meaning that was not intended—but these occasions merely serve as glowing reminders that all communication is sometimes open to misinterpretation. To clarify, let's consider some specific illustrations of what we are talking about.

Suppose you have entered a fairly crowded public place, a waiting room or a lobby, and you look for a place to sit and wait. If you are like most of us, you make a quick survey of the seating choices, hoping to find some place that is relatively comfortable without intruding on the personal space and privacy of others. You will probably decide not to sit next to the young woman who appears to be writing something and who has placed her books in the chair next to her. It looks as though she prefers her relative isolation. You could sit by the couple who are talking over in the corner, but their postures seem a little bit stiff and their faces look rather serious. Sitting too close to them might make you feel like an eavesdropper. There's a possibility of sitting beside the man who is calmly watching the people come and go; it doesn't seem as though you would be interfer-

* Albert Mehrabian, *Nonverbal Communication* (Chicago, 1972), pp. 2-3.

ing with him. On the other hand, another person who is reading a magazine looks up briefly at you, smiles, and then looks back at the magazine. Either of these last two options is likely to seem most comfortable, and you would probably select one of them, given these four choices. Your whole survey of the room and your decision might take place in less time than it takes to read about it; you have attached some meaning to people's nonverbal behavior and that behavior has influenced your own.

In the case of people we are well acquainted with, we can often sense some things about their moods, even when they try to conceal this information from us. When someone is uneasy or preoccupied, postures, movements, and certainly facial expressions can reveal this fact to a close friend, even though there may be nothing in the words that reveal the emotional state. Indeed, sometimes the nonverbal messages about a person's mood almost completely obscure what is being said! The same is true, of course, when someone we know well is extremely pleased or excited. No doubt there are millions of loyal watchers of Johnny Carson, for example, who have become so familiar with his routine nonverbal patterns that they can reliably tell when he is uneasy, relaxed, irritated, or exhilarated.

If you think about a speaker who is addressing an audience, you know that as a listener you often form judgments about the nonverbal elements of the speech. If the speaker happens to be a fairly familiar one, such as an instructor you listen to daily, you may know enough about his or her basic nonverbal style so that you feel pretty confident in your ability to perceive any departure from it. In fact, it is often through being sensitive to certain of their instructors' nonverbal cues that students learn what is important for them to remember. But even if none of us have ever seen the speaker before in our lives, we are still inclined to make use of nonverbal clues. Although we may not always attach the correct meaning to them, the speaker's facial expression, movements, and postures can help us form impressions about such things as sincerity, interest, enthusiasm, and trustworthiness. Most likely, when the speaker is not familiar to us, we will rely on the general expectations we have about the ways that speakers ought to behave nonverbally, and we will notice if the speaker departs too drastically from these expectations. We may not spend much time thinking about the general nonverbal standards we have for people we listen to, but we do have them.

*

An assignment that asks you to watch a little television can't be all bad, and this time we want to look very closely at the screen—with the volume off. Pick a program featuring a single speaker—an educational program or one on the Sunday morning schedule where one person is in the picture for long periods of time. Watch one of these communicators intently for ten to fifteen minutes. What nonverbal messages do you pick up? What is the range of meaningful expression you can detect? What judgments can you make about the kinds of feeling and emotions displayed? If you watch long enough, you should find some recurring nonverbal patterns. Can you identify and describe some of them? Finally, if you could watch *yourself* for ten or fifteen minutes with your volume off, how would you respond to the questions we have asked here?

*

Now that we have seen some examples of the ways that people can and do communicate without words, you can no doubt think of countless other instances. They are everywhere. They probably most often occur on the fringes of your awareness and, once they are pointed out, you "rediscover" them. If you are at all inclined toward studying the human being as communicator, nonverbal communication can become a rich and fascinating source of material for you to examine. Indeed, the experience of the two of us and the testimony of many of our students is that once you put your mind to noticing the silent messages we all use it is hard to stop. And yet it is important to be aware that the meanings we attach to the nonverbal behavior of others may be in error.

Even though much of this behavior is involuntary, it can be misread. A blush may creep over a face; the pupils of the eyes may dilate; tension or nervousness may produce random activity; what seems to be a look of joy, or surprise, or anger, or grief appears. All these signs can be misinterpreted. The frown that we take personally turns out to be the result of concentration on a problem that doesn't involve us at all. Nevertheless, these involuntary responses are the ones that we trust the most, because we feel that they are spontaneous and natural. At the same time, because the nonverbal environment is often inseparable from the verbal one that our culture imposes on us, we learn to trust other kinds of nonverbal patterns. We learn a great deal about how and when to stand, smile, wave, nod, look, move—and a great deal about how and when not to. Despite any individual differences, we adjust to the larger cultural patterns, and we learn to rely on these patterns, learn to use them in helping us interpret the meaning of spoken messages. We make use of them whether sending or receiving, and they form an important part of the meaning assigned when we listen to a speaker.

Of course, these acquired characteristics probably have the greatest potential for misinterpretation. All of us gain some skill in masking our true feelings, and some people develop the conscious ability to display the kinds of nonverbal behavior that we consider to be involuntary. No doubt this skill helps to explain why some people are better actors than others, and it also helps to explain why so much ambiguity exists in this aspect of communication.

Five specific aspects

Clearly, a speaker should be most interested in nonverbal elements as they contribute to the meaning of the verbal message, and for the listener, these elements can both clarify and intensify what is being said. As we have already suggested, however, the nonverbal can play an important role in the other direction, creating feedback and making the sender a receiver as the communication process occurs. We will expand on both these functions when we turn to the actual presentation of speeches, but here, we want to take a more detailed look at one approach to nonverbal meaning. The approach is that of Paul Ekman and Wallace Friesen, who have devoted considerable effort to the study of the subject. They describe a system of five categories: *adaptors, emblems, illustrators, affect displays,* and *regulators.* °

Not all are of great importance to the public speaker. *Adaptors,* for example, are related to the satisfaction of bodily needs, and in social situations only fragments of these behaviors are likely to be found. We observe them when people touch their faces, scratch an arm, or groom their hair. These actions add little to meaning, but the excessive use of them may indicate uneasiness or become distracting to the audience. So we can say little more than that a speaker ought to avoid such excess.

Nor do *emblems* appear often in public speaking. Ekman and Friesen identify them as those nonverbal acts that have a rather clear and direct verbal equivalent in a given social system. In this category we find the handshake, the clenched fist, the V-for-victory sign. In other words, emblems are learned behaviors that tend to have specific meanings, gestures that can be readily translated into words. When people use emblems, they ordinarily are quite aware of the fact that they are using them, and they do so with the intent to communicate. Very specialized emblems can be seen in the signals of the football referee or the baseball umpire. In these last instances and others, the emblem may be accompanied by words, and there are occasions when a speaker might use emblems. Ordinarily, however, the other three categories are most important for the public speaker.

Illustrators are directly related to speaking behavior. All of us use them to illustrate, to enhance, to emphasize, to complement what we are saying orally. Movements of the head, arms, and hands can be used, for instance, to accent or emphasize our words or phrases. This type of illustrator becomes a kind of nonverbal punctuation. Other

° Paul Ekman and Wallace V. Friesen, "The Repertoire of Nonverbal Behavior: Categories, Origins, Usage, and Coding," *Semiotica,* Vol. 1, No. 1 (1969), pp. 49-98.

types of illustrators, such as pointing, describing a sequential or spatial relationship, depicting something being talked about through a gesture or movement that resembles the thing, and even the use of hands to "trace ideas" are all examples of commonly-used illustrator behavior. We all know people who talk with their bodies almost as much as they talk with their vocal mechanisms; if you have ever experimented with trying to talk without the use of your hands, you have probably found the experience frustrating and enlightening. Indeed, it is hard to imagine trying to describe an exciting bit of action in a basketball game without using your hands, or to give a set of directions on just about anything without using the appropriate movements to illustrate what you are talking about.

Like emblems, illustrators are learned behaviors, and it seems clear that some nationalities and cultures rely more heavily on them than others. One of the central concerns of the old elocution courses was training in the use of appropriate and effective illustrators. In those days there was a great deal of concern for the *way* in which a person made a speech and there was an abundance of rules and recipes for appropriate movement and gesture. In some of those classes, delivery received too much emphasis, but there is no denying that the basic reasons for the study of elocution were legitimate, as the use of illustrators is a most important part of our communicative behavior.

*

Two observation exercises. First, observe other speakers and note how effectively they use illustrators. Their uses may be instructive to you. Second, observe yourself and try to discover your own habits. Do you point, count off important points on your fingers, use expansive arm gestures in conversations, clasp your hands? Whatever illustrations you naturally use, they are part of your communication style, and some of them should be carried over into your speechmaking.

*

As to *affect displays*, these acts involve the nonverbal communication of emotion and feeling. Although other parts of the body can convey information about a person's emotional state, the primary source of meaning is the face. It appears that certain facial expressions of emotion—such as anger, happiness, fear, and surprise—are culture free, that is, they are perhaps our only universal language. Yet there are cultural differences in the ways these facial expressions are used. Ekman and Friesen have distinguished four "display rules" for the facial expression of motion: overintensifying, deintensifying, neutralizing, and masking. Depending on our cultural conditioning and the circumstances of a given moment, we can act more sad than we really are (overintensifying); we can act less sad (deintensifying); we can feel sad but not convey any emotion (neutralizing); or we can feel sad but put on a happy face (masking). In this respect, then, a speaker's facial expression can reinforce or modify or contradict the verbal behavior. Typically we put most trust in the spontaneous behavior of another because it seems natural and involuntary, and all of us have learned to be wary of the expression that appears to have been pasted on. All this is a rather subjective business, but despite the occasional error, we manage to develop a pretty reliable set of standards, even though they may be almost impossible to describe. Certainly we learn to rely on facial expression in interpreting emotion. If you were to ask people what they consider to be the most important aspect of another person's nonverbal behavior, facial cues almost invariably will rank first.

*

We won't suggest that you learn to put on a face, happy or otherwise. In the first place, we wouldn't know where to start, and in the second, most speakers don't find themselves in situations that call for strong emotional utterance. Most of the time, it is enough to demonstrate some concern for the subject and the audience. We are back to control again, because the speaker who is in command of materials, self, and situation is most likely to evince that facial expression that confirms what the words say.

*

Regulators, the last category, are the kinds of behavior that help regulate and sustain interaction between two or more parties in communication. These are the cues that a listener may use to tell a speaker to go on, to slow down, to repeat, to stop, and so forth. They are the cues a speaker may use to tell the listeners to pay attention, to wait a minute before interrupting, to respond now, and so forth. Probably the most commonly used regulator is the nod of the head, usually interpreted to mean, "Keep sending. I'm still with you." Others include eye contact, raising the eyebrows, tilting the head, and a variety of subtle physical postures and slight movements. These acts are pretty much culturally determined, and they may not require any conscious effort. In ordinary communication, in fact, we may be aware of regulators only when they are absent altogether or when we try not to provide them for some other party. They are perhaps most important in conversations and at other times when the size of the group is limited, but they also apply in the public-speaking situation. Without regulators, there would be no nonverbal feedback between the participants, from audience to speaker or speaker to audience.

We will return to these categories in the next chapter, but as we conclude here, we should note once again that nonverbal communication is a rich and complicated subject. Obviously, the five categories we have been talking about are not clear, distinct types, nor are they mutually exclusive. Nonverbal communication has been the subject of increasing study in recent years, and the main contribution of this study seems to be the clarification of issues for students of communication.

*

Another observation task. Test the usefulness of Ekman and Friesen's five kinds of nonverbal acts by noting the occurrence of these acts in other people. Notice them in informal conversations, and compare your findings with observations of people in public-speaking situations. Can you provide the same study of your own nonverbal communication? Where do you have difficulty sorting your behavior into the five categories? Can you suggest additions to or refinements of these categories?

*

SUGGESTED READINGS

Aristotle, *Rhetoric* (especially 1356a, 1377b-1378a, 1404b, and 1417a). The most influential work in the history of communication study. The treatise is a bit ponderous in places, but it is filled with insights, and it gives perspective to everything that has been done since.

Albert Mehrabian, *Silent Messages* (Belmont, Cal., 1971). This readable treatment of nonverbal communication incorporates a great deal of the research on the subject. The material is discussed in a useful, practical manner.

Harry C. Triandis, *Attitude and Attitude Change* (New York, 1971). Chapter 7, "The Source," deals in detail with the current theory and research that relates to the study of message-senders, but the entire book is useful background for the reader interested in the study of attitudes.

PREVIEW: CHAPTER 11

Chapter 11 concerns the actual delivery of your speech. The topics are:

The memorized speech
The impromptu speech
The manuscript speech
    Writing the speech
    Reading the speech
The extemporaneous speech
    Rehearsal
    Delivery
    Evaluation

Most of the chapter is devoted to the extemporaneous speech and we offer some concrete suggestions, which you will, of course, adapt to your own particular style. However, we open the chapter with a discussion of other kinds of speeches, with special attention to the writing and reading of the manuscript speech, because it is a mode that you may want to use for speeches longer than those you will be giving in class. Finally, we close with some observations that should help you become a better judge both of your own speeches and those of others.

speakers

PRESENTING THE SPEECH

11

"Speak the speech, I pray you, as I pronounced it to you, trippingly on the tongue. But if you mouth it, as many of your players do, I had as lief the town crier spoke my lines."

Hamlet, Act III, Scene 2

Throughout this book we have been assuming that you would be working with the extemporaneous mode of presentation—that you would be preparing and rehearsing for most of your speeches, but leaving your exact wording to the moment of utterance. This is the mode we will concentrate on in this chapter, but three others deserve comment: the memorized, the impromptu, and the manuscript speech.

THE MEMORIZED SPEECH

Obviously, the memorized speech is one that is committed to memory, and there are times when this is a useful approach. Conwell, for example, adapted "Acres of Diamonds" to time and place, but he included large swatches of the same material in each performance. On a more limited scale, Boyd does the same thing in "Shoes." Few people, however, find themselves giving the same speech over and over again, and memorization is something that the novice speaker ordinarily ought to avoid. Memorization may tempt you, particularly at first before you get used to the speaking situation, but although we have avoided prescriptive advice, we do urge that you resist the temptation.

Of course, it is possible to memorize a speech simply by rehearsing it over and over until it is the same every time, but the inexperienced speaker who is seduced by memorization usually writes out the speech. But this is an inexperienced speaker, someone who doesn't know that oral and written styles differ, as we tried to suggest in our euphemism example. The greater formality and larger vocabulary that are natural to writing will cramp and strain the speaker's natural *speaking* expertise. Furthermore, the very task of memorization imposes constraints that produce further strain; the mind is occupied with remembering rather than with communicating, with the result that the speech very likely will seem artificial. The listeners may not be able to say exactly why, but they will know that the presentation is somehow stilted and mechanical. So we advise you as Hamlet advises the players later in the passage we quoted above, "Pray you, avoid it."

THE IMPROMPTU SPEECH

At the other extreme, in terms of preparation, is the impromptu speech —the speech given on the spur of the moment, without prior preparation and rehearsal. The impromptu speech is a useful way to get accustomed to extemporaneous speaking, for it is in some ways the most direct extension of our expertise as communicators. In conversations and in meetings with specific agendas, we are all impromptu speakers. An impromptu speech may be stimulated by a timely event, a collection of objects, a general topic, a specific question relating to a subject you have been investigating, or by some other technique that works for you and your instructor. Such exercises give you little or no time to do anything more than quickly consider what you are going to say. And it isn't like a conversation or a meeting where you can choose not to participate, sitting there with a smile on your face and keeping your mouth shut.

An impromptu speech calls for you to gather your thoughts rapidly and to express them, often within some rather challenging constraints that are called for by the occasion. Perhaps you have seen —even envied—people who can appear organized, reasonable, and fluent on the spur of the moment. That is a rare skill, indeed, and it is usually the result of a great deal of speaking experience. In fact, the experience that comes from planning and presenting an extemporaneous speech may be the best training that a good impromptu speaker can get.

Of course it is essential for speakers to know what they are talking about. It is important, too, to know that you can learn to make use of some of the basic ingredients found in a good extemporaneous speech in any kind of formal or informal communication situation that you may encounter. The same general principles apply. As with other skills, though, practice and experience are the keys. It is worth noting, in the meantime, that listeners tend to be more tolerant of various little shortcomings in speeches in the impromptu situation than they might be in more formal settings. A number of shortcomings in organization and fluency can be forgiven when people know that you are speaking without any time for preparation. This knowledge should make it easier for you to try an impromptu speech when you get the chance.

THE MANUSCRIPT SPEECH

Far removed from the impromptu speech is the manuscript speech, the speech written out and read aloud. Once a speaker has established control of the extemporaneous mode, the manuscript approach may prove to be another logical extension. Even in extemporaneous speaking, the goal is control, and the manuscript simply specifies that control on a more precise basis. You have heard many speeches delivered from manuscript, whether on television, at a public meeting, maybe in church, and certainly in classroom lectures.

*

By way of anticipating what we will say about the presentation of manuscript speeches, we ask that you try to remember the last time you heard a speech read from manuscript. What were your general impressions? Did the speaker use the manuscript so well that you were hardly aware of the mode? Or, on the other hand, were you so aware of the manuscript that it got in the way of the message? What made for the differences?

*

What happens with manuscript speeches? Under the best conditions, what happens is that the speaker may make the manuscript a vehicle for real communication. That is what Lincoln and Agnew did. But, as you surely know, a speaker may let the manuscript interfere. This interference is most obvious when the manuscript becomes a real barrier, when the speaker concentrates on the written words to the exclusion of any communication contact with the audience. We suggested another facet of interference when we talked about the literary style that probably would attend the memorized speech. After all, the speaker who sets out to prepare a manuscript for a speech runs the same risks that we mentioned concerning vocabulary and syntax. That's why we say that manuscript speaking should be an extension of the extemporaneous, and the extension applies to both the construction of the message and its delivery.

Writing the speech

Skill in extemporaneous speaking requires an extension and a refinement of our natural competence as communicators. This skill is equally applicable in writing the manuscript speech. Once speakers have learned to assess the audience feedback they get in the speaking situation, they can apply this knowledge in the writing of a manuscript speech. That is, the projected speech can be said and then written, rather than being written and then said. "My Grandfather" is a case in point. What we are suggesting is that, given the demands of the manuscript, you use your speaking style as the basis for the speech. And make no mistake, you may well find yourself in circumstances where a manuscript will give you control over the speaking situation that the extemporaneous approach does not offer. It is not accidental that we hear so many speeches delivered from manuscript; too many times, a speaker needs the greater control that a manuscript provides. A written text enables the speaker to determine wording, time spent on the ideas developed, and the entire allotment of time with greater precision. It is one thing to talk extemporaneously for seven or eight minutes, quite another to do so for forty-five minutes or an hour. Not that the latter is impossible—you undoubtedly have encountered instructors who do a very effective job of lecturing extemporaneously. Nevertheless, it is possible that you may find yourself, one day, in a speaking situation that suggests the use of a manuscript. In fact, such an assignment appears in some introductory speech courses, but regardless of when it might happen, the writing and the presentation merit special attention.

We said that the manuscript should be an extension of the extemporaneous mode, that it should be said and then written. That suggestion can be pressed too far, of course, and we are not indicating that you sit down with a tape recorder, rattle off something in stream-of-consciousness fashion, then type it out. We're simply suggesting that your basis should be what you are in your oral style. But having warned you about getting too literary with the writing, we have to note some possible advantages in this regard: the manuscript does provide the opportunity for refining and polishing your oral style. Perhaps there is a word teetering on the tip of your tongue, ready to become part of your speaking vocabulary; extemporaneous practice may produce that word, but the manuscript almost surely will. Similarly, the manuscript permits more conscious planning in all aspects of wording. It may be the use of just one word—such as Boyd's use of "well" that we commented on—but the possibilities extend throughout, including the entire message as a unit. Can you imagine, for example, that Lincoln could have achieved such careful development had he been speaking extemporaneously? Notice, for instance, his adroit use of the refrain "our fathers who framed the government under which we live" during his mock debate with the Southern position; this is only one illustration of many that might be cited in that speech. Now, it may be that you will never run for national political office, so you won't spend weeks laboring over a manuscript the way Lincoln did. Yet, given the decision to use the manuscript mode, you will find that some hours of labor will be both needed and rewarding.

Reading the speech

Lincoln having become a myth, it is easy to forget that he was just as human as the rest of us, and there probably is a tendency to treat the "Cooper Institute Address" as a terribly serious document. It is that, surely, but there is humor—even though it is rather sarcastic humor—and now we have arrived at the matter of delivering the manuscript speech. All texts of Lincoln's speech indicate a conscious mimicking of Douglas's "gur-reat pur-rinciple" of Popular Sovereignty, and even in the absence of a videotape, it can hardly be doubted that Lincoln gave special emphasis to expressions such as "Senator Douglas and his *peculiar* adherents" or "And does not such affirmation become impudently absurd when coupled with the *other* affirmation, from the *same* mouth?" (our italics). Now it happens that Lincoln did not have a bland voice like the ones you hear on the evening news. He had a marked accent, and the voice quality was not rich and strong; furthermore, he was physically awkward. Nevertheless, he had a direct and forceful communicative style, and newspaper accounts of his speech report both laughter and applause breaking out during the speech. Lincoln's delivery surely contributed to these reactions.

Lincoln had long experience in extemporaneous speaking, in courts and in the legislature, and the Lincoln-Douglas Debates alone constituted an extensive chapter in that experience. In short, he learned to talk not just to, but *with* people in public, and he maintained that same directness when using a manuscript. Directness is the key, and it is in presentation that many manuscript speeches founder. There is, however, no reason why they must. Some speakers find it psychologically more comfortable to bury their noses in the manuscript—to avoid looking at all those scary faces out there in the audience—and you have doubtless heard such speakers. The purposes of communication aren't served very well by this kind of speaking behavior.

If you write out a speech in what is your basic style of oral communication, if you get it down on paper in a form that is easy to read, and if you practice until you are thoroughly at ease with it, the liveliness and spontaneity that we associate with extemporaneous delivery can be yours with the manuscript. Your eyes must give some attention to the page, certainly, but you will find memory operating, and you can be physically direct with your audience.

We would also point out that a manuscript need not be entirely inflexible in regard to substance. We have indicated that a memorized speech can be adapted at times, and even a long manuscript presentation can be altered on the spot. In a short one, you can make minor alterations in wording, and in a longer one, you can deliberately plan for some places along the way where seemingly ad-lib remarks may be appropriate. A question from the audience or feedback that suggests a repeating of some segment may take time that you can compensate for by later deletions. You may have to compress an example or illustration, or entirely suppress a minor idea, but all these things can be done if you place the manuscript in a proper perspective. It should be your vehicle for the purpose of effective human communication, not an end in itself, and you should use it in any way that serves that purpose.

THE EXTEMPORANEOUS SPEECH

Rehearsal

In what follows about the rehearsal of extemporaneous speeches, we assume you will allow yourself time for that purpose. In the introductory speech course, the notion of staying ahead of the game has special meaning. We are not referring to assigned reading, because that usually creates no special problems. We are referring to the speeches you will be giving. One of the reasons that college or university life can seem so demanding and so exhausting is that there are so terribly many choices to be made. Even the extremely diligent student is constantly juggling priorities, priorities that may involve a field trip in archeology, an impending examination in mathematics, a paper on Renaissance diplomacy, and any number of other tasks.

Everyone knows, of course, that it is possible to let assigned reading slip by, cram it down the night before, and somehow survive the examination the next day. But that is an especially hazardous route in speech preparation, particularly for the inexperienced speaker. If you have ever taken the slip-by-cram-it-down-and-survive approach, recall the physical and mental strain and drain. Now project that strain and drain into the public-speaking situation, and ask yourself if that's the way you want to approach it, even if you are one of those students who can bring off the last-minute effort. A bit later we will acknowledge the fact that some speakers need very little rehearsal time. You may be one but, for the moment at least, we suggest that you let others' experience be your guide. That's why we suggested you create an inventory of possible topics, subjects that seem worth exploring with an audience. That's also why we suggested the possibility (with your instructor's permission) of using a single topic for more than one speech. You might concentrate on the effect of understanding in one of them, and acceptance in another, but the job of finding a topic is simplified.

Let's assume now that you are past all the preliminaries, have chosen a topic, gathered materials, and have sketched out the pattern of development. It's time now to start your oral rehearsal, time to start saying the words aloud. Where you do this doesn't much matter. You might begin while sitting at your desk, lying in bed, or taking a shower. Eventually, however, you should practice in the posture of the actual speaking situation. If you will be standing in front of the audience with no podium, then you should rehearse in that posture. If you will have a podium, try turning a wastebasket or some other object upside down on a desk or table when you practice.

And though a friend can be pressed into service as a (perhaps reluctant) sample audience, don't limit your imagination to an audience of one. Try to imagine, as you practice, the very room and the audience that will be present. Try, in short, to make the experience as close as possible to the real thing. How much of this practice is needed will vary from one individual to the next, and it is something that you will have to learn for yourself.

Your first objective is to gain control of the verbal message, but that control should be such that it encourages the vitality and directness we associate with the ordinary uses of language. We suggested that you might want to know rather precisely how you would start and how you would stop, but even the starting and stopping should permit some flexibility in language, and that flexibility should be maintained throughout. Too much rehearsal may lead to a speech that risks the "canned" flavor of memorization. You can usually tell, though, with a little practice, when you have rehearsed too much. If you don't write out the speech and if you permit yourself to be satisfied with various ways of saying generally the same thing, you at least lay the foundation for extending your natural expertise into the public-speaking situation.

Certainly, what you do naturally may not be best. Late in the sixteenth century, Stephano Guazzo addressed himself to the matter in *The Civil Conversation* and remarked that "the rude speech of the country Clown is as natural to him, as the fine and polished is to the Citizen and Gentleman." Consequently, he argues that "it is needful

"Hard to believe he flunked public speaking."

to aid our selves with a little Art." And at the verbal level, you might try a "little Art." Although the manuscript speech offers more potential in this regard, there is no reason why the extemporaneous speaker should forget about the precise nuance of meaning that a particular word may provide, should ignore the possibilities in metaphorical uses, or should neglect any expressions that might give special force to the message.

*

Almost everyone has access to recording equipment these days, and a tape recorder can be used as an excellent tool for speech rehearsal. When you hear your speech on tape you can listen to it with much more objectivity than when you are giving it.

Try recording a speech that you are about to give and observe the way you develop your ideas and support them. Pay attention to your manner of expression as well. Could your style be more clear, or more appropriate, or more vivid? Now listen mainly to your delivery. How is your speaking rate? How about variety in tone of voice and force of presentation? Does your voice convey an interest in the subject?

Tape your speech on one day and listen to it the next day. It may sound different after this delay.

*

Nonverbal rehearsal. Then there are the nonverbal aspects of the message, and although this topic is an extremely nettlesome one, we again suggest that you consider using a little art. If you did the exercise in which we asked that you contemplate your own nonverbal behavior, you have a basis from which to work. No speaker gestures when speaking in a way that corresponds exactly with the gestures used when sitting in a chair or when stretched out on a couch. In addition, nonverbal communication is tremendously varied within and across cultures. Wherever you are within that varied range, you won't move and gesture when giving a speech in the same way you do in conversation. But if you determine your natural tendencies, you can build on them. Let's use an animated conversation as a point of departure.

Standing in a group of people, everyone makes general physical adjustments to the flow of communication, turning the head and eyes and adjusting the entire trunk of the body. But circumstances prevent the public speaker from making some of the larger adjustments, the physical arrangements preventing much freedom to move about. But when movement is possible it seems quite natural, as long as it does not become a sign of nervous pacing, and a speaker is never so confined that the body and head cannot turn to encompass the entire audience. This physical activity can perform several functions.

Though there may not be a spoken interchange between speaker and audience, there are still some nonverbal regulators of the type we mentioned in the preceding chapter that are likely to be operating here. The nods, the glances, the pauses, the movements, and such, serve as a kind of "nonverbal punctuation" which makes it easier for the audience to listen and comprehend. In general, the audience simply will be more responsive to the speaker who establishes physical directness. Part of the explanation is the very nature of the process. We learn to talk in face-to-face situations. This fact also helps explain why we like to see as well as hear a speaker. We all do a great deal of speech reading—that is, we quite literally *see* differences in pronunciation; the sound may not be that distinct, but if we can see the speaker's mouth, the difference between "first" and "worst" or "mine" and "nine" becomes visible.

Physical activity can also help you get used to the public-speaking situation, in which there is often more adrenalin in your system than you really need. Physical action, even of a limited sort, can help use up this nervous excess and make you more at ease. More specific gestures of hands and arms help here, too, in addition to their primary function as illustrators.

Again, start with the nonverbal illustrators that seem most naturally your own, and build on them. This can be harder than it sounds, because it is difficult to become conscious of one's gestures without becoming *self*-conscious at the same time, but it can be done.

The goal is to project your natural use of illustrators into your public speaking, and this goal supports the idea that you practice your speech aloud in a physical posture like that you will actually use. Don't plan any special gestures or force yourself into any that seem uncomfortable. On the other hand, don't restrict your natural tendency to extend an arm, point with a finger, or use any other gesture that is a part of your nonverbal style. Occasionally, an inexperienced speaker will come on too strong, but the other extreme is far more common, and the thing to do is nurture your existing patterns. This advice assumes that you don't have repetitious and otherwise distracting patterns, but if you do, you will find it out soon enough; on the whole, it is better to get a little involved physically than to stand in front of your audience like a robot. And remember that whatever you do with your hands and arms in gesturing, when you finish the gesture, they will always come right back down to the same place by your side. That posture, too, is perfectly natural and acceptable.

Rehearsing aloud. We have made only a few passing references to the use of the voice in speaking, and although it may seem ironic, we aren't going to say too much here. Probably none of us are ever happy with that strange-sounding voice that emerges from a tape recording; it always seems higher and thinner than we think it is. The body is to blame. When we produce sound, the vibrations travel through flesh and bone, as well as through the air, and the inner ear is agitated by all these vibrations. The recording machine, regardless of its fidelity, misses these vibrations so we just do not hear ourselves as others hear us. That is no great matter, for when you come to think of it, how many voices can you recall that have truly gotten in the way of the message? You can certainly think of speakers whose delivery was ineffective, but seldom will you find that some vocal characteristic was the primary cause. Having a wide latitude of acceptance for nonverbal behavior in speaking, we have the same wide latitude for the voice we hear.

The voice can make a difference, of course, but the evidence indicates that variety of tone and inflection is the most important element in determining whether or not we respond favorably to a voice, and few voices lack such variety. At the extreme would be the absolute monotone—no change in pitch, no inflections, no changes in rate, and none in force. Any problems in these four areas may be increased in the public-speaking situation, so you will have to be alert to the possibilities. If you find that you are hurrying, speaking too softly, or restricting the scope of your normal inflectional pattern, then it follows that you should work on these things during rehearsal. There is no solution other than rehearsing and gaining experience in the actual speaking process. If you have some persistent difficulty, however, a course in voice and articulation or one in the oral interpretation of literature may be the answer, or your instructor may be able to recommend a book with some vocal drills for you to do on your own. If we don't go into a lot of detail here, it is not because the voice is unimportant, but because serious problems in this area are very few, and there aren't many that effort and experience will not overcome.

> **V.** I have never considered myself to be a very dramatic interpreter of our language and, I must confess, I have never been especially interested in acquiring that skill. Although I have always respected the interest of those who take courses in oral interpretation, it just wasn't for me. I learned something about my voice, though, by reading stories to my kids when they were little. In the privacy of our living room, I portrayed all the various characters in my children's books with different voices and I read the narrations with as much drama and gusto as I could provide. Truthfully, I would have melted away in embarrassment if I had been observed by other adults. The kids didn't complain though —in fact I think they rather enjoyed it, which is probably why I kept it up. It wasn't until I had been doing this reading for two or three months that I realized that, even in ordinary speaking situations, my voice had undergone some changes. I could actually *feel* a greater control over my pitch range, my vocal force and my articulation.
>
> Moral: George Bernard Shaw may have believed that reading rots the mind, but I'll bet he didn't know that reading aloud strengthens the vocal mechanism.

Delivery

In extemporaneous speaking, the precise wording of the message waits until the moment of presentation, but there are different ways to approach this mode of delivery. You might, for example, use a rather complete outline. Or you might use a card on which you do no more than list the main headings of the speech. Or you might be extremely bold and heroic, standing up with no notes at all. For a speech running to thirty minutes or an hour, outline and notes may be quite necessary. On the other hand, notes are not really necessary when you are giving a speech that is only a few minutes in length.

Notes may seem to offer immediate security, but they can become an impediment, and if you think about it for a minute, you will know why. Your natural expertise with the language does not include speaking from notes, and when you use them, you introduce one more complication in your efforts to master the public-speaking situation. That complication may prove to be a distraction as you seek to gain control. Once you have established some degree of control, you will find it much easier to use notes skillfully. This argument works both in theory and in practice. The two of us prohibit notes for the first short speeches in our classes, and our students manage extremely well, finding it easier to handle notes later with no loss of the directness that should be a goal throughout the study of extemporaneous speaking.

As we noted, the impromptu speech is the most direct extension of our expertise with language, and the extemporaneous speech merely takes that expertise further, but its added dimensions are crucial. They allow for the development of more complex ideas, for more complicated arguments, and for a much richer development of all the uses of public speaking. Yet the impromptu and the extemporaneous speech exercise are at one in attempting to cultivate a spontaneous, direct, and lively style in delivery. You should try to avoid anything that will prevent or hinder that kind of presentation. Throughout the history of rhetorical studies, this projection of a lively and seemingly natural manner of presentation has been the goal. Toward that end, writers have offered exhaustive analyses of every gesture and every possible facial expression. In Quintilian's *Institutio Oratoria,* for example, you can find a long section on how the speaker ought to manage his toga! We won't go that far, but we have already suggested that, like a good scout, you Be Prepared. We further suggest that you do anything else that will contribute to your ease and confidence. And when the time arrives, be neither overly eager nor overly laconic, for the physical pace you set for yourself is important, even as you move into position.

When you haved moved into position, and are facing your audience in the introductory speech class, you will see a variety of faces. One may be quite sleepy, another distracted because it is the face that will be speaking next, still another distracted because it is the face that has just finished speaking, and so on through many possibilities. But students in an introductory class are usually extremely sympathetic and helpful. They care because they know exactly how you feel. They have many beautiful faces, and you should concentrate on those faces. Take in all the audience with your movement, posture, gestures, and looks, but give special attention to those who seem receptive or responsive. It would be unrealistic to expect that every member of your audience will be attentive and interested, so why not concentrate on those who are? That is what we do in ordinary situations, and that is precisely why you should do it when speaking in public. If you focus on responsive faces, even though they sometimes look puzzled or inquiring, you will be reinforcing fundamental elements in your uses of language. Consequently, you are more likely to react in a manner that is both direct and lively. You can talk to the neutral-looking and passive faces as well, even though their feedback is harder to read. Many people are quite passive as listeners, but this doesn't mean that they aren't following you. Your visual contact with them is one way of including them as audience members and keeping their minds on your presentation. All these matters of delivery will become easier as you gain additional experience, but the experience will be most instructive if you do everything you can to make each speech as real as possible.

M. When the rest of our lathing crew moved on to the new job, Ellie Mosley and I, his helper, stayed behind to finish up the work. Then we rejoined the others, but on Friday, we returned for our pay. (I must add that this was the South of the late 1950s, that the crew consisted entirely of blacks, except for their lowly helper, and that Mose was president of the local union.) Well, the contractor told us he could not pay us: we hadn't completed the work, hadn't done it properly, and shouldn't expect our checks until an inspection had been made. I started to protest, but Mose took over.

Watching and listening, I did not know whether to laugh or cry. I had worked with Mose for two months and knew him to be an intelligent, articulate human being. Suddenly, he changed. Oh, his arguments were good: local union rules stipulated that contractors who did not pay on Friday became liable for eight hours a day until payment was made, whether any work was done or not. And, of course, the president of the local union had a special responsibility in such matters.

But as Mose made these points and repeated them, he became almost inarticulate. He seemed to have lost control of grammar and syntax, and his accent became so pronounced that I had trouble understanding him. Furthermore, he added negative physical reinforcement. Slumping from his normally upright posture, he fidgeted nervously with his hands, and avoiding all eye contact, he looked down at the ground or off to one side. In voice, posture, and gesture, Mose became another person, became the very personification of Uncle Tom. The contractor simply could not deal with the situation. He tried, certainly, but Mose merely slouched a bit more, scratched slowly along a forearm, looked off toward the horizon, and repeated his arguments in an even more unintelligible accent. We took our checks with us to the car.

Evaluation

At various places, we have talked about feedback during the speech, about audience behavior that indicates the response to a speaker's efforts. After the speech, however, you will usually get special feedback in the form of oral or written comments on your performance. These comments may come from the students, from your instructor, or both, but whatever the source you should attend to them. The "good news"-"bad news" distinction is appropriate, because the inexperienced speaker especially needs to know what things about the presentation were well received and what things weren't as effective as they might have been.

The good news, of course, is when everything works out exactly as you had hoped. Presenting the speech, you observe positive reaction, and when you have finished, you are satisfied with your efforts. Even then, it is good to learn that the audience can testify that all went well, can comment favorably on general structure, a particular unit of structure, a metaphor, or an example introduced. After all, meaning is in the audience, and a speaker can never be certain until the audience has provided some reaction.

Of course, if the reaction is not all that positive, the bad news may be hard to live with, but what doesn't work can be as instructive as what does. In the first place, you may expend considerable effort on a speech, and know at the time you are speaking that it is not going over well. You ask yourself why, and there seems to be no good answer. Maybe, all things considered, you would go about it in much the same way if you had to do it all over again. The chances are good, however, that something is awry when a speech fails to generate any positive reaction. No matter how painful that may be to your ego, you will improve as you learn to accept constructive criticism. You should, in this regard, make real demands on yourself, on others in the class, and on your instructor. Even a speech that is good may have room for improvement, and you should never be satisfied with the notion that your latest speech was better than the last one. What else should you expect!

Given regular speech assignments, most speakers show definite improvement, and much of the obvious improvement involves greater control in delivery. That control is a most important objective, but don't be misled into thinking that it is the most important factor. Delivery is, after all, just delivery, and whatever the word used to describe the presentation, the ideas are what count most. Be happy that you gain control, but resist the temptation of believing that control is everything.

And resist the temptation to comment on other speeches exclusively in terms of delivery. Criticism in the introductory speech class is a two-way street, and if you want help from other students, you should reply in kind. You will spend most of your time in class as a receiver rather than as a sender of messages, and this can be a useful learning opportunity for you as well as for those who are speaking at the time. A speech being a speech, delivery is an obvious point of reference, so of course you should not ignore it. Nevertheless, your criticism will be most profitable when you focus your attention on the entire meaning of the message. Most people will demonstrate increasing control of the speaking situation as the course progresses, but to observe that fact is not the end of evaluation. As a critic, you should do more—you should let other students know when they hit or miss the mark. We don't suggest that you throw tact aside. Your response may be most productive immediately, or the speaker may receive your criticism more receptively after a day or so has passed, and this may be true even when your remarks are mostly positive.

The notion of your being not only a speaker, but an audience member and critic, is terribly important. By accepting this responsibility, you can make the entire public-speaking experience much more interesting and profitable. It isn't just a matter of listening to others because they have to listen to you; it is a matter of learning from what others do. Not all the things that work for one speaker will work for you, but by concentrating on the ways in which others develop and present their ideas, you increase the options available in developing and presenting your own ideas.

SUGGESTED READINGS

Gilbert Austin, *Chironomia* (1806; reprinted Carbondale, Ill., 1966). This book is best remembered for the notational system Austin developed for use in teaching oratory, but it also has historical interest because Austin surveys the writings of his predecessors. Beyond the historical attraction, however, you will find that there is a wealth of sensible advice sensibly presented.

G. P. Mohrmann, *Composition and Style in the Writing of Speeches* (Dubuque, Iowa, 1970). This little book is devoted exclusively to the preparation and presentation of manuscript speeches.

PREVIEW: CHAPTER 12

In this final chapter, we discuss just two topics:

Assessing your communication
Your growth as a speaker

As the headings suggest, we have come full circle from the Emerson quotation with which we began, but his notion of self-reliance is more than ever the point here. We want this chapter to serve as a reminder that *you* are the one who must eventually assume full responsibility for your improvement as a speaker. Others can and will help, but the doing must be yours.

a final word

LEARNING FROM EXPERIENCE

12

No matter where the two of us go, within or outside the academic community, we continually encounter people who are interested in better communication. Sometimes, frankly, they are more than interested—they are almost desperate. They share their specific problems with us; they tell their stories; they frequently express their concern and frustration. They would like to be better communicators themselves, and they would like to see better communication from others in both their private and professional lives. They ask for answers and insights; they want a bit of advice on a specific problem; they want to know what they can do about the problem and what they can read on the subject. Although communication has been studied and written about for as long as we have records, it seems as though only in recent years has almost everyone come to realize its importance. And, happily, more and more people appear to be willing to confront their problems with communication. No agency, no group, no individual person, after all, can exist outside the communication framework.

So, given this pervasive need, what can any of us do to respond to it? There are no specific answers to such a general question, but a good general answer involves learning. Not the kind of "learning" that enables you to identify the correct answer in a multiple-choice test. And not the kind of "learning" that enables you to reproduce information or instructions at some later time. These kinds of learning can be helpful—even for gaining insights about speech communication—but the kind of learning we are talking about involves deeper and more substantive changes in your image and, thus, in your day-to-day behavior. It is the kind of learning that tends most often to come from experience—the learning you do, for example, when you put your hand on a hot stove and discover painfully that you had better never repeat the experience. Or, better still, the learning you do when you discover that, in order to take your hands off the handlebars, you have to take your eyes off the handlebars too, and focus them on the street ahead where they belong; and you have to relax the rest of your body as if your hands were still there.

We are talking about experience. You have learned from *experience* to communicate the way you do; in some respects this has been an unconscious process, and in others it has been a conscious one. Your culture has "programmed" you in some important ways; here your learning was essentially unconscious. In other instances, you experimented with some kind of communication through trial and error, and your particular social environment provided the appropriate rewards or punishments; here your learning was conscious. At times, specific prescriptions may have been there for you to follow, especially as you worked on some form of communication during your early formal education. We discussed this business very early in the book, but important points are worth repeating: much of who and what you are at the moment is the net effect of your previous communication experiences. There is no denying, then, that you can learn to be a better communicator and, specifically, a better public speaker by continuing the same basic processes you have been using all your life.

ASSESSING YOUR COMMUNICATION

We all seem to have acquired an intuitive system for evaluating the outcome of our communication transactions. We may have trouble explaining it very clearly if someone asks us to, but most of us actually make some judgments about whether things have gone fairly well or whether they haven't. We tend to become consciously aware of the fact

V. All teachers have some things they say to their students on the first day of class, and I'm certainly no exception. I talk about such things as expectations, ground rules, assignments, and grading. Usually, too, I try to find some things to say to generate enthusiasm and interest. In this connection, about every second time I teach the introductory speech course, I tell my new students that a personal commitment to the course can significantly change their lives. The reason I don't make this point every time is that it rather embarrasses me to say it—it sounds too much like some kind of a sales pitch for a miracle cure. Nonetheless, I believe it. If people are really committed to becoming better communicators they can do it. I have yet to find an exception.

that we are evaluating a communication experience only when that situation is personally important to us. Then we are inclined to play the scene back in our heads after it is over, thinking something like, "Wow, I got off easy that time—I thought it would be worse," or, "Now I know what I should have told her when she asked . . . ," or perhaps, "Boy, I think they really went for my explanation of. . . ." The point is that we do have some internal standards for our own communication experiences and we commonly apply them. For most of us our internal standards operate in public-speaking situations as well as in informal settings. We have a pretty good idea about how well we were received, how well we achieved whatever it was we set out to achieve. Nevertheless, most of us tend to be more aware of our shortcomings than our listeners are, and most of us—even experienced speakers—will sometimes underrate the acceptability of our efforts in public speaking.

It is possible, of course to check your intuitive reaction against other judgments, and the evaluation process of the last chapter applies here. Certainly it makes good sense to start with the audience in your speech class as you begin to assess your influence and try to become more objective in your assessment. An obvious point of departure would be the five effects of awareness, willingness, understanding, acceptance, and behavior. Using any one of these general effects, you can key your analysis to some specific point or points in a particular speech you give. In the relatively ideal conditions of the classroom, you could devise a test that would indicate whether you achieved the desired effect. For example, some kind of attitude scale could help you determine whether you had made your audience more willing and receptive. If you wanted to test the extent of your listeners' understanding, you might figure out a way to measure their retention of information. Even better, you could devise a measure of what your listeners know and how much they care about your subject before you speak, and then you could compare these findings with those from a similar test given after they have listened to you. Then you would be in a much better position to assess the influence of your presentation.

*

Perhaps you will be provided with a critique form in class, but even if you are, you will find it helpful to devise an evaluation sheet for a speech that you plan to give. Be sure that it permits reactions that will be helpful to you in determining the effect or effects your speech may have on your listeners in the various areas we have been discussing. You might want to include some specific questions about the methods/strategies/approaches that you plan to try, to get some indication of how they are received.

If you are able to, give the evaluation sheet to your listeners. If this isn't possible, fill it out yourself, being as honest as you can in estimating the responses you would get. Actually, you should fill out a sheet yourself in any case, so that you can compare it with whatever other reactions are available.

*

These techniques of evaluation that we have been talking about can become extremely elaborate, so elaborate as to be usable only in carefully controlled research. Nevertheless, versions of all these techniques are appropriate to the introductory speech class, and you should take advantage of the opportunity to use one or more of them. Outside the classroom, your opportunities will be severely restricted, for while your listeners will want you to do well, they are not listening to you for the purpose of studying communication, so they ordinarily will not offer advice that will help you perform better the next time. You may be able to get an honest evaluation from a friend, but all you may be able to do is watch your audience carefully to see what nonverbal cues of listener attentiveness and comprehension you can pick up. Occasionally, too, remarks and questions from your listeners can be helpful in revealing how your speech was received. Instead of a pretest for the audience, if you really want to do well, you will probably have to come up with a rather thorough audience analysis along the lines we discussed in Chapter 4. Good preparation, of course, will increase the likelihood that your evaluation of a given communication experience will yield the kind of results you would like to see.

There are two other considerations that should guide you in your assessment of a speaking experience. These are, first, what the audience thinks of you yourself, and second, what the audience thinks of your presentation, the speech itself. Strictly speaking, these three components of the speech—the subject/purpose, the speaker, and the presentation—are interrelated. Each component may add to or detract from the total experience in various ways. Your listeners may indicate, for instance, that they understand your subject and they find you to be an acceptable, credible source, but they may still rate your presentation on the low side. It may be dull or it may be too long. Instructors fairly often find that their lectures have this kind of mixed effect on their students. Obviously in such cases the news isn't all bad.

But there are other times when the three components may interact in such a way that a poor presentation may interfere with or even destroy some other desired effect, such as understanding. Then the presentation would become a matter of crucial importance. So you can see how valuable it is for you to find out, whenever possible, how your audience views you as a speaker and how it regards the speech itself.

YOUR GROWTH AS A SPEAKER

We could end this book with one simple sentence: *It's mainly up to you.* If you have read the text with some thoughtfulness and if you have worked on or at least seriously considered the exercises and applications, we are confident that your awareness of audiences, messages, and speakers is heightened and sharpened. Awareness is an essential ingredient in your growth as a speaker. In this regard, we are satisfied that we have given you a generous measure of both broadly theoretical and specifically applied means for increasing your awareness.

We have also given you a number of guidelines and tools for effective speaking. It is up to you to adapt and develop these tools according to your own communication needs and your own personal style. This will certainly call for some practice and experimentation, but we can assure you that there is ample opportunity for both in our society. Because human interaction is so important, many people would like to become better communicators, better speakers, but they lose their enthusiasm when they discover that a certain amount of effort is involved. It's rather like wanting to play the piano very well, but not really being interested in all that time spent in practice.

But, for good or ill, we practice communication all the time. Since the practice is unavoidable, all you need to add to your awareness and understanding of speaking is your personal commitment to improving your abilities. Without your commitment to growth as a speaker, the awareness and the tools are a means to a mere academic exercise. But with your commitment, they are the basis for a more rewarding and fulfilling life.

It's mainly up to you.

index